FAMILIAR STUDIES

OF

MEN AND BOOKS

BY

ROBERT LOUIS STEVENSON

PETER FENELON COLLIER, PUBLISHER

To

THOMAS STEVENSON

CIVIL ENGINEER

BY WHOSE DEVICES THE GREAT SEA LIGHTS IN EVERY QUARTER

OF THE WORLD NOW SHINE MORE BRIGHTLY

THIS VOLUME IS IN LOVE AND GRATITUDE

DEDICATED BY HIS SON

THE AUTHOR

3978

PREFACE

BY WAY OF CRITICISM

THESE studies are collected from the monthly press. One appeared in the "New Quarterly," one in "Macmillan's," and the rest in the "Cornhill Magazine." To the "Cornhill" I owe a double debt of thanks; first, that I was received there in the very best society, and under the eye of the very best of editors; and second, that the proprietors have allowed me to republish so considerable an amount of copy.

These nine worthies have been brought together from many different ages and countries. Not the most erudite of men could be perfectly prepared to deal with so many and such various sides of human life and manners. To pass a true judgment upon Knox and Burns implies a grasp upon the very deepest strain of thought in Scotland—a country far more essentially different from England than many parts of America; for, in a sense, the first of these men re-created Scotland, and the second is its most essentially national production. To treat fitly of Hugo and Villon would involve yet wider knowledge, not only of a country foreign to the author by race, history, and religion, but of the growth and liberties of art. Of the two Americans, Whitman and Thoreau, each is the type of something not so much realized as widely sought after among the late generations of their countrymen; and to see them clearly in a nice relation to the society that brought them forth, an author would require a large habit of life among modern Americans. As for Yoshida, I have already disclaimed responsibility; it was but my hand that held the pen.

In truth, these are but the readings of a literary vagrant. One book led to another, one study to another. The first was published with trepidation. Since no bones were broken the second was launched with greater confidence. So, by insensible degrees, a young man of our generation acquires, in his own eyes, a kind of roving judicial commission through the ages; and, having once escaped the perils of the Freemans and the Furnivalls, sets himself up to right the wrongs of universal history and criticism. Now, it is one thing to write with enjoyment on a subject while the story is hot in your mind from recent reading, colored with recent prejudice; and it is quite another business to put these writings coldly forth again in a bound volume. We are most of us attached to our opinions; that is one of the "natural affections" of which we hear so much in youth; but few of us are altogether free from paralyzing doubts and scruples. For my part, I have a small idea of the degree of accuracy possible to man, and I feel sure these studies teem with error. One and all were written with genuine interest in the subject; many, however, have been conceived and finished with imperfect knowledge; and all have lain, from beginning to end, under the disadvantages inherent in this style of writing.

Of these disadvantages a word must here be said. The writer of short studies, having to condense in a few pages the events of a whole lifetime, and the effect on his own mind of many various volumes, is bound, above all things, to make that condensation logical and striking. For the only justification of his writing at all is that he shall present a brief, reasoned, and memorable view. By the necessity of the case, all the more neutral circumstances are omitted from his narrative; and that of itself, by the negative exaggeration of which I have spoken in the text, lends to the matter in hand a certain false and specious glitter. By the necessity of the case, again, he is forced to view his subject throughout in a particular illumination, like a studio artifice. Like Hales with Pepys, he must nearly break his sitter's neck to get the proper shadows on the portrait. It is from one side only that he has

time to represent his subject. The side selected will either be
the one most striking to himself, or the one most obscured by
controversy; and in both cases that will be the one most liable
to strained and sophisticated reading. In a biography, this
and that is displayed; the hero is seen at home, playing the
flute; the different tendencies of his work come, one after
another, into notice; and thus something like a true general
impression of the subject may at last be struck. But in the
short study, the writer, having seized his "point of view,"
must keep his eye steadily to that. He seeks, perhaps, rather
to differentiate than truly to characterize. The proportions
of the sitter must be sacrificed to the proportions of the portrait; the lights are heightened, the shadows overcharged;
the chosen expression, continually forced, may degenerate at
length into a grimace; and we have at best something of a
caricature, at worst a calumny. Hence, if they be readable
at all, and hang together by their own ends, the peculiar convincing force of these brief representations. They take so
little a while to read, and yet in that little while the subject
is so repeatedly introduced in the same light and with the
same expression, that, by sheer force of repetition, that view
is imposed upon the reader. The two English masters of the
style, Macaulay and Carlyle, largely exemplify its dangers.
Carlyle, indeed, had so much more depth and knowledge of
the heart, his portraits of mankind are felt and rendered with
so much more poetic comprehension, and he, like his favorite
Ram Dass, had a fire in his belly so much more hotly burning than the patent reading lamp by which Macaulay studied,
that it seems at first sight hardly fair to bracket them together. But the "point of view" was imposed by Carlyle on
the men he judged of in his writings with an austerity not
only cruel but almost stupid. They are too often broken
outright on the Procrustean bed; they are probably always
disfigured. The rhetorical artifice of Macaulay is easily
spied; it will take longer to appreciate the moral bias of
Carlyle. So with all writers who insist on forcing some
significance from all that comes before them; and the writer

of short studies is bound, by the necessity of the case, to write entirely in that spirit. What he cannot vivify he should omit.

Had it been possible to rewrite some of these papers, I hope I should have had the courage to attempt it. But it is not possible. Short studies are, or should be, things woven like a carpet, from which it is impossible to detach a strand. What is perverted has its place there forever as a part of the technical means by which what is right has been presented. It is only possible to write another study, and then, with a new "point of view," would follow new perversions and perhaps a fresh caricature. Hence, it will be, at least, honest to offer a few grains of salt to be taken with the text; and as some words of apology, addition, correction, or amplification fall to be said on almost every study in the volume, it will be most simple to run them over in their order. But this must not be taken as a propitiatory offering to the gods of shipwreck; I trust my cargo unreservedly to the chances of the sea; and do not, by criticising myself, seek to disarm the wrath of other and less partial critics.

Hugo's Romances.—This is an instance of the "point of view." The five romances studied with a different purpose might have given different results, even with a critic so warmly interested in their favor. The great contemporary master of wordmanship, and indeed of all literary arts and technicalities, had not unnaturally dazzled a beginner. But it is best to dwell on merits, for it is these that are most often overlooked.

Burns.—I have left the introductory sentences on Principal Shairp, partly to explain my own paper, which was merely supplemental to his amiable but imperfect book, partly because that book appears to me truly misleading both as to the character and the genius of Burns. This seems ungracious, but Mr. Shairp has himself to blame; so good a Wordsworthian was out of character upon that stage.

This half apology apart, nothing more falls to be said except upon a remark called forth by my study in the columns of a literary Review. The exact terms in which that sheet disposed of Burns I cannot now recall; but they were to this effect—that Burns was a bad man, the impure vehicle of fine verses; and that this was the view to which all criticism tended. Now I knew, for my own part, that it was with the profoundest pity, but with a growing esteem, that I studied the man's desperate efforts to do right; and the more I reflected, the stranger it appeared to me that any thinking being should feel otherwise. The complete letters shed, indeed, a light on the depths to which Burns had sunk in his character of Don Juan, but they enhance in the same proportion the hopeless nobility of his marrying Jean. That I ought to have stated this more noisily I now see; but that any one should fail to see it for himself, is to me a thing both incomprehensible and worthy of open scorn. If Burns, on the facts dealt with in this study, is to be called a bad man, I question very much whether either I or the writer in the Review have ever encountered what it would be fair to call a good one. All have some fault. The fault of each grinds down the hearts of those about him, and—let us not blink the truth—hurries both him and them into the grave. And when we find a man persevering indeed, in his fault, as all of us do, and openly overtaken, as not all of us are, by its consequences, to gloss the matter over, with too polite biographers, is to do the work of the wrecker disfiguring beacons on a perilous seaboard; but to call him bad, with a self-righteous chuckle, is to be talking in one's sleep with Heedless and Too-bold in the arbor.

Yet it is undeniable that much anger and distress is raised in many quarters by the least attempt to state plainly, what every one well knows, of Burns's profligacy, and of the fatal consequences of his marriage. And for this there are perhaps two subsidiary reasons. For, first, there is, in our drunken land, a certain privilege extended to drunkenness. In Scotland, in particular, it is almost respectable, above all when compared with any "irregularity between the sexes." The selfishness of the one, so much more gross in essence, is so much less immediately conspicuous in its results that our demiurgeous Mrs. Grundy smiles apologetically on its victims. It is often said—I have heard it with these ears—that drunkenness "may lead to vice." Now I did not think it at all proved that Burns was what is called a drunkard; and I was obliged to dwell very plainly on the irregularity and the too frequent vanity and meanness of his relations to women. Hence, in the eyes of many, my study was a step toward the demonstration of Burns's radical badness.

But second, there is a certain class, professors of that low morality so greatly more distressing than the better sort of vice, to whom you must never represent an act that was virtuous in itself, as attended by any other consequences than a large family and fortune. To hint that Burns's marriage had an evil influence is, with this class, to deny the moral law. Yet such is the fact. It was bravely done; but he had presumed too far on his strength. One after another the lights of his life went out, and he fell from circle to circle to the dishonored sickbed of the end. And surely for any one that has a thing to call a soul he shines out tenfold more nobly in the failure of that frantic effort to do right, than if he had turned on his heel with Worldly Wiseman, married a congenial spouse, and lived orderly and died reputably an old man. It is his chief title that he refrained from "the wrong that amendeth wrong." But the common, trashy mind of our generation is still aghast, like the Jews of old, at any word of an unsuccessful virtue. Job has been written and read; the tower of Siloam fell nineteen hundred years ago; yet we have still to desire a little Christianity, or, failing that, a little even of that rude, old, Norse nobility of soul, which saw virtue and vice alike go unrewarded, and was yet not shaken in its faith.

Walt Whitman.—This is a case of a second difficulty which lies continually before the writer of critical studies: that he has to mediate between the author whom he loves and the public who are certainly indifferent and frequently averse. Many articles had been written on this notable man. One after another had leaned, in my eyes, either to praise or blame unduly. In the last case, they helped to blindfold our fastidious public to an inspiring writer; in the other, by an excess of unadulterated praise, they moved the more candid to revolt. I was here on the horns of a dilemma; and between these horns I squeezed myself with perhaps some loss to the substance of the paper. Seeing so much in Whitman that was merely ridiculous, as well as so much more that was unsurpassed in force and fitness—seeing the true prophet doubled, as I thought, in places with the Bull in a China Shop—it appeared best to steer a middle course, and to laugh with the scorners when I thought they had any excuse, while I made haste to rejoice with the rejoicers over what is imperishably good, lovely, human, or divine, in his extraordinary poems. That was perhaps the right road; yet I cannot help feeling that in this attempt to trim my sails between an author whom I love and honor and a public too averse to recognize his merit, I have been led into a tone unbecoming from one of my stature to one of Whitman's. But the good and the great man will go on his way not vexed with my little shafts of merriment. He, first of any one, will understand how, in the attempt to explain him credibly to Mrs. Grundy, I have been led into certain airs of the man of the world, which are merely ridiculous in me, and were not intentionally discourteous to himself. But there is a worse side to the question; for in my eagerness to be all things to all men, I am afraid I may have sinned against proportion. It will be enough to say here that Whitman's faults are few and unimportant when they are set beside his surprising merits. I had written another paper full of gratitude for the help that had been given me in my life, full of enthusiasm for the intrinsic merit of the poems, and conceived in the noisiest extreme of youthful eloquence. The present study was a rifacimento. From it, with the design already mentioned, and in a fit of horror at my old excess, the big words and emphatic passages were ruthlessly excised. But this sort of prudence is frequently its own punishment; along with the exaggeration, some of the truth is sacrificed; and the result is cold, constrained, and grudging. In short, I might almost everywhere have spoken more strongly than I did.

Thoreau.—Here is an admirable instance of the "point of view" forced throughout, and of too earnest reflection on imperfect facts. Upon me this pure, narrow, sunnily-ascetic Thoreau had exercised a great charm. I have scarce written ten sentences since I was introduced to him, but his influence might be somewhere detected by a close observer. Still it was as a writer that I had made his acquaintance; I took him on his own explicit terms; and when I learned details of his life, they were, by the nature of the case and my own *parti-pris*, read even with a certain violence in terms of his writings. There could scarce be a perversion more justifiable than that; yet it was still a perversion. The study, indeed, raised so much ire in the breast of Dr. Japp (H. A. Page), Thoreau's sincere and learned disciple, that had either of us been men, I please myself with thinking, of less temper and justice, the difference might have made us enemies instead of making us friends. To him who knew the man from the inside, many of my statements sounded like inversions made on purpose; and yet when we came to talk of them together, and he had understood how I was looking at the man through the books, while he had long since learned to read the books through the man, I believe he understood the spirit in which I had been led astray.

On two most important points, Dr. Japp added to my knowledge, and with the same blow fairly demolished that part of my criticism. First, if Thoreau were content to dwell by Walden Pond, it was not merely with designs of self-improvement, but to serve mankind in the highest sense. Hither came the fleeing slave; thence was he dispatched along the road to freedom. That shanty in the woods was a station in the great Underground Railroad; that adroit and philosophic solitary was an ardent worker, soul and body, in that so much more than honorable movement, which, if atonement were possible for nations, should have gone far to wipe away the guilt of slavery. But in history sin always meets with condign punishment; the generation passes, the offense remains, and the innocent must suffer. No underground railroad could atone for slavery, even as no bills in Parliament can redeem the ancient wrongs of Ireland. But here at least is a new light shed on the Walden episode.

Second, it appears, and the point is capital, that Thoreau was once fairly and manfully in love, and, with perhaps too much aping of the angel, relinquished the woman to his brother. Even though the brother were like to die of it, we have not yet heard the last opinion of the woman. But be that as it may, we have here the explanation of the "rarefied and freezing air" in which I complained that he had taught himself to breathe. Reading the man through the books, I took his professions in good faith. He made a dupe of me, even as he was seeking to make a dupe of himself, wresting philosophy to the needs of his own sorrow. But in the light of this new fact, those pages, seemingly so cold, are seen to be alive with feeling. What appeared to be a lack of interest in the philosopher turns out to have been a touching insincerity of the man to his own heart; and that fine-spun airy theory of friendship, so devoid, as I complained, of any quality of flesh and blood, a mere anodyne to lull his pains. The most temperate of living critics once marked a passage of my own with a cross and the words, "This seems nonsense." It not only seemed; it was so. It was a private bravado of my own, which I had so often repeated to keep up my spirits that I had grown at last wholly to believe it, and had ended by setting it down as a contribution to the theory of life. So with the more icy parts of this philosophy of Thoreau's. He was affecting the Spartanism he had not; and the old sentimental wound still bled afresh, while he deceived himself with reasons.

Thoreau's theory, in short, was one thing and himself

another : of the first, the reader will find what I believe to be a pretty faithful statement and a fairly just criticism in the study; of the second he will find but a contorted shadow. So much of the man as fitted nicely with his doctrines, in the photographer's phrase, came out. But that large part which lay outside and beyond, for which he had found or sought no formula, on which perhaps his philosophy even looked askance, is wanting in my study, as it was wanting in the guide I followed. In some ways a less serious writer, in all ways a nobler man, the true Thoreau still remains to be depicted.

Villon.—I am tempted to regret that I ever wrote on this subject, not merely because the paper strikes me as too picturesque by half, but because I regarded Villon as a bad fellow. Others still think well of him, and can find beautiful and human traits where I saw nothing but artistic evil; and by the principle of the art, those should have written of the man, and not I. Where you see no good, silence is the best. Though this penitence comes too late, it may be well, at least, to give it expression.

The spirit of Villon is still living in the literature of France. Fat Peg is oddly of a piece with the work of Zola, the Goncourts, and the infinitely greater Flaubert; and, while similar in ugliness, still surpasses them in native power. The old author, breaking with an eclat de voix, out of his tongue-tied century, has not yet been touched on his own ground, and still gives us the most vivid and shocking impression of reality. Even if that were not worth doing at all, it would be worth doing as well as he has done it; for the pleasure we take in the author's skill repays us, or at least reconciles us to the baseness of his attitude. Fat Peg ("La Grosse Margot") is typical of much; it is a piece of experience that has nowhere else been rendered into literature; and a kind of gratitude for the author's plainness mingles, as we read, with the nausea proper to the business. I shall quote here a verse of an old students' song, worth laying side by side with Villon's startling ballade. This singer, also, had an unworthy mistress, but he did not choose to share the wages

of dishonor; and it is thus, with both wit and pathos, that
he laments her fall:

> Nunc plango florem
>   Ætatis teneræ
> Nitidiorem
>   Veneris sidere:
> Tunc columbinam
>   Mentis dulcedinem,
> Nunc serpentinam
>   Amaritudinem.
> Verbo rogantes
>   Removes ostio,
> Munera dantes
>   Foves cubiculo,
>   Illos abire præcipis
>   A quibus nihil accipis,
>   Cæcos claudosque recipis,
>   Viros illustres decipis
>   Cum melle venenosa.*

But our illustrious writer of ballades it was unnecessary to
deceive; it was the flight of beauty alone, not that of honesty
or honor, that he lamented in his song; and the nameless
mediæval vagabond has the best of the comparison.

There is now a Villon Society in England; and Mr. John
Payne has translated him entirely into English, a task of unusual difficulty. I regret to find that Mr. Payne and I are
not always at one as to the author's meaning; in such cases
I am bound to suppose that he is in the right, although the
weakness of the flesh withholds me from anything beyond a
formal submission. He is now upon a larger venture, promising us at last that complete Arabian Nights to which we
have all so long looked forward.

Charles of Orleans.—Perhaps I have done scanty justice to the charm of the old Duke's verses, and certainly he
is too much treated as a fool. The period is not sufficiently
remembered. What that period was, to what a blank of

---

* *Gaudeamus: Carmina vagorum selecta.* Leipsic. Trübner. 1879.

imbecility the human mind had fallen, can only be known to
those who have waded in the chronicles.   Excepting Comines
and La Salle and Villon, I have read no author who did not
appall me by his torpor; and even the trial of Joan of Arc,
conducted as it was by chosen clerks, bears witness to a
dreary, sterile folly—a twilight of the mind peopled with
childish phantoms.   In relation to his contemporaries, Charles
seems quite a lively character.

It remains for me to acknowledge the kindness of Mr.
Henry Pyne, who, immediately on the appearance of the
study, sent me his edition of the Debate between the Heralds :
a courtesy from the expert to the amateur only too uncommon in these days.

Knox.—Knox, the second in order of interest among the
reformers, lies dead and buried in the works of the learned
and unreadable M'Crie.   It remains for some one to break
the tomb and bring him forth, alive again and breathing, in
a human book.   With the best intentions in the world, I
have only added two more flagstones, ponderous like their
predecessors, to the mass of obstruction that buries the reformer from the world; I have touched him in my turn with
that "mace of death," which Carlyle has attributed to Dryas-
dust; and my two dull papers are, in the matter of dullness,
worthy additions to the labors of M'Crie.   Yet I believe they
are worth reprinting in the interest of the next biographer of
Knox.   I trust his book may be a masterpiece; and I indulge
the hope that my two studies may lend him a hint or perhaps
spare him a delay in its composition.

Of the *Pepys* I can say nothing; for it has been too recently through my hands; and I still retain some of the heat
of composition.   Yet it may serve as a text for the last remark I have to offer.   To Pepys I think I have been amply
just; to the others, to Burns, Thoreau, Whitman, Charles of
Orleans, even Villon, I have found myself in the retrospect
ever too grudging of praise, ever too disrespectful in manner.
It is not easy to see why I should have been most liberal to
the man of least pretensions.   Perhaps some cowardice with

held me from the proper warmth of tone; perhaps it is easier to be just to those nearer us in rank of mind. Such at least is the fact, which other critics may explain. For these were all men whom, for one reason or another, I loved; or when I did not love the men, my love was the greater to their books. I had read them and lived with them; for months they were continually in my thoughts; I seemed to rejoice in their joys and to sorrow with them in their griefs; and behold, when I came to write of them, my tone was sometimes hardly courteous and seldom wholly just.

R. L. S.

CONTENTS

VOLUME SEVEN

(19)

VICTOR HUGO'S ROMANCES

Après le roman pittoresque mais prosaïque de Walter Scott il restera un autre roman à créer, plus beau et plus complet encore selon nous. C'est le roman, à la fois drame et épopée, pittoresque mais poétique, réel mais idéal, vrai mais grand, qui enchâssera Walter Scott dans Homère.—Victor Hugo on "Quentin Durward."

VICTOR HUGO'S romances occupy an important position in the history of literature; many innovations, timidly made elsewhere, have in them been carried boldly out to their last consequences; much that was indefinite in literary tendencies has attained to definite maturity; many things have come to a point and been distinguished one from the other; and it is only in the last romance of all, "Quatre Vingt Treize," that this culmination is most perfect. This is in the nature of things. Men who are in any way typical of a stage of progress may be compared more justly to the hand upon the dial of the clock, which continues to advance as it indicates, than to the stationary milestone, which is only the measure of what is past. The movement is not arrested. That significant something by which the work of such a man differs from that of his predecessors, goes on disengaging itself and becoming more and more articulate and cognizable. The same principle of growth that carried his first book beyond the books of previous writers, carries his last book beyond his

first. And just as the most imbecile production of any
literary age gives us sometimes the very clew to comprehension we have sought long and vainly in contemporary masterpieces, so it may be the very weakest
of an author's books that, coming in the sequel of
many others, enables us at last to get hold of what
underlies the whole of them—of that spinal marrow of
significance that unites the work of his life into something organic and rational. This is what has been done
by "Quatre Vingt Treize" for the earlier romances of
Victor Hugo, and, through them, for a whole division
of modern literature. We have here the legitimate con-
tinuation of a long and living literary tradition; and
hence, so far, its explanation. When many lines di-
verge from each other in direction so slightly as to
confuse the eye, we know that we have only to produce them to make the chaos plain: this is continually
so in literary history; and we shall best understand
the importance of Victor Hugo's romances if we think
of them as some such prolongation of one of the main
lines of literary tendency.

When we compare the novels of Walter Scott with
those of the man of genius who preceded him, and
whom he delighted to honor as a master in the art—I
mean Henry Fielding—we shall be somewhat puzzled,
at the first moment, to state the difference that there
is between these two. Fielding has as much human
science; has a far firmer hold upon the tiller of his
story; has a keen sense of character, which he draws
(and Scott often does so too) in a rather abstract and
academical manner; and finally, is quite as humorous

and quite as good-humored as the great Scotchman.
With all these points of resemblance between the men,
it is astonishing that their work should be so different.
The fact is, that the English novel was looking one
way and seeking one set of effects in the hands of
Fielding; and in the hands of Scott it was looking
eagerly in all ways and searching for all the effects
that by any possibility it could utilize. The difference
between these two men marks a great enfranchisement.
With Scott the Romantic movement, the movement of
an extended curiosity and an enfranchised imagination,
has begun. This is a trite thing to say; but trite
things are often very indefinitely comprehended: and
this enfranchisement, in as far as it regards the technical change that came over modern prose romance, has
never perhaps been explained with any clearness.

To do so, it will be necessary roughly to compare
the two sets of conventions upon which plays and romances are respectively based. The purposes of these
two arts are so much alike, and they deal so much
with the same passions and interests, that we are apt
to forget the fundamental opposition of their methods.
And yet such a fundamental opposition exists. In the
drama the action is developed in great measure by
means of things that remain outside of the art; by
means of real things, that is, and not artistic conventions for things. This is a sort of realism that is not
to be confounded with that realism in painting of which
we hear so much. The realism in painting is a thing
of purposes; this, that we have to indicate in the
drama, is an affair of method. We have heard a story,
indeed, of a painter in France who, when he wanted

to paint a sea-beach, carried realism from his ends to
his means, and plastered real sand upon his canvas;
and that is precisely what is done in the drama. The
dramatic author has to paint his beaches with real
sand: real live men and women move about the stage;
we hear real voices; what is feigned merely puts a
sense upon what is; we do actually see a woman go
behind a screen as Lady Teazle, and, after a certain
interval, we do actually see her very shamefully produced again. Now all these things, that remain as
they were in life, and are not transmuted into any
artistic convention, are terribly stubborn and difficult to
deal with; and hence there are for the dramatist many
resultant limitations in time and space. These limitations in some sort approximate toward those of painting: the dramatic author is tied down, not indeed to
a moment, but to the duration of each scene or act;
he is confined to the stage, almost as the painter is
confined within his frame. But the great restriction
is this, that a dramatic author must deal with his
actors, and with his actors alone. Certain moments of
suspense, certain significant dispositions of personages, a
certain logical growth of emotion, these are the only
means at the disposal of the playwright. It is true
that, with the assistance of the scene-painter, the cos-
tumier and the conductor of the orchestra, he may add
to this something of pageant, something of sound and
fury; but these are, for the dramatic writer, beside the
mark, and do not come under the vivifying touch of
his genius. When we turn to romance, we find this
no longer. Here nothing is reproduced to our senses
directly. Not only the main conception of the work,

but the scenery, the appliances, the mechanism by which this conception is brought home to us, have been put through the crucible of another man's mind, and come out again, one and all, in the form of written words. With the loss of every degree of such realism as we have described, there is for art a clear gain of liberty and largeness of competence. Thus, painting, in which the round outlines of things are thrown on to a flat board, is far more free than sculpture, in which their solidity is preserved. It is by giving up these identities that art gains true strength. And so in the case of novels as compared with the stage. Continuous narration is the flat board on to which the novelist throws everything. And from this there results for him a great loss of vividness, but a great compensating gain in his power over the subject; so that he can now subordinate one thing to another in importance, and introduce all manner of very subtle detail, to a degree that was before impossible. He can render just as easily the flourish of trumpets before a victorious emperor and the gossip of country market women, the gradual decay of forty years of a man's life and the gesture of a passionate moment. He finds himself equally unable, if he looks at it from one point of view—equally able, if he looks at it from another point of view—to reproduce a color, a sound, an outline, a logical argument, a physical action. He can show his readers, behind and around the personages that for the moment occupy the foreground of his story, the continual suggestion of the landscape; the turn of the weather that will turn with it men's lives and fortunes, dimly foreshadowed on the horizon; the fatality of

distant events, the stream of national tendency, the
salient framework of causation. And all this thrown
upon the flat board—all this entering, naturally and
smoothly, into the texture of continuous intelligent narration.

This touches the difference between Fielding and
Scott. In the work of the latter, true to his character
of a modern and a romantic, we become suddenly conscious of the background. Fielding, on the other hand,
although he had recognized that the novel was nothing
else than an epic in prose, wrote in the spirit not of
the epic, but of the drama. This is not, of course, to
say that the drama was in any way incapable of a
regeneration similar in kind to that of which I am
now speaking with regard to the novel. The notorious
contrary fact is sufficient to guard the reader against
such a misconstruction. All that is meant is, that
Fielding remained ignorant of certain capabilities which
the novel possesses over the drama; or, at least, neglected and did not develop them. To the end he continued to see things as a playwright sees them. The
world with which he dealt, the world he had realized
for himself and sought to realize and set before his
readers, was a world of exclusively human interest. As
for landscape, he was content to underline stage directions, as it might be done in a play-book: Tom and
Molly retire into a practicable wood. As for nationality
and public sentiment, it is curious enough to think that
Tom Jones is laid in the year forty-five, and that the
only use he makes of the rebellion is to throw a troop of
soldiers into his hero's way. It is most really important,
however, to remark the change which has been intro-

duced into the conception of character by the beginning of the romantic movement and the consequent introduction into fiction of a vast amount of new material. Fielding tells us as much as he thought necessary to account for the actions of his creatures; he thought that each of these actions could be decomposed on the spot into a few simple personal elements, as we decompose a force in a question of abstract dynamics. The larger motives are all unknown to him; he had not understood that the nature of the landscape or the spirit of the times could be for anything in a story; and so, naturally and rightly, he said nothing about them. But Scott's instinct, the instinct of the man of an age profoundly different, taught him otherwise; and, in his work, the individual characters begin to occupy a comparatively small proportion of that canvas on which armies maneuver, and great hills pile themselves upon each other's shoulders. Fielding's characters were always great to the full stature of a perfectly arbitrary will. Already in Scott we begin to have a sense of the subtle influences that moderate and qualify a man's personality; that personality is no longer thrown out in unnatural isolation, but is resumed into its place in the constitution of things.

It is this change in the manner of regarding men and their actions first exhibited in romance, that has since renewed and vivified history. For art precedes philosophy and even science. People must have noticed things and interested themselves in them before they begin to debate upon their causes or influence. And it is in this way that art is the pioneer of knowledge; those predilections of the artist he knows not why,

those irrational acceptations and recognitions, reclaim,
out of the world that we have not yet realized, ever
another and another corner; and after the facts have
been thus vividly brought before us and have had time
to settle and arrange themselves in our minds, some
day there will be found the man of science to stand
up and give the explanation. Scott took an interest in
many things in which Fielding took none; and for this
reason, and no other, he introduced them into his
romances. If he had been told what would be the
nature of the movement that he was so lightly initiat-
ing, he would have been very incredulous and not a
little scandalized. At the time when he wrote, the
real drift of this new manner of pleasing people in
fiction was not yet apparent; and, even now, it is only
by looking at the romances of Victor Hugo that we are
enabled to form any proper judgment in the matter.
These books are not only descended by ordinary generation from the Waverley novels, but it is in them
chiefly that we shall find the revolutionary tradition of
Scott carried further; that we shall find Scott himself,
in so far as regards his conception of prose fiction and
its purposes, surpassed in his own spirit instead of
tamely followed. We have here, as I said before, a
line of literary tendency produced, and by this production definitely separated from others. When we come
to Hugo, we see that the deviation, which seemed
slight enough and not very serious between Scott and
Fielding, is indeed such a great gulf in thought and
sentiment as only successive generations can pass over:
and it is but natural that one of the chief advances
that Hugo has made upon Scott is an advance in self-

consciousness. Both men follow the same road; but where the one went blindly and carelessly, the other advances with all deliberation and forethought. There never was artist much more unconscious than Scott; and there have been not many more conscious than Hugo. The passage at the head of these pages shows how organically he had understood the nature of his own changes. He has, underlying each of the five great romances (which alone I purpose here to examine), two deliberate designs: one artistic, the other consciously ethical and intellectual. This is a man living in a different world from Scott, who professes sturdily (in one of his introductions) that he does not believe in novels having any moral influence at all; but still Hugo is too much of an artist to let himself be hampered by his dogmas; and the truth is that the artistic result seems, in at least one great instance, to have very little connection with the other, or directly ethical result.

The artistic result of a romance, what is left upon the memory by any really powerful and artistic novel, is something so complicated and refined that it is difficult to put a name upon it; and yet something as simple as nature. These two propositions may seem mutually destructive, but they are so only in appearance. The fact is that art is working far ahead of language as well as of science, realizing for us, by all manner of suggestions and exaggerations, effects for which as yet we have no direct name; nay, for which we may never perhaps have a direct name, for the reason that these effects do not enter very largely into the necessities of life. Hence alone is that suspicion of

vagueness that often hangs about the purpose of a romance: it is clear enough to us in thought; but we
are not used to consider anything clear until we are
able to formulate it in words, and analytical language
has not been sufficiently shaped to that end. We all
know this difficulty in the case of a picture, simple
and strong as may be the impression that it has left
with us; and it is only because language is the medium of romance, that we are prevented from seeing that
the two cases are the same. It is not that there is
anything blurred or indefinite in the impression left
with us, it is just because the impression is so very
definite after its own kind, that we find it hard to fit
it exactly with the expressions of our philosophical
speech.

It is this idea which underlies and issues from a
romance, this something which it is the function of
that form of art to create, this epical value, that I
propose chiefly to seek and, as far as may be, to
throw into relief, in the present study. It is thus, I
believe, that we shall see most clearly the great stride
that Hugo has taken beyond his predecessors, and how,
no longer content with expressing more or less abstract
relations of man to man, he has set before himself the
task of realizing, in the language of romance, much of
the involution of our complicated lives.

This epical value is not to be found, let it be understood, in every so-called novel. The great majority
are not works of art in anything but a very secondary
signification. One might almost number on one's fingers
the works in which such a supreme artistic intention
has been in any way superior to the other and lesser

aims, themselves more or less artistic, that generally go hand in hand with it in the conception of prose romance. The purely critical spirit is, in most novels, paramount. At the present moment we can recall one man only, for whose works it would have been equally possible to accomplish our present design: and that man is Hawthorne. There is a unity, an unwavering creative purpose, about some at least of Hawthorne's romances, that impresses itself on the most indifferent reader; and the very restrictions and weaknesses of the man served perhaps to strengthen the vivid and single impression of his works. There is nothing of this kind in Hugo: unity, if he attains to it, is indeed unity out of multitude; and it is the wonderful power of subordination and synthesis thus displayed, that gives us the measure of his talent. No amount of mere discussion and statement, such as this, could give a just conception of the greatness of this power. It must be felt in the books themselves, and all that can be done in the present essay is to recall to the reader the more general features of each of the five great romances, hurriedly and imperfectly, as space will permit, and rather as a suggestion than anything more complete.

The moral end that the author had before him in the conception of "Notre Dame de Paris" was (he tells us) to "denounce" the external fatality that hangs over men in the form of foolish and inflexible superstition. To speak plainly, this moral purpose seems to have mighty little to do with the artistic conception; moreover it is very questionably handled, while the artistic conception is developed with the most consum-

mate success. Old Paris lives for us with newness of
life: we have ever before our eyes the city cut into
three by the two arms of the river, the boat-shaped
island "moored" by five bridges to the different shores,
and the two unequal towns on either hand. We forget
all that enumeration of palaces and churches and con-
vents which occupies so many pages of admirable description, and the thoughtless reader might be inclined
to conclude from this that they were pages thrown
away; but this is not so: we forget, indeed, the details, as we forget or do not see the different layers of
paint on a completed picture; but the thing desired has
been accomplished, and we carry away with us a sense
of the "Gothic profile" of the city, of the "surprising
forest of pinnacles and towers and belfries," and we
know not what of rich and intricate and quaint. And
throughout, Notre Dame has been held up over Paris
by a height far greater than that of its twin towers:
the Cathedral is present to us from the first page to
the last; the title has given us the clew, and already
in the Palace of Justice the story begins to attach itself
to that central building by character after character. It
is purely an effect of mirage; Notre Dame does not,
in reality, thus dominate and stand out above the city;
and any one who should visit it, in the spirit of the
Scott-tourists to Edinburgh or the Trossachs, would be
almost offended at finding nothing more than this old
church thrust away into a corner. It is purely an
effect of mirage, as we say; but it is an effect that
permeates and possesses the whole book with astonishing consistency and strength. And then, Hugo has peopled this Gothic city, and, above all, this Gothic church,

with a race of men even more distinctly Gothic than
their surroundings. We know this generation already;
we have seen them clustered about the worn capitals
of pillars, or craning forth over the church-leads with
the open mouths of gargoyles. About them all there is
that sort of stiff quaint unreality, that conjunction of
the grotesque, and even of a certain bourgeois snugness,
with passionate contortion and horror, that is so characteristic of Gothic art. Esmeralda is somewhat an exception; she and the goat traverse the story like two
children who have wandered in a dream. The finest
moment of the book is when these two share with the
two other leading characters, Dom Claude and Quasimodo, the chill shelter of the old cathedral. It is here
that we touch most intimately the generative artistic
idea of the romance: are they not all four taken out
of some quaint molding, illustrative of the Beatitudes,
or the Ten Commandments, or the seven deadly sins?
What is Quasimodo but an animated gargoyle? What
is the whole book but the reanimation of Gothic art?

It is curious that in this, the earliest of the five
great romances, there should be so little of that ex-
travagance that latterly we have come almost to identify
with the author's manner. Yet even here we are dis-
tressed by words, thoughts, and incidents that defy belief and alienate the sympathies. The scene of the *in
pace*, for example, in spite of its strength, verges dangerously on the province of the penny novelist. I do
not believe that Quasimodo rode upon the bell; I should
as soon imagine that he swung by the clapper. And
again the following two sentences, out of an otherwise
admirable chapter, surely surpass what it has ever en-

tered into the heart of any other man to imagine (vol.
ii., p. 180): "Il souffrait tant que par instants il s'ar-
rachait des poignees de cheveux, *pour voir s'ils ne
blanchissaient pas.*" And, p. 181: "Ses pensees etaient
si insupportables qu'il prenait sa tête à deux mains et
tâchait de l'arracher de ses epaules *pour la briser sur
le pave.*"

One other fault, before we pass on. In spite of the
horror and misery that pervade all of his later work,
there is in it much less of actual melodrama than here,
and rarely, I should say never, that sort of brutality,
that useless insufferable violence to the feelings, which is
the last distinction between melodrama and true tragedy.
Now, in "Notre Dame," the whole story of Esmeralda's
passion for the worthless archer is unpleasant enough;
but when she betrays herself in her last hiding-place,
herself and her wretched mother, by calling out to this
sordid hero who has long since forgotten her—well, that
is just one of those things that readers will not forgive; they do not like it, and they are quite right;
life is hard enough for poor mortals, without having it
indefinitely imbittered for them by bad art.

We look in vain for any similar blemish in "Les
Miserables." Here, on the other hand, there is perhaps
the nearest approach to literary restraint that Hugo has
ever made: there is here certainly the ripest and most
easy development of his powers. It is the moral intention of this great novel to awaken us a little, if it
may be—for such awakenings are unpleasant—to the
great cost of this society that we enjoy and profit by,
to the labor and sweat of those who support the litter,

civilization, in which we ourselves are so smoothly carried forward. People are all glad to shut their eyes;
and it gives them a very simple pleasure when they
can forget that our laws commit a million individual
injustices, to be once roughly just in the general; that
the bread that we eat, and the quiet of the family,
and all that embellishes life and makes it worth having, have to be purchased by death—by the deaths of
animals, and the deaths of men wearied out with labor,
and the deaths of those criminals called tryants and
revolutionaries, and the deaths of those revolutionaries
called criminals. It is to something of all this that
Victor Hugo wishes to open men's eyes in "Les Miserables"; and this moral lesson is worked out in masterly
coincidence with the artistic effect. The deadly weight
of civilization to those who are below presses sensibly
on our shoulders as we read. A sort of mocking indignation grows upon us as we find Society rejecting,
again and again, the services of the most serviceable;
setting Jean Valjean to pick oakum, casting Galileo
into prison, even crucifying Christ. There is a haunt-
ing and horrible sense of insecurity about the book.
The terror we thus feel is a terror for the machinery
of law, that we can hear tearing, in the dark, good
and bad between its formidable wheels with the iron
stolidity of all machinery, human or divine. This terror incarnates itself sometimes and leaps horribly out
upon us; as when the crouching mendicant looks up,
and Jean Valjean, in the light of the street lamp,
recognizes the face of the detective; as when the lantern of the patrol flashes suddenly through the darkness
of the sewer; or as when the fugitive comes forth at

last at evening, by the quiet riverside, and finds the police there also, waiting stolidly for vice and stolidly satisfied to take virtue instead. The whole book is full of oppression, and full of prejudice, which is the great cause of oppression. We have the prejudices of M. Gillenormand, the prejudices of Marius, the prejudices in revolt that defend the barricade, and the throned prejudices that carry it by storm. And then we have the admirable but ill-written character of Javert, the man who had made a religion of the police, and would not survive the moment when he learned that there was another truth outside the truth of laws; a just creation, over which the reader will do well to ponder.

With so gloomy a design this great work is still full of life and light and love. The portrait of the good Bishop is one of the most agreeable things in modern literature. The whole scene at Montfermeil is full of the charm that Hugo knows so well how to throw about children. Who can forget the passage where Cosette, sent out at night to draw water, stands in admiration before the illuminated booth, and the huckster behind "lui faisait un peu l'effet d'être le Pere eternel?" The pathos of the forlorn sabot laid trustingly by the chimney in expectation of the Santa Claus that was not, takes us fairly by the throat; there is nothing in Shakespeare that touches the heart more nearly. The loves of Cosette and Marius are very pure and pleasant, and we cannot refuse our affection to Gavroche, although we may make a mental reservation of our profound disbelief in his existence. Take it for all in all, there are few books in the world that can be compared with it. There is as much calm and serenity as Hugo has ever attained to; the melodramatic coarsenesses that dis-figured "Notre Dame" are no longer present.   There is certainly much that is painfully improbable; and again, the story itself is a little too well constructed; it produces on us the effect of a puzzle, and we grow incredulous as we find that every character fits again and again into the plot, and is, like the child's cube, serviceable on six faces; things are not so well arranged in life as all that comes to.   Some of the digressions, also, seem out of place, and do nothing but interrupt and irritate.   But when all is said, the book remains of masterly conception and of masterly development, full of pathos, full of truth, full of a high eloquence.

Superstition and social exigency having been thus dealt with in the first two members of the series, it remained for "Les Travailleurs de la Mer" to show man hand to hand with the elements, the last form of external force that is brought against him.   And here once more the artistic effect and the moral lesson are worked out together, and are, indeed, one.   Gilliat, alone upon the reef at his herculean task, offers a type of human industry in the midst of the vague "diffusion of forces into the illimitable," and the visionary develop-ment of "wasted labor" in the sea, and the winds, and the clouds.   No character was ever thrown into such strange relief as Gilliat.   The great circle of sea-birds that come wonderingly around him on the night of his arrival, strikes at once the note of his pre-eminence and isolation.   He fills the whole reef with his indefati-gable toil; this solitary spot in the ocean rings with the clamor of his anvil; we see him as he comes and

goes, thrown out sharply against the clear background
of the sea. And yet his isolation is not to be compared with the isolation of Robinson Crusoe, for example; indeed, no two books could be more instructive
to set side by side than "Les Travailleurs" and this
other of the old days before art had learned to occupy
itself with what lies outside of human will. Crusoe
was one sole center of interest in the midst of a nature utterly dead and utterly unrealized by the artist;
but this is not how we feel with Gilliat; we feel that
he is opposed by a "dark coalition of forces," that an
"immense animosity" surrounds him; we are the witnesses of the terrible warfare that he wages with "the
silent inclemency of phenomena going their own way,
and the great general law, implacable and passive":
"a conspiracy of the indifferency of things" is against
him. There is not one interest on the reef, but two.
Just as we recognize Gilliat for the hero, we recognize,
as implied by this indifferency of things, this direction
of forces to some purpose outside our purposes, yet
another character who may almost take rank as the
villain of the novel, and the two face up to one another
blow for blow, feint for feint, until, in the storm, they
fight it epically out, and Gilliat remains the victor;—a
victor, however, who has still to encounter the octopus.
I need say nothing of the gruesome, repulsive excellence
of that famous scene; it will be enough to remind the
reader that Gilliat is in pursuit of a crab when he is
himself assaulted by the devil fish, and that this, in
its way, is the last touch to the inner significance of
the book; here, indeed, is the true position of man in
the universe.

But in "Les Travailleurs," with all its strength, with all its eloquence, with all the beauty and fitness of its main situations, we cannot conceal from ourselves that there is a thread of something that will not bear calm scrutiny. There is much that is disquieting about the storm, admirably as it begins. I am very doubtful whether it would be possible to keep the boat from foundering in such circumstances, by any amount of breakwater and broken rock. I do not understand the way in which the waves are spoken of, and prefer just to take it as a loose way of speaking, and pass on. And lastly, how does it happen that the sea was quite calm next day? Is this great hurricane a piece of scene-painting after all? And when we have forgiven Gilliat's prodigies of strength (although, in soberness, he reminds us more of Porthos in the Vicomte de Brage-lonne than is quite desirable), what is to be said to his suicide, and how are we to condemn in adequate terms that unprincipled avidity after effect, which tells us that the sloop disappeared over the horizon, and the head under the water, at one and the same moment? Monsieur Hugo may say what he will, but we know better; we know very well that they did not; a thing like that raises up a despairing spirit of opposition in a man's readers; they give him the lie fiercely, as they read. Lastly, we have here already some beginning of that curious series of English blunders, that makes us wonder if there are neither proof sheets nor judicious friends in the whole of France, and affects us some-times with a sickening uneasiness as to what may be our own exploits when we touch upon foreign countries and foreign tongues. It is here that we shall find the

famous "first of the fourth," and many English words
that may be comprehensible perhaps in Paris. It is
here that we learn that "laird" in Scotland is the same
title as "lord" in England. Here, also, is an account
of a Highland soldier's equipment, which we recommend
to the lovers of genuine fun.

In "L'Homme qui Rit," it was Hugo's object to
"denounce" (as he would say himself) the aristocratic
principle as it was exhibited in England; and this purpose, somewhat more unmitigatedly satiric than that of
the two last, must answer for much that is unpleasant
in the book. The repulsiveness of the scheme of the
story, and the manner in which it is bound up with
impossibilities and absurdities, discourage the reader at
the outset, and it needs an effort to take it as seriously
as it deserves. And yet when we judge it deliberately,
it will be seen that, here again, the story is admirably
adapted to the moral. The constructive ingenuity exhibited throughout is almost morbid. Nothing could be
more happily imagined, as a *reductio ad absurdum* of
the aristocratic principle, than the adventures of Gwyn-
plaine, the itinerant mountebank, snatched suddenly out
of his little way of life, and installed without preparation as one of the hereditary legislators of a great
country. It is with a very bitter irony that the paper,
on which all this depends, is left to float for years at
the will of wind and tide. What, again, can be finer
in conception than that voice from the people heard suddenly in the House of Lords, in solemn arraignment of
the pleasures and privileges of its splendid occupants?
The horrible laughter, stamped forever "by order of

the king" upon the face of this strange spokesman of democracy, adds yet another feature of justice to the scene; in all time, travesty has been the argument of oppression; and, in all time, the oppressed might have made this answer: "If I am vile, is it not your system that has made me so?" This ghastly laughter gives occasion, moreover, for the one strain of tenderness running through the web of this unpleasant story: the love of the blind girl Dea for the monster. It is a most benignant providence that thus harmoniously brings together these two misfortunes; it is one of those compensations, one of those afterthoughts of a relenting destiny, that reconcile us from time to time to the evil that is in the world; the atmosphere of the book is purified by the presence of this pathetic love; it seems to be above the story somehow, and not of it, as the full moon over the night of some foul and feverish city.

There is here a quality in the narration more intimate and particular than is general with Hugo; but it must be owned, on the other hand, that the book is wordy, and even, now and then, a little wearisome. Ursus and his wolf are pleasant enough companions; but the former is nearly as much an abstract type as the latter. There is a beginning, also, of an abuse of conventional conversation, such as may be quite pardonable in the drama where needs must, but is without excuse in the romance. Lastly, I suppose one must say a word or two about the weak points of this not immaculate novel; and if so, it will be best to distinguish at once. The large family of English blunders, to which we have alluded already in speaking of "Les

Travailleurs," are of a sort that is really indifferent in art. If Shakespeare makes his ships cast anchor by some seaport of Bohemia, if Hugo imagines Tom-Tim-Jack to be a likely nickname for an English sailor, or if either Shakespeare, or Hugo, or Scott, for that matter, be guilty of "figments enough to confuse the march of a whole history—anachronisms enough to overset all chronology," * the life of their creations, the artistic truth and accuracy of their work, is not so much as compromised. But when we come upon a passage like the sinking of the "Ourque" in this romance, we can do nothing but cover our face with our hands: the conscientious reader feels a sort of disgrace in the very reading. For such artistic falsehoods, springing from what I have called already an unprincipled avidity after effect, no amount of blame can be exaggerated; and above all, when the criminal is such a man as Victor Hugo. We cannot forgive in him what we might have passed over in a third-rate sensation novelist. Little as he seems to know of the sea and nautical affairs, he must have known very well that vessels do not go down as he makes the "Ourque" go down; he must have known that such a liberty with fact was against the laws of the game, and incompatible with all appearance of sincerity in conception or workmanship.

In each of these books, one after another, there has been some departure from the traditional canons of romance; but taking each separately, one would have feared to make too much of these departures, or to

---

* Prefatory letter to "Peveril of the Peak."

found any theory upon what was perhaps purely acci-
dental. The appearance of "Quatre Vingt Treize" has
put us out of the region of such doubt. Like a doctor
who has long been hesitating how to classify an epidemic malady, we have come at last upon a case so
well marked that our uncertainty is at an end. It is
a novel built upon "a sort of enigma," which was at
that date laid before revolutionary France, and which
is presented by Hugo to Tellmarch, to Lantenac, to
Gauvain, and very terribly to Cimourdain, each of whom
gives his own solution of the question, clement or stern,
according to the temper of his spirit. That enigma was
this: "Can a good action be a bad action? Does not
he who spares the wolf kill the sheep?" This question,
as I say, meets with one answer after another during
the course of the book, and yet seems to remain un-
decided to the end. And something in the same way,
although one character, or one set of characters, after
another comes to the front and occupies our attention
for the moment, we never identify our interest with
any of these temporary heroes nor regret them after
they are withdrawn. We soon come to regard them
somewhat as special cases of a general law; what we
really care for . is something that they only imply and
body forth to us. We know how history continues
through century after century; how this king or that
patriot disappears from its pages with his whole generation, and yet we do not cease to read, nor do we
even feel as if we had reached any legitimate conclusion,
because our interest is not in the men, but in the
country that they loved or hated, benefited or injured.
And so it is here: Gauvain and Cimourdain pass away,

and we regard them no more than the lost armies of which we find the cold statistics in military annals; what we regard is what remains behind; it is the principle that put these men where they were, that filled them for a while with heroic inspiration, and has the power, now that they are fallen, to inspire others with the same courage. The interest of the novel centers about revolutionary France: just as the plot is an abstract judicial difficulty, the hero is an abstract historical force. And this has been done, not, as it would have been before, by the cold and cumbersome machinery of allegory, but with bold, straightforward realism, dealing only with the objective materials of art, and dealing with them so masterfully that the palest abstractions of thought come before us, and move our hopes and fears, as if they were the young men and maidens of customary romance.

The episode of the mother and children in "Quatre Vingt Treize" is equal to anything that Hugo has ever written There is one chapter in the second volume, for instance, called "Sein gueri, cœur saignant," that is full of the very stuff of true tragedy, and nothing could be more delightful than the humors of the three children on the day before the assault. The passage on La Vendee is really great, and the scenes in Paris have much of the same broad merit. The book is full, as usual, of pregnant and splendid sayings. But when thus much is conceded by way of praise, we come to the other scale of the balance, and find this, also, somewhat heavy. There is here a yet greater over-employment of conventional dialogue than in "L'Homme qui Rit"; and much that should have been said by the author himself, if it were to be said at all, he has most unwarrantably put into the mouths of one or other of his characters. We should like to know what becomes of the main body of the troop in the wood of La Saudraie during the thirty pages or so in which the foreguard lays aside all discipline, and stops to gossip over a woman and some children. We have an unpleasant idea forced upon us at one place, in spite of all the good-natured incredulity that we can summon up to resist it. Is it possible that Monsieur Hugo thinks they ceased to steer the corvette while the gun was loose? Of the chapter in which Lantenac and Halmalho are alone together in the boat, the less said the better; of course, if there were nothing else, they would have been swamped thirty times over during the course of Lantenac's harangue. Again, after Lantenac has landed, we have scenes of almost inimitable workmanship that suggest the epithet "statuesque" by their clear and trenchant outline; but the tocsin scene will not do, and the tocsin unfortunately pervades the whole passage, ringing continually in our ears with a taunting accusation of falsehood. And then, when we come to the place where Lantenac meets the Royalists, under the idea that he is going to meet the Republicans, it seems as if there were a hitch in the stage mechanism. I have tried it over in every way, and I cannot conceive any disposition that would make the scene possible as narrated.

Such then, with their faults and their signal excellences, are the five great novels.

Romance is a language in which many persons learn to speak with a certain appearance of fluency; but there

are few who can ever bend it to any practical need,
few who can ever be said to express themselves in it.
It has become abundantly plain in the foregoing examination that Victor Hugo occupies a high place among
those few. He has always a perfect command over his
stories; and we see that they are constructed with a
high regard to some ulterior purpose, and that every
situation is informed with moral significance and grandeur. Of no other man can the same thing be said in
the same degree. His romances are not to be confused
with "the novel with a purpose" as familiar to the
English reader: this is generally the model of incompe-
tence; and we see the moral clumsily forced into every
hole and corner of the story, or thrown externally over
it like a carpet over a railing. Now the moral significance, with Hugo, is of the essence of the romance;
it is the organizing principle. If you could somehow
despoil "Les Miserables" or "Les Travailleurs" of their
distinctive lesson, you would find that the story had
lost its interest and the book was dead.

Having thus learned to subordinate his story to an
idea, to make his art speak, he went on to teach it to
say things heretofore unaccustomed. If you look back
at the five books of which we have now so hastily
spoken, you will be astonished at the freedom with
which the original purposes of story-telling have been
laid aside and passed by. Where are now the two
lovers who descended the main watershed of all the
Waverley novels, and all the novels that have tried to
follow in their wake? Sometimes they are almost lost
sight of before the solemn isolation of a man against
the sea and sky, as in "Les Travailleurs"; sometimes,

as in "Les Miserables," they merely figure for a while,
as a beautiful episode in the epic of oppression; sometimes they are entirely absent, as in "Quatre Vingt
Treize." There is no hero in "Notre Dame": in "Les
Miserables" it is an old man: in "L'Homme qui Rit"
it is a monster: in "Quatre Vingt Treize" it is the
Revolution. Those elements that only began to show
themselves timidly, as adjuncts, in the novels of Walter
Scott, have usurped ever more and more of the canvas;
until we find the whole interest of one of Hugo's
romances centering around matter that Fielding would
have banished from his altogether, as being out of the
field of fiction. So we have elemental forces occupying
nearly as large a place, playing (so to speak) nearly as
important a role, as the man, Gilliat, who opposes and
overcomes them. So we find the fortunes of a nation
put upon the stage with as much vividness as ever
before the fortunes of a village maiden or a lost heir;
and the forces that oppose and corrupt a principle holding the attention quite as strongly as the wicked barons
or dishonest attorneys of the past. Hence those individual interests that were supreme in Fielding, and even
in Scott, stood out over everything else and formed, as
it were, the spine of the story, figure here only as
one set of interests among many sets, one force among
many forces, one thing to be treated out of a whole
world of things equally vivid and important. So that,
for Hugo, man is no longer an isolated spirit without
antecedent or relation here below, but a being involved
in the action and reaction of natural forces, himself a
center of such action and reaction; or a unit in a great
multitude, chased hither and thither by epidemic terrors

and aspirations, and, in all seriousness, blown about by every wind of doctrine. This is a long way that we have traveled: between such work and the work of Fielding is there not, indeed, a great gulf in thought and sentiment?

Art, thus conceived, realizes for men a larger portion of life, and that portion one that it is more difficult for them to realize unaided; and besides helping them to feel more intensely those restricted personal interests which are patent to all, it awakes in them some consciousness of those more general relations that are so strangely invisible to the average man in ordinary moods. It helps to keep man in his place in nature, and, above all, it helps him to understand more intelligently the responsibilities of his place in society. And in all this generalization of interest, we never miss those small humanities that are at the opposite pole of excellence in art; and while we admire the intellect that could see life thus largely, we are touched with another sentiment for the tender heart that slipped the piece of gold into Cosette's sabot, that was virginally troubled at the fluttering of her dress in the spring wind, or put the blind girl beside the deformity of the laughing man. This, then, is the last praise that we can award to these romances. The author has shown a power of just subordination hitherto unequaled; and as, in reaching forward to one class of effects, he has not been forgetful or careless of the other, his work is more nearly complete work, and his art, with all its imperfections, deals more comprehensively with the materials of life than that of any of his otherwise more sure and masterly predecessors.

These five books would have made a very great

fame for any writer, and yet they are but one façade
of the monument that Victor Hugo has erected to his
genius. Everywhere we find somewhat the same greatness, somewhat the same infirmities. In his poems and
plays there are the same unaccountable protervities that
have already astonished us in the romances. There, too,
is the same feverish strength, welding the fiery iron of
his idea under forge-hammer repetitions—an emphasis
that is somehow akin to weakness—a strength that is a
little epileptic. He stands so far above all his contemporaries, and so incomparably excels them in richness,
breadth, variety, and moral earnestness, that we almost
feel as if he had a sort of right to fall oftener and
more heavily than others; but this does not reconcile
us to seeing him profit by the privilege so freely. We
like to have, in our great men, something that is above
question; we like to place an implicit faith in them,
and see them always on the platform of their greatness; and this, unhappily, cannot be with Hugo. As
Heine said long ago, his is a genius somewhat deformed; but, deformed as it is, we accept it gladly;
we shall have the wisdom to see where his foot slips,
but we shall have the justice also to recognize in him
one of the greatest artists of our generation, and, in
many ways, one of the greatest artists of time. If we
look back, yet once, upon these five romances, we see
blemishes such as we can lay to the charge of no other
man in the number of the famous; but to what other
man can we attribute such sweeping innovations, such a
new and significant presentment of the life of man, such
an amount, if we merely think of the amount, of equally
consummate performance?

SOME ASPECTS OF ROBERT BURNS

To write with authority about another man, we must have fellow-feeling and some common ground of experience with our subject. We may praise or blame according as we find him related to us by the best or worst in ourselves; but it is only in virtue of some relationship that we can be his judges, even to condemn. Feelings which we share and understand enter for us into the tissue of the man's character; those to which we are strangers in our own experience we are inclined to regard as blots, exceptions, inconsistencies, and excursions of the diabolic; we conceive them with repugnance, explain them with difficulty, and raise our hands to heaven in wonder when we find them in conjunction with talents that we respect or virtues that we admire. David, king of Israel, would pass a sounder judgment on a man than either Nathaniel or David Hume. Now, Principal Shairp's recent volume, although I believe no one will read it without respect and interest, has this one capital defect—that there is imperfect sympathy between the author and the subject, between the critic and the personality under criticism. Hence an inorganic, if not an incoherent, presentation of both the poems and the man. Of "Holy Willie's Prayer," Principal Shairp remarks that "those who have loved most what was best in Burns's poetry must have regretted that it was ever written." To the "Jolly Beggars," so far as my memory serves me, he refers but once; and then only to remark on the "strange, not to say painful," circumstance that the same hand which wrote the "Cotter's Saturday Night" should have stooped to write the "Jolly Beggars." The "Saturday Night" may or may not be an admirable poem; but its significance is trebled, and the power and range of the poet first appears, when it is set beside the "Jolly Beggars." To take a man's work piecemeal, except with the design of elegant extracts, is the way to avoid, and not to perform, the critic's duty. The same defect is displayed in the treatment of Burns as a man, which is broken, apologetical, and confused. The man here presented to us is not that Burns, teres atque rotundus—a burly figure in literature, as, from our present vantage of time, we have begun to see him. This, on the other hand, is Burns as he may have appeared to a contemporary clergyman, whom we shall conceive to have been a kind and indulgent but orderly and orthodox person, anxious to be pleased, but too often hurt and disappointed by the behavior of his red-hot protege, and solacing himself with the explanation that the poet was "the most inconsistent of men." If you are so sensibly pained by the misconduct of your subject, and so paternally delighted with his virtues, you will always be an excellent gentleman, but a somewhat questionable biographer. Indeed, we can only be sorry and surprised that Principal Shairp should have chosen a theme so uncongenial. When we find a man writing on Burns, who likes neither "Holy Willie," nor the "Beggars," nor the "Ordination," nothing is

adequate to the situation but the old cry of Geronte:
"Que diable allait-il faire dans cette galere?" And
every merit we find in the book, which is sober and
candid in a degree unusual with biographies of Burns,
only leads us to regret more heartily that good work
should be so greatly thrown away.

It is far from my intention to tell over again a
story that has been so often told; but there are certainly some points in the character of Burns that will
bear to be brought out, and some chapters in his life
that demand a brief rehearsal. The unity of the man's
nature, for all its richness, has fallen somewhat out of
sight in the pressure of new information and the apologetical ceremony of biographers. Mr. Carlyle made an
inimitable bust of the poet's head of gold; may I not
be forgiven if my business should have more to do
with the feet, which were of clay?

YOUTH

Any view of Burns would be misleading which
passed over in silence the influences of his home and
his father. That father, William Burnes, after having
been for many years a gardener, took a farm, married, and, like an emigrant in a new country, built
himself a house with his own hands. Poverty of the
most distressing sort, with sometimes the near prospect
of a jail, imbittered the remainder of his life. Chill,
backward, and austere with strangers, grave and imperious in his family, he was yet a man of very unusual
parts and of an affectionate nature. On his way through
life he had remarked much upon other men, with more

result in theory than practice; and he had reflected upon many subjects as he delved the garden. His great delight was in solid conversation; he would leave his work to talk with the schoolmaster Murdoch; and Robert, when he came home late at night, not only turned aside rebuke but kept his father two hours beside the fire by the charm of his merry and vigorous talk. Nothing is more characteristic of the class in general, and William Burnes in particular, than the pains he took to get proper schooling for his boys, and, when that was no longer possible, the sense and resolution with which he set himself to supply the deficiency by his own influence. For many years he was their chief companion; he spoke with them seriously on all subjects as if they had been grown men; at night, when work was over, he taught them arithmetic; he borrowed books for them on history, science, and theology; and he felt it his duty to supplement this last —the trait is laughably Scottish—by a dialogue of his own composition, where his own private shade of orthodoxy was exactly represented. He would go to his daughter as she stayed afield herding cattle, to teach her the names of grasses and wild flowers, or to sit by her side when it thundered. Distance to strangers, deep family tenderness, love of knowledge, a narrow, precise, and formal reading of theology—everything we learn of him hangs well together, and builds up a popular Scotch type. If I mention the name of Andrew Fairservice, it is only as I might couple for an instant Dugald Dalgetty with old Marshal Loudon, to help out the reader's comprehension by a popular but unworthy instance of a class. Such was the influence

of this good and wise man that his household became
a school to itself, and neighbors who came into the
farm at meal time would find the whole family, father,
brothers, and sisters, helping themselves with one hand,
and holding a book in the other. We are surprised at
the prose style of Robert; that of Gilbert need surprise
us no less; even William writes a remarkable letter for
a young man of such slender opportunities. One anec-
dote marks the taste of the family. Murdoch brought
"Titus Andronicus," and, with such dominie elocution
as we may suppose, began to read it aloud before this
rustic audience; but when he had reached the passage
where Tamora insults Lavinia, with one voice and "in
an agony of distress" they refused to hear it to an
end. In such a father and with such a home, Robert
had already the making of an excellent education; and
what Murdoch added, although it may not have been
much in amount, was in character the very essence of
a literary training. Schools and colleges, for one great
man whom they complete, perhaps unmake a dozen;
the strong spirit can do well upon more scanty fare.

Robert steps before us, almost from the first, in his
complete character—a proud, headstrong, impetuous lad,
greedy of pleasure, greedy of notice; in his own phrase
"panting after distinction," and in his brother's "cher-
ishing a particular jealousy of people who were richer
or of more consequence than himself": with all this,
he was emphatically of the artist nature. Already he
made a conspicuous figure in Tarbolton church, with
the only tied hair in the parish, "and his plaid, which
was of a particular color, wrapped in a particular manner round his shoulders." Ten years later, when a

married man, the father of a family, a farmer, and an officer of Excise, we shall find him out fishing in masquerade, with fox-skin cap, belted greatcoat, and great Highland broadsword. He liked dressing up, in fact, for its own sake. This is the spirit which leads to the extravagant array of Latin Quarter students, and the proverbial velveteen of the English landscape-painter; and, though the pleasure derived is in itself merely personal, it shows a man who is, to say the least of it, not pained by general attention and remark. His father wrote the family name *Burnes;* Robert early adopted the orthography *Burness* from his cousin in the Mearns; and in his twenty-eighth year changed it once more to *Burns.* It is plain that the last trans-formation was not made without some qualm; for in addressing his cousin he adheres, in at least one more letter, to spelling number two. And this, again, shows a man preoccupied about the manner of his appearance even down to the name, and little willing to follow custom. Again, he was proud, and justly proud, of his powers in conversation. To no other man's have we the same conclusive testimony from different sources and from every rank of life. It is almost a common-place that the best of his works was what he said in talk. Robertson, the historian, "scarcely ever met any man whose conversation displayed greater vigor"; the Duchess of Gordon declared that he "carried her off her feet"; and, when he came late to an inn, the servants would get out of bed to hear him talk. But, in these early days at least, he was determined to shine by any means. He made himself feared in the village for his tongue. He would crush weaker men to

their faces, or even perhaps —for the statement of Sillar
is not absolute—say cutting things of his acquaintances
behind their back. At the church door, between sermons, he would parade his religious views amid hisses.
These details stamp the man. He had no genteel timidities in the conduct of his life. He loved to force his
personality upon the world. He would please himself,
and shine. Had he lived in the Paris of 1830, and
joined his lot with the Romantics, we can conceive him
writing *Jehan* for *Jean*, swaggering in Gautier's red
waistcoat, and horrifying Bourgeois in a public cafe
with paradox and gasconnade.

A leading trait throughout his whole career was his
desire to be in love. *Ne fait pas ce tour qui veut.*
His affections were often enough touched, but perhaps
never engaged. He was all his life on a voyage of
discovery, but it does not appear conclusively that he
ever touched the happy isle. A man brings to love a
deal of ready-made sentiment, and even from childhood
obscurely prognosticates the symptoms of this vital
malady. Burns was formed for love; he had passion,
tenderness, and a singular bent in the direction; he
could foresee, with the intuition of an artist, what love
ought to be; and he could not conceive a worthy life
without it. But he had ill-fortune, and was besides so
greedy after every shadow of the true divinity, and so
much the slave of a strong temperament, that perhaps
his nerve was relaxed and his heart had lost the power
of self-devotion before an opportunity occurred. The circumstances of his youth doubtless counted for something in the result. For the lads of Ayrshire, as soon
as the day's work was over and the beasts were

stabled, would take the road, it might be in a winter
tempest, and travel perhaps miles by moss and moorland to spend an hour or two in courtship. Rule 10
of the Bachelor's Club at Tarbolton provides that "every
man proper for a member of this Society must be a
professed lover of *one or more* of the female sex." The
rich, as Burns himself points out, may have a choice
of pleasurable occupations, but these lads had nothing
but their "cannie hour at e'en. ' It was upon love and
flirtation that this rustic society was built; gallantry
was the essence of life among the Ayrshire hills as
well as in the Court of Versailles; and the days were
distinguished from each other by love-letters, meetings,
tiffs, reconciliations, and expansions to the chosen confidant, as in a comedy of Marivaux. Here was a field
for a man of Burns's indiscriminate personal ambition,
where he might pursue his voyage of discovery in quest
of true love, and enjoy temporary triumphs by the way.
He was "constantly the victim of some fair enslaver"
—at least, when it was not the other way about; and
there were often underplots and secondary fair enslavers
in the background. Many—or may we not say most?
—of these affairs were entirely artificial. One, he tells
us, he began out of "a vanity of showing his parts in
courtship," for he piqued himself on his ability at a
love-letter. But, however they began, these flames of
his were fanned into a passion ere the end; and he
stands unsurpassed in his power of self-deception, and
positively without a competitor in the art, to use his
own words, of "battering himself into a warm affection"—a debilitating and futile exercise. Once he had
worked himself into the vein, "the agitations of his

mind and body" were an astonishment to all who knew him. Such a course as this, however pleasant to a thirsty vanity, was lowering to his nature. He sank more and more toward the professional Don Juan. With a leer of what the French call fatuity, he bids the belles of Mauchline beware of his seductions; and the same cheap self-satisfaction finds a yet uglier vent when he plumes himself on the scandal at the birth of his first bastard. We can well believe what we hear of his facility in striking up an acquaintance with women: he would have conquering manners; he would bear down upon his rustic game with the grace that comes of absolute assurance—the Richelieu of Lochlea or Mossgiel. In yet another manner did these quaint ways of courtship help him into fame. If he were great as principal, he was unrivaled as confidant. He could enter into a passion; he could counsel wary moves, being, in his own phrase, so old a hawk; nay, he could turn a letter for some unlucky swain, or even string a few lines of verse that should clinch the business and fetch the hesitating fair one to the ground. Nor, perhaps, was it only his "curiosity, zeal, and intrepid dexterity" that recommended him for a second in such affairs; it must have been a distinction to have the assistance and advice of "Rab the Ranter"; and one who was in no way formidable by himself might grow dangerous and attractive through the fame of his associate.

I think we can conceive him, in these early years, in that rough moorland country, poor among the poor with his seven pounds a year, looked upon with doubt by respectable elders, but for all that the best talker,

the best letter-writer, the most famous lover and confidant, the laureate poet, and the only man who wore
his hair tied in the parish. He says he had then as
high a notion of himself as ever after; and I can well
believe it. Among the youth he walked *facile princeps*,
an apparent god; and even if, from time to time, the
Reverend Mr. Auld should swoop upon him with the
thunders of the Church, and, in company with seven
others, Rab the Ranter must figure some fine Sunday
on the stool of repentance, would there not be a sort
of glory, an infernal apotheosis, in so conspicuous a
shame? Was not Richelieu in disgrace more idolized
than ever by the dames of Paris? and when was the
highwayman most acclaimed but on his way to Tyburn?
Or, to take a simile from nearer home, and still more
exactly to the point, what could even corporal punish
ment avail, administered by a cold, abstract, unearthly
schoolmaster, against the influence and fame of the
school's hero?

And now we come to the culminating point of Burns's
early period. He began to be received into the unknown upper world. His fame soon spread from among
his fellow-rebels on the benches, and began to reach
the ushers and monitors of this great Ayrshire academy.
This arose in part from his lax views about religion;
for at this time that old war of the creeds and con-
fessors, which is always grumbling from end to end of
our poor Scotland, brisked up in these parts into a hot
and virulent skirmish; and Burns found himself iden-
tified with the opposition party—a clique of roaring
lawyers and half heretical divines, with wit enough to
appreciate the value of the poet's help, and not sufficient

taste to moderate his grossness and personality. We
may judge of their surprise when "Holy Willie" was
put into their hand; like the amorous lads of Tarbolton,
they recognized in him the best of seconds. His sa-
tires began to go the round in manuscript; Mr. Aiken,
one of the lawyers, "read him into fame"; he himself
was soon welcome in many houses of a better sort,
where his admirable talk, and his manners, which he
had direct from his Maker, except for a brush he gave
them at a country dancing school, completed what his
poems had begun. We have a sight of him at his first
visit to Adamhill, in his plowman's shoes, coasting
around the carpet as though that were sacred ground.
But he soon grew used to carpets and their owners;
and he was still the superior of all whom he encountered, and ruled the roost in conversation. Such was
the impression made, that a young clergyman, himself
a man of ability, trembled and became confused when
he saw Robert enter the church in which he was to
preach. It is not surprising that the poet determined
to publish: he had now stood the test of some publicity,
and under this hopeful impulse he composed in six
winter months the bulk of his more important poems.
Here was a young man who, from a very humble
place, was mounting rapidly; from the cynosure of a
parish, he had become the talk of a county; once the
bard of rural courtships, he was now about to appear
as a bound and printed poet in the world's bookshops.
A few more intimate strokes are necessary to complete the sketch. This strong young plowman, who
feared no competitor with the flail, suffered like a fine
lady from sleeplessness and vapors; he would fall into

the blackest melancholies, and be filled with remorse for
the past and terror for the future. He was still not
perhaps devoted to religion, but haunted by it; and at
a touch of sickness prostrated himself before God in
what I can only call unmanly penitence. As he had
aspirations beyond his place in the world, so he had
tastes, thoughts, and weaknesses to match. He loved to
walk under a wood to the sound of a winter tempest;
he had a singular tenderness for animals; he carried a
book with him in his pocket when he went abroad,
and wore out in this service two copies of the "Man
of Feeling." With young people in the field at work
he was very long-suffering; and when his brother Gilbert spoke sharply to them—"O man, ye are no for
young folk," he would say, and give the defaulter a
helping hand and a smile. In the hearts of the men
whom he met, he read as in a book; and, what is yet
more rare, his knowledge of himself equaled his knowledge of others. There are no truer things said of Burns
than what is to be found in his own letters. Country Don Juan as he was, he had none of that blind
vanity which values itself on what it is not; he knew
his own strength and weakness to a hair: he took himself boldly for what he was, and, except in moments of
hypochondria, declared himself content.

THE LOVE STORIES

On the night of Mauchline races, 1785, the young
men and women of the place joined in a penny ball,
according to their custom. In the same set danced
Jean Armour, the master-mason's daughter, and our

dark-eyed Don Juan. His dog (not the immortal Luath, but a successor unknown to fame, *caret quia vate sacro*), apparently sensible of some neglect, followed his master to and fro, to the confusion of the dancers. Some mirthful comments followed; and Jean heard the poet say to his partner—or, as I should imagine, laughingly launch the remark to the company at large—that "he wished he could get any of the lasses to like him as well as his dog." Some time after, as the girl was bleaching clothes on Mauchline green, Robert chanced to go by, still accompanied by his dog; and the dog, "scouring in long excursion," scampered with four black paws across the linen. This brought the two into conversation; when Jean, with a somewhat hoydenish advance, inquired if "he had yet got any of the lasses to like him as well as his dog?" It is one of the misfortunes of the professional Don Juan that his honor forbids him to refuse battle; he is in life like the Roman soldier upon duty, or like the sworn physician who must attend on all diseases. Burns accepted the provocation; hungry hope reawakened in his heart; here was a girl—pretty, simple at least, if not honestly stupid, and plainly not averse to his attentions: it seemed to him once more as if love might here be waiting him. Had he but known the truth! for this facile and empty-headed girl had nothing more in view than a flirtation; and her heart, from the first and on to the end of her story, was engaged by another man. Burns once more commenced the celebrated process of "battering himself into a warm affection"; and the proofs of his success are to be found in many verses of the period. Nor did he succeed with himself only; Jean, with her

heart still elsewhere, succumbed to his fascination, and
early in the next year the natural consequence became
manifest. It was a heavy stroke for this unfortunate
couple. They had trifled with life, and were now rudely
reminded of life's serious issues. Jean awoke to the
ruin of her hopes; the best she had now to expect was
marriage with a man who was a stranger to her dear-
est thoughts; she might now be glad if she could get
what she would never have chosen. As for Burns, at
the stroke of the calamity he recognized that his voyage of discovery had led him into a wrong hemisphere
—that he was not, and never had been, really in love
with Jean. Hear him in the pressure of the hour.
"Against two things," he writes, "I am as fixed as
fate—staying at home, and owning her conjugally. The
first, by heaven, I will not do!—the last, by hell, I will
never do!" And then he adds, perhaps already in a
more relenting temper: "If you see Jean, tell her I
will meet her, so God help me in my hour of need."
They met accordingly; and Burns, touched with her
misery, came down from these heights of independence,
and gave her a written acknowledgment of marriage.
It is the punishment of Don Juanism to create continually false positions—relations in life which are wrong
in themselves, and which it is equally wrong to break
or to perpetuate. This was such a case. Worldly Wiseman would have laughed and gone his way; let us be
glad that Burns was better counseled by his heart.
When we discover that we can be no longer true,
the next best is to be kind. I daresay he came away
from that interview not very content, but with a glorious conscience; and as he went homeward, he would

sing his favorite, "How are Thy servants blest, O
Lord!" Jean, on the other hand, armed with her
"lines," confided her position to the master-mason, her
father, and his wife. Burns and his brother were then
in a fair way to ruin themselves in their farm; the
poet was an execrable match for any well-to-do country
lass; and perhaps old Armour had an inkling of a
previous attachment on his daugther's part. At least,
he was not so much incensed by her slip from virtue
as by the marriage which had been designed to cover
it. Of this he would not hear a word. Jean, who had
besought the acknowledgment only to appease her parents, and not at all from any violent inclination to
the poet, readily gave up the paper for destruction; and
all parties imagined, although wrongly, that the marriage was thus dissolved. To a proud man like Burns
here was a crushing blow. The concession which had
been wrung from his pity was now publicly thrown
back in his teeth. The Armour family preferred disgrace to his connection. Since the promise, besides, he
had doubtless been busy "battering himself" back again
into his affection for the girl; and the blow would not
only take him in his vanity, but wound him at the
heart.

He relieved himself in verse; but for such a smarting affront manuscript poetry was insufficient to console
him. He must find a more powerful remedy in good
flesh and blood, and after this discomfiture, set forth
again at once upon his voyage of discovery in quest of
love. It is perhaps one of the most touching things in
human nature, as it is a commonplace of psychology,
that when a man has just lost hope or confidence in

one love, he is then most eager to find and lean upon
another. The universe could not be yet exhausted;
there must be hope and love waiting for him somewhere; and so, with his head down, this poor, insulted
poet ran once more upon his fate. There was an innocent and gentle Highland nursery maid at service in a
neighboring family; and he had soon battered himself
and her into a warm affection and a secret engagement. Jean's marriage lines had not been destroyed
till March 13, 1786; yet all was settled between Burns
and Mary Campbell by Sunday, May 14, when they met
for the last time, and said farewell with rustic solemnities upon the banks of Ayr. They each wet their
hands in a stream, and, standing one on either bank,
held a Bible between them as they vowed eternal faith.
Then they exchanged Bibles, on one of which Burns,
for greater security, had inscribed texts as to the binding nature of an oath; and surely, if ceremony can do
aught to fix the wandering affections, here were two
people united for life. Mary came of a superstitious
family, so that she perhaps insisted on these rites; but
they must have been eminently to the taste of Burns
at this period; for nothing would seem superfluous, and
no oath great enough, to stay his tottering constancy.

Events of consequence now happened thickly in the
poet's life. His book was announced; the Armours
sought to summon him at law for the aliment of the
child; he lay here and there in hiding to correct the
sheets; he was under an engagement for Jamaica, where
Mary was to join him as his wife; now, he had "orders within three weeks at latest to repair aboard the
'Nancy,' Captain Smith;" now his chest was already

on the road to Greenock; and now, in the wild autumn weather on the moorland, he measures verses of farewell:

> "The bursting tears my heart declare;
> Farewell the bonny banks of Ayr!"

But the great master dramatist had secretly another intention for the piece; by the most violent and complicated solution, in which death and birth and sudden fame all play a part as interposing deities, the act-drop fell upon a scene of transformation. Jean was brought to bed of twins, and, by an amicable arrangement, the Burnses took the boy to bring up by hand, while the girl remained with her mother. The success of the book was immediate and emphatic; it put £20 at once into the author's purse; and he was encouraged upon all hands to go to Edinburgh and push his success in a second and larger edition. Third and last in these series of interpositions, a letter came one day to Mossgiel Farm for Robert. He went to the window to read it; a sudden change came over his face, and he left the room without a word. Years afterward, when the story began to leak out, his family understood that he had then learned the death of Highland Mary. Except in a few poems and a few dry indications purposely misleading as to date, Burns himself made no reference to this passage of his life; it was an adventure of which, for I think sufficient reasons, he desired to bury the details. Of one thing we may be glad: in after years he visited the poor girl's mother, and left her with the impression that he was "a real warm-hearted chield."

Perhaps a month after he received this intelligence, he set out for Edinburgh on a pony he had borrowed from a friend. The town that winter was "agog with the plowman poet." Robertson, Dugald Stewart, Blair, "Duchess Gordon and all the gay world," were of his acquaintance. Such a revolution is not to be found in literary history. He was now, it must be remembered, twenty-seven years of age; he had fought since his early boyhood an obstinate battle against poor soil, bad seed, and inclement seasons, wading deep in Ayrshire mosses, guiding the plow in the furrow, wielding "the thresher's weary flingin'-tree"; and his education, his diet, and his pleasures, had been those of a Scotch countryman. Now he stepped forth suddenly among the polite and learned. We can see him as he then was, in his boots and buckskins, his blue coat and waistcoat striped with buff and blue, like a farmer in his Sunday best; the heavy plowman's figure firmly planted on its burly legs; his face full of sense and shrewdness, and with a somewhat melancholy air of thought, and his large dark eye "literally glowing" as he spoke. "I never saw such another eye in a human head," says Walter Scott, "though I have seen the most distinguished men of my time." With men, whether they were lords or omnipotent critics, his manner was plain, dignified, and free from bashfulness or affectation. If he made a slip, he had the social courage to pass on and refrain from explanation. He was not embarrassed in this society, because he read and judged the men; he could spy snobbery in a titled lord; and, as for the critics, he dismissed their system in an epigram. "These gentlemen," said he, "remind me of some spinsters in

my country who spin their thread so fine that it is
neither fit for weft nor woof." Ladies, on the other
hand, surprised him; he was scarce commander of himself in their society; he was disqualified by his acquired
nature as a Don Juan; and he, who had been so much
at his ease with country lasses, treated the town dames
to an extreme of deference. One lady, who met him
at a ball, gave Chambers a speaking sketch of his
demeanor. "His manner was not prepossessing—scarcely, she thinks, manly or natural. It seemed as if he
affected a rusticity or *landertness*, so that when he
said the music was 'bonnie, bonnie,' it was like the
expression of a child." These would be company manners; and doubtless on a slight degree of intimacy the
affectation would grow less. And his talk to women
had always "a turn either to the pathetic or humorous,
which engaged the attention particularly."

The Edinburgh magnates (to conclude this episode at
once) behaved well to Burns from first to last. Were
heaven-born genius to revisit us in similar guise, I am
not venturing too far when I say that he need expect
neither so warm a welcome nor such solid help. Although Burns was only a peasant, and one of no very
elegant reputation as to morals, he was made welcome
to their homes. They gave him a great deal of good
advice, helped him to some five hundred pounds of
ready money, and got him, as soon as he asked it, a
place in the Excise. Burns, on his part, bore the ele-
vation with perfect dignity; and with perfect dignity
returned, when the time had come, into a country
privacy of life. His powerful sense never deserted him,
and from the first he recognized that his Edinburgh

popularity was but an ovation and the affair of a day. He wrote a few letters in a high-flown, bombastic vein of gratitude; but in practice he suffered no man to intrude upon his self-respect. On the other hand, he never turned his back, even for a moment, on his old associates; and he was always ready to sacrifice an acquaintance to a friend, although the acquaintance were a duke. He would be a bold man who should promise similar conduct in equally exacting circumstances. It was, in short, an admirable appearance on the stage of life—socially successful, intimately self-respecting, and like a gentleman from first to last.

In the present study, this must only be taken by the way, while we return to Burns's love affairs. Even on the road to Edinburgh he had seized upon the opportunity of a flirtation, and had carried the "battering" so far that when next he moved from town, it was to steal two days with this anonymous fair one. The exact importance to Burns of this affair may be gathered from the song in which he commemorated its occurrence. "I love the dear lassie," he sings, "because she loves me;" or, in the tongue of prose: "Finding an opportunity, I did not hesitate to profit by it; and even now if it returned, I should not hesitate to profit by it again." A love thus founded has no interest for mortal man. Meantime, early in the winter, and only once, we find him regretting Jean in his correspondence. "Because"—such is his reason—"because he does not think he will ever meet so delicious an armful again;" and then, after a brief excursion into verse, he goes straight on to describe a new episode in the voyage of discovery with the daughter of a Lothian

farmer for a heroine. I must ask the reader to follow
all these references to his future wife; they are essential to the comprehension of Burns's character and fate.
In June, we find him back at Mauchline, a famous
man. There, the Armour family greeted him with a
"mean, servile compliance," which increased his former
disgust. Jean was not less compliant; a second time the
poor girl submitted to the fascination of the man whom
she did not love, and whom she had so cruelly insulted
little more than a year ago; and, though Burns took advantage of her weakness, it was in the ugliest and most
cynical spirit, and with a heart absolutely indifferent.
Judge of this by a letter written some twenty days
after his return—a letter to my mind among the most
degrading in the whole collection—a letter which seems
to have been inspired by a boastful, libertine bagman.
"I am afraid," it goes, "I have almost ruined one
source, the principal one, indeed, of my former happiness—the eternal propensity I always had to fall in
love. My heart no more glows with feverish rapture;
I have no paradisiacal evening interviews." Even the
process of "battering" has failed him, you perceive.
Still he had some one in his eye—a lady, if you
please, with a fine figure and elegant manners, and
who had "seen the politest quarters in Europe." "I
frequently visited her," he writes, "and after passing
regularly the intermediate degrees between the distant
formal bow and the familiar grasp round the waist, I
ventured, in my careless way, to talk of friendship in
rather ambiguous terms; and after her return to ——,
I wrote her in the same terms. Miss, construing my
remarks further than even I intended, flew off in a

tangent of female dignity and reserve, like a mounting
lark in an April morning; and wrote me an answer
which measured out very completely what an immense
way I had to travel before I could reach the climate
of her favors. But I am an old hawk at the sport,
and wrote her such a cool, deliberate, prudent reply, as
brought my bird from her aerial towerings, pop, down
to my foot, like Corporal Trim's hat." I avow a carnal
longing, after this transcription, to buffet the Old Hawk
about the ears. There is little question that to this lady
he must have repeated his addresses, and that he was
by her (Miss Chalmers) eventually, though not at all
unkindly, rejected. One more detail to characterize the
period. Six months after the date of this letter, Burns,
back in Edinburgh, is served with a writ *in medita-
tione fugæ*, on behalf of some Edinburgh fair one,
probably of humble rank, who declared an intention of
adding to his family.

About the beginning of December (1787), a new
period opens in the story of the poet's random affections.
He met at a tea party one Mrs. Agnes M'Lehose, a
married woman of about his own age, who, with her
two children, had been deserted by an unworthy husband. She had wit, could use her pen, and had read
"Werther" with attention. Sociable, and even somewhat frisky, there was a good, sound, human kernel
in the woman; a warmth of love, strong dogmatic religious feeling, and a considerable, but not authorita-
tive, sense of the proprieties. Of what biographers refer
to daintily as "her somewhat voluptuous style of beauty,"
judging from the silhouette in Mr. Scott Douglas's invaluable edition, the reader will be fastidious if he does

not approve. Take her for all in all, I believe she was the best woman Burns encountered. The pair took a fancy for each other on the spot; Mrs. M'Lehose, in her turn, invited him to tea; but the poet, in his character of the Old Hawk, preferred a tête-à-tête, excused himself at the last moment, and offered a visit instead. An accident confined him to his room for nearly a month, and this led to the famous Clarinda and Sylvander correspondence. It was begun in simple sport; they are already at their fifth or sixth exchange, when Clarinda writes: "It is really curious so much *fun* passing between two persons who saw each other only *once;*" but it is hardly safe for a man and woman in the flower of their years to write almost daily, and sometimes in terms too ambiguous, sometimes in terms too plain, and generally in terms too warm, for mere acquaintance. The exercise partakes a little of the nature of battering, and danger may be apprehended when next they meet. It is difficult to give any account of this remarkable correspondence; it is too far away from us, and perhaps, not yet far enough, in point of time and manner; the imagination is baffled by these stilted literary utterances, warming, in bravura passages, into downright truculent nonsense. Clarinda has one famous sentence in which she bids Sylvander connect the thought of his mistress with the changing phases of the year; it was enthusiastically admired by the swain, but on the modern mind produces mild amazement and alarm. "Oh, Clarinda," writes Burns, "shall we not meet in a state—some yet unknown state—of being, where the lavish hand of Plenty shall minister to the highest wish of Benevolence, and where

the chill north wind of Prudence shall never blow over
the flowery field of Enjoyment?" The design may be
that of an Old Hawk, but the style is more suggestive of a Bird of Paradise. It is sometimes hard to
fancy they are not gravely making fun of each other
as they write. Religion, poetry, love, and charming
sensibility, are the current topics. "I am delighted,
charming Clarinda, with your honest enthusiasm for religion," writes Burns; and the pair entertained a fiction
that this was their "favorite subject." "This is Sunday," writes the lady, "and not a word on our favorite subject. Oh, fie! 'divine Clarinda!'" I suspect, although quite unconsciously on the part of the lady,
who was bent on his redemption, they but used the
favorite subject as a stalking-horse. In the meantime,
the sportive acquaintance was ripening steadily into a
genuine passion. Visits took place, and then became
frequent. Clarinda's friends were hurt and suspicious;
her clergyman interfered; she herself had smart attacks
of conscience; but her heart had gone from her control; it was altogether his, and she "counted all things
but loss—heaven excepted—that she might win and keep
him." Burns himself was transported while in her
neighborhood, but his transports somewhat rapidly declined during an absence. I am tempted to imagine
that, womanlike, he took on the color of his mistress's
feeling; that he could not but heat himself at the
fire of her unaffected passion; but that, like one who
should leave the hearth upon a winter's night, his
temperature soon fell when he was out of sight, and
in a word, though he could share the symptoms, that
he had never shared the disease. At the same time,

amid the fustian of the letters there are forcible and true expressions, and the love verses that he wrote upon Clarinda are among the most moving in the language.

We are approaching the solution. In mid winter, Jean, once more in the family way, was turned out of doors by her family; and Burns had her received and cared for in the house of a friend. For he remained to the last imperfect in his character of Don Juan, and lacked the sinister courage to desert his victim. About the middle of February (1788), he had to tear himself from his Clarinda and make a journey into the southwest on business. Clarinda gave him two shirts for his little son. They were daily to meet in prayer at an appointed hour. Burns, too late for the post at Glasgow, sent her a letter by parcel that she might not have to wait. Clarinda on her part writes, this time with a beautiful simplicity: "I think the streets look deserted-like since Monday; and there's a certain insipidity in good kind folks I once enjoyed not a little. Miss Wardrobe supped here on Monday. She once named you, which kept me from falling asleep. I drank your health in a glass of ale—as the lasses do at Hallowe'en—'in to myself'.'" Arrived at Mauchline, Burns installed Jean Armour in a lodging, and prevailed on Mrs. Armour to promise her help and countenance in the approaching confinement. This was kind at least; but hear his expressions: "I have taken her a room; I have taken her to my arms; I have given her a mahogany bed; I have given her a guinea. . . . I swore her privately and solemnly never to attempt any claim on me as a husband, even though anybody should persuade her she had such a claim—which she has not, neither during my life nor after my death. She did all this like a good girl." And then he took advantage of the situation. To Clarinda he wrote: "I this morning called for a certain woman. I am disgusted with her; I cannot endure her;" and he accused her of "tasteless insipidity, vulgarity of soul, and mercenary fawning." This was already in March; by the thirteenth of that month he was back in Edinburgh. On the 17th, he wrote to Clarinda: "Your hopes, your fears, your cares, my love, are mine; so don't mind them. I will take you in my hand through the dreary wilds of this world, and scare away the ravening bird or beast that would annoy you." Again on the 21st: "Will you open, with satisfaction and delight, a letter from a man who loves you, who has loved you, and who will love you, to death, through death, and forever. . . . How rich am I to have such a treasure as you! . . . 'The Lord God knoweth,' and, perhaps, 'Israel he shall know,' my love and your merit. Adieu, Clarinda! I am going to remember you in my prayers." By the 7th of April, seventeen days later, he had already decided to make Jean Armour publicly his wife.

A more astonishing stage-trick is not to be found. And yet his conduct is seen, upon a nearer examination, to be grounded both in reason and in kindness. He was now about to embark on a solid worldly career; he had taken a farm; the affair with Clarinda, however gratifying to his heart, was too contingent to offer any great consolation to a man like Burns, to whom marriage must have seemed the very dawn of hope and

self-respect. This is to regard the question from its lowest aspect; but there is no doubt that he entered on
this new period of his life with a sincere determination
to do right. He had just helped his brother with a loan
of a hundred and eighty pounds; should he do nothing
for the poor girl whom he had ruined? It was true
he could not do as he did without brutally wounding
Clarinda; that was the punishment of his bygone fault;
he was, as he truly says, "damned with a choice only
of different species of error and misconduct." To be
professional Don Juan, to accept the provocation of any
lively lass upon the village green, may thus lead a
man through a series of detestable words and actions,
and land him at last in an undesired and most unsuit-
able union for life. If he had been strong enough to
refrain or bad enough to persevere in evil; if he had
only not been Don Juan at all, or been Don Juan altogether, there had been some possible road for him
throughout this troublesome world; but a man, alas!
who is equally at the call of his worse and better instincts, stands among changing events without foundation or resource.*

DOWNWARD COURSE

It may be questionable whether any marriage could
have tamed Burns; but it is at least certain that there
was no hope for him in the marriage he contracted.
He did right, but then he had done wrong before; it
was, as I said, one of those relations in life which it

---

* For the love affairs see, in particular, Mr. Scott Douglas's edition
under the different dates.

seems equally wrong to break or to perpetuate. He
neither loved nor respected his wife. "God knows," he
writes, "my choice was as random as blind man's
buff." He consoles himself by the thought that he has
acted kindly to her; that she "has the most sacred enthusiasm of attachment to him;" that she has a good
figure; that she has a "wood-note wild," "her voice
rising with ease to B natural," no less. The effect on
the reader is one of unmingled pity for both parties
concerned. This was not the wife who (in his own
words) could "enter into his favorite studies or relish
his favorite authors;" this was not even a wife, after
the affair of the marriage lines, in whom a husband
could joy to place his trust. Let her manage a farm
with sense, let her voice rise to B natural all day
long, she would still be a peasant to her lettered lord,
and an object of pity rather than of equal affection.
She could now be faithful, she could now be forgiving,
she could now be generous even to a pathetic and touching degree; but coming from one who was unloved,
and who had scarce shown herself worthy of the sentiment, these were all virtues thrown away, which could
neither change her husband's heart nor affect the in
herent destiny of their relation. From the outset, it
was a marriage that had no root in nature; and we
find him, ere long, lyrically regretting Highland Mary,
renewing correspondence with Clarinda in the warmest
language, on doubtful terms with Mrs. Riddel, and on
terms unfortunately beyond any question with Anne
Park.

Alas! this was not the only ill circumstance in his
future. He had been idle for some eighteen months,

superintending his new edition, hanging on to settle
with the publisher, traveling in the Highlands with
Willie Nichol, or philandering with Mrs. M'Lehose; and
in this period the radical part of the man had suffered
irremediable hurt. He had lost his habits of industry,
and formed the habit of pleasure. Apologetical biographers assure us of the contrary; but from the first,
he saw and recognized the danger for himself; his
mind, he writes, is "enervated to an alarming degree"
by idleness and dissipation; and again, "my mind has
been vitiated with idleness." It never fairly recovered.
To business he could bring the required diligence and
attention without difficulty; but he was thenceforward
incapable, except in rare instances, of that superior
effort of concentration which is required for serious
literary work. He may be said, indeed, to have worked
no more, and only amused himself with letters. The
man who had written a volume of masterpieces in six
months, during the remainder of his life rarely found
courage for any more sustained effort than a song.
And the nature of the songs is itself characteristic of
these idle later years; for they are often as polished
and elaborate as his earlier works were frank, and
headlong, and colloquial; and this sort of verbal elabo-
ration in short flights is, for a man of literary turn,
simply the most agreeable of pastimes. The change in
manner coincides exactly with the Edinburgh visit. In
1786 he had written the "Address to a Louse," which
may be taken as an extreme instance of the first manner; and already, in 1787, we come upon the rosebud
pieces to Miss Cruikshank, which are extreme examples
of the second. The change was, therefore, the direct

and very natural consequence of his great change in life; but it is not the less typical of his loss of moral courage that he should have given up all larger ventures, nor the less melancholy that a man who first attacked literature with a hand that seemed capable of moving mountains, should have spent his later years in whittling cherry-stones.

Meanwhile, the farm did not prosper; he had to join to it the salary of an exciseman; at last he had to give it up, and rely altogether on the latter resource. He was an active officer; and, though he sometimes tempered severity with mercy, we have local testimony oddly representing the public feeling of the period, that, while "in everything else he was a perfect gentleman, when he met with anything seizable he was no better than any other gauger."

There is but one manifestation of the man in these last years which need delay us: and that was the sudden interest in politics which arose from his sympathy with the great French Revolution. His only political feeling had been hitherto a sentimental Jacobitism, not more or less respectable than that of Scott, Aytoun, and the rest of what George Borrow has nicknamed the "Charlie over the water" Scotchmen. It was a sentiment almost entirely literary and picturesque in its origin, built on ballads and the adventures of the Young Chevalier; and in Burns it is the more excusable, because he lay out of the way of active politics in his youth. With the great French Revolution, something living, practical, and feasible appeared to him for the first time in this realm of human action. The young plowman who had desired so earnestly to rise

now reached out his sympathies to a whole nation animated with the same desire. Already in 1788 we find
the old Jacobitism hand in hand with the new popular
doctrine, when, in a letter of indignation against the
zeal of a Whig clergyman, he writes: "I daresay the
American Congress in 1776 will be allowed to be as
able and as enlightened as the English Convention was
in 1688; and that their posterity will celebrate the cen-
tenary of their deliverance from us, as duly and sincerely as we do ours from the oppressive measures of
the wrong-headed house of Stuart." As time wore on,
his sentiments grew more pronounced and even violent;
but there was a basis of sense and generous feeling to
his hottest excess. What he asked was a fair chance
for the individual in life; an open road to success and
distinction for all classes of men. It was in the same
spirit that he had helped to found a public library in
the parish where his farm was situated, and that he
sang his fervent snatches against tyranny and tyrants.
Witness, were it alone, this verse:

> "Here's freedom to him that wad read,
>   Here's freedom to him that wad write;
>   There's nane ever feared that the truth
>   should be heard
>   But them wham the truth wad indite."

Yet his enthusiasm for the cause was scarce guided by
wisdom. Many stories are preserved of the bitter and
unwise words he used in country coteries; how he proposed Washington's health as an amendment to Pitt's,
gave as a toast "the last verse of the last chapter of
Kings," and celebrated Dumouriez in a doggerel im-

promptu full of ridicule and hate. Now his sympathies
would inspire him with "Scots, wha hae"; now involve
him in a drunken broil with a loyal officer, and consequent apologies and explanations, hard to offer for a
man of Burns's stomach. Nor was this the front of
his offending. On February 27, 1792, he took part in
the capture of an armed smuggler, bought at the subsequent sale four carronades, and dispatched them with
a letter to the French Assembly. Letter and guns
were stopped at Dover by the English officials; there
was trouble for Burns with his superiors; he was reminded firmly, however delicately, that, as a paid official, it was his duty to obey and to be silent; and all
the blood of this poor, proud, and falling man must
have rushed to his head at the humiliation. His letter to Mr. Erskine, subsequently Earl of Mar, testifies,
in its turgid, turbulent phrases, to a perfect passion of
alarmed self-respect and vanity. He had been muzzled,
and muzzled, when all was said, by his paltry salary
as an exciseman; alas! had he not a family to keep?
Already, he wrote, he looked forward to some such
judgment from a hackney scribbler as this: "Burns,
notwithstanding the fanfaronnade of independence to be
found in his works, and after having been held forth
to view and to public estimation as a man of some
genius, yet, quite destitute of resources within himself
to support his borrowed dignity, he dwindled into a paltry
exciseman, and shrunk out the rest of his insignificant
existence in the meanest of pursuits, and among the
vilest of mankind." And then on he goes, in a style
of rhodomontade, but filled with living indignation, to
declare his right to a political opinion, and his willing-

ness to shed his blood for the political birthright of his sons. Poor, perturbed spirit! he was indeed exercised in vain; those who share and those who differ from his sentiments about the Revolution, alike understand and sympathize with him in this painful strait; for poetry and human manhood are lasting like the race, and politics, which are but a wrongful striving after right, pass and change from year to year and age to age. The "Twa Dogs" has already outlasted the constitution of Sieyes and the policy of the Whigs; and Burns is better known among English-speaking races than either Pitt or Fox.

Meanwhile, whether as a man, a husband, or a poet, his steps led downward. He knew, knew bitterly, that the best was out of him; he refused to make another volume, for he felt that it would be a disappointment; he grew petulantly alive to criticism, unless he was sure it reached him from a friend. For his songs, he would take nothing; they were all that he could do; the proposed Scotch play, the proposed series of Scotch tales in verse, all had gone to water; and in a fling of pain and disappointment, which is surely noble with the nobility of a viking, he would rather stoop to borrow than to accept money for these last and inadequate efforts of his muse. And this desperate abnegation rises at times near to the height of madness; as when he pretended that he had not written, but only found and published, his immortal "Auld Lang Syne." In the same spirit he became more scrupulous as an artist; he was doing so little, he would fain do that little well; and about two months before his death, he asked Thomson to send back all his manuscripts for revisal,

saying that he would rather write five songs to his
taste than twice that number otherwise. The battle of
his life was lost; in forlorn efforts to do well, in desperate submissions to evil, the last years flew by. His
temper is dark and explosive, launching epigrams, quarrel-
ing with his friends, jealous of young puppy officers.
He tries to be a good father; he boasts himself a
libertine. Sick, sad, and jaded, he can refuse no occasion of temporary pleasure, no opportunity to shine; and
he who had once refused the invitations of lords and
ladies is now whistled to the inn by any curious
stranger. His death (July 21, 1796), in his thirty-
seventh year, was indeed a kindly dispensation. It is
the fashion to say he died of drink; many a man has
drunk more and yet lived with reputation and reached
a good age. That drink and debauchery helped to de-
stroy his constitution, and were the means of his unconscious suicide, is doubtless true; but he had failed
in life, had lost his power of work, and was already
married to the poor, unworthy, patient Jean, before he
had shown his inclination to convivial nights, or at
least before that inclination had become dangerous either
to his health or his self-respect. He had trifled with
life, and must pay the penalty. He had chosen to be
Don Juan, he had grasped at temporary pleasures, and
substantial happiness and solid industry had passed him
by. He died of being Robert Burns, and there is no
levity in such a statement of the case; for shall we
not, one and all, deserve a similar epitaph?

WORKS

The somewhat cruel necessity which has lain upon me throughout this paper only to touch upon those points in the life of Burns where correction or amplification seemed desirable, leaves me little opportunity to speak of the works which have made his name so famous. Yet, even here, a few observations seem necessary.

At the time when the poet made his appearance and great first success, his work was remarkable in two ways. For, first, in an age when poetry had become abstract and conventional, instead of continuing to deal with shepherds, thunderstorms, and personifications, he dealt with the actual circumstances of his life, however matter-of-fact and sordid these might be. And, second, in a time when English versification was particularly stiff, lame, and feeble, and words were used with ultra-academical timidity, he wrote verses that were easy, racy, graphic, and forcible, and used language with absolute tact and courage as it seemed most fit to give a clear impression. If you take even those English authors whom we know Burns to have most admired and studied, you will see at once that he owed them nothing but a warning. Take Shenstone, for instance, and watch that elegant author as he tries to grapple with the facts of life. He has a description, I remember, of a gentleman engaged in sliding or walking on thin ice, which is a little miracle of incompe-

tence. You see my memory fails me, and I positively
cannot recollect whether his hero was sliding or walking;
as though a writer should describe a skirmish, and the
reader, at the end, be still uncertain whether it were
a charge of cavalry or a slow and stubborn advance of
foot. There could be no such ambiguity in Burns; his
work is at the opposite pole from such indefinite and
stammering performances; and a whole lifetime passed
in the study of Shenstone would only lead a man
further and further from writing the "Address to a
Louse." Yet Burns, like most great artists, proceeded
from a school and continued a tradition; only the school
and tradition were Scotch, and not English. While the
English language was becoming daily more pedantic and
inflexible, and English letters more colorless and slack,
there was another dialect in the sister country, and a
different school of poetry tracing its descent, through
King James I., from Chaucer. The dialect alone accounts for much; for it was then written colloquially,
which kept it fresh and supple; and, although not
shaped for heroic flights, it was a direct and vivid
medium for all that had to do with social life. Hence,
whenever Scotch poets left their laborious imitations of
bad English verses, and fell back on their own dialect,
their style would kindle, and they would write of their
convivial and somewhat gross existences with pith and
point. In Ramsay, and far more in the poor lad
Fergusson, there was mettle, humor, literary courage,
and a power of saying what they wished to say definitely and brightly, which in the latter case should have
justified great anticipations. Had Burns died at the
same age as Fergusson, he would have left us literally

nothing worth remark. To Ramsay and to Fergusson, then, he was indebted in a very uncommon degree, not only following their tradition and using their measures, but directly and avowedly imitating their pieces. The same tendency to borrow a hint, to work on some one else's foundation, is notable in Burns from first to last, in the period of song-writing as well as in that of the early poems; and strikes one oddly in a man of such deep originality, who left so strong a print on all he touched, and whose work is so greatly distinguished by that character of "inevitability" which Wordsworth denied to Goethe.

When we remember Burns's obligations to his predecessors, we must never forget his immense advances on them. They had already "discovered" nature; but Burns discovered poetry—a higher and more intense way of thinking of the things that go to make up nature, a higher and more ideal key of words in which to speak of them. Ramsay and Fergusson excelled at making a popular—or shall we say vulgar?—sort of society verses, comical and prosaic, written, you would say, in taverns while a supper party waited for its laureate's word; but on the appearance of Burns, this coarse and laughing literature was touched to finer issues, and learned gravity of thought and natural pathos. What he had gained from his predecessors was a direct, speaking style, and to walk on his own feet instead of on academical stilts. There was never a man of letters with more absolute command of his means; and we may say of him, without excess, that his style was his slave. Hence that energy of epithet, so concise and telling, that a foreigner is tempted to explain it by some special richness or aptitude in the dialect he wrote. Hence that Homeric justice and completeness of description which gives us the very physiognomy of nature, in body and detail, as nature is. Hence, too, the unbroken literary quality of his best pieces, which keeps him from any slip into the weariful trade of word-painting, and presents everything, as everything should be presented by the art of words, in a clear, continuous medium of thought. Principal Shairp, for instance, gives us a paraphrase of one tough verse of the original; and for those who know the Greek poets only by paraphrase, this has the very quality they are accustomed to look for and admire in Greek. The contemporaries of Burns were surprised that he should visit so many celebrated mountains and waterfalls, and not seize the opportunity to make a poem. Indeed, it is not for those who have a true command of the art of words, but for peddling, professional amateurs, that these pointed occasions are most useful and inspiring. As those who speak French imperfectly are glad to dwell on any topic they may have talked upon or heard others talk upon before, because they know appropriate words for it in French, so the dabbler in verse rejoices to behold a waterfall, because he has learned the sentiment and knows appropriate words for it in poetry. But the dialect of Burns was fitted to deal with any subject; and whether it was a stormy night, a shepherd's collie, a sheep struggling in the snow, the conduct of cowardly soldiers in the field, the gait and cogitations of a drunken man, or only a village cock-crow in the morning, he could find language to give it freshness, body, and relief. He was always ready to borrow the hint of a design, as though he had a difficulty in commencing—a difficulty, let us say, in choosing a subject out of a world which seemed all equally living and significant to him; but once he had the subject chosen, he could cope with nature single-handed, and make every stroke a triumph. Again, his absolute mastery in his art enabled him to express each and all of his different humors, and to pass smoothly and congruously from one to another. Many men invent a dialect for only one side of their nature—perhaps their pathos or their humor, or the delicacy of their senses—and, for lack of a medium, leave all the others unexpressed. You meet such a one, and find him in conversation full of thought, feeling, and experience, which he has lacked the art to employ in his writings. But Burns was not thus hampered in the practice of the literary art; he could throw the whole weight of his nature into his work, and impregnate it from end to end. If Doctor Johnson, that stilted and accomplished stylist, had lacked the sacred Boswell, what should we have known of him? and how should we have delighted in his acquaintance as we do? Those who spoke with Burns tell us how much we have lost who did not. But I think they exaggerate their privilege: I think we have the whole Burns in our possession set forth in his consummate verses.

It was by his style, and not by his matter, that he affected Wordsworth and the world. There is, indeed, only one merit worth considering in a man of letters—that he should write well; and only one damning fault—that he should write ill. We are little the better for the reflections of the sailor's parrot in the story. And so, if Burns helped to change the course of literary history, it was by his frank, direct, and masterly utterance, and not by his homely choice of subjects. That was imposed upon him, not chosen upon a principle. He wrote from his own experience, because it was his nature so to do, and the tradition of the school from which he proceeded was fortunately not opposed to homely subjects. But to these homely subjects he communicated the rich commentary of his nature; they were all steeped in Burns; and they interest us not in themselves, but because they have been passed through the spirit of so genuine and vigorous a man. Such is the stamp of living literature; and there was never any more alive than that of Burns.

What a gust of sympathy there is in him sometimes flowing out in byways hitherto unused, upon mice, and flowers, and the devil himself; sometimes speaking plainly between human hearts; sometimes ringing out in exultation like a peal of beals! When we compare the "Farmer's Salutation to his Auld Mare Maggie," with the clever and inhumane production of half a century earlier, "The Auld Man's Mare's dead," we see in a nutshell the spirit of the change introduced by Burns. And as to its manner, who that has read it can forget how the collie, Luath, in the "Twa Dogs," describes and enters into the merry-making in the cottage?

> "The luntin' pipe an' sneeshin' mill,
>   Are handed round wi' richt guid will;
>   The canty auld folks crackin' crouse,
>   The young anes rantin' through the house—
>   My heart has been sae fain to see them
>   That I for joy hae barkit wi' them."

It was this ardent power of sympathy that was fatal
to so many women, and, through Jean Armour, to himself at last. His humor comes from him in a stream
so deep and easy that I will venture to call him the
best of humorous poets. He turns about in the midst
to utter a noble sentiment or a trenchant remark on
human life, and the style changes and rises to the occasion. I think it is Principal Shairp who says, happily,
that Burns would have been no Scotchman if he had
not loved to moralize; neither, may we add, would he
have been his father's son; but (what is worthy of note)
his moralizings are to a large extent the moral of his
own career. He was among the least impersonal of
artists. Except in the "Jolly Beggars," he shows no
gleam of dramatic instinct. Mr. Carlyle has complained
that "Tam o' Shanter" is, from the absence of this
quality, only a picturesque and external piece of work;
and I may add that in the "Twa Dogs" it is precisely
in the infringement of dramatic propriety that a great
deal of the humor of the speeches depends for its existence and effect. Indeed, Burns was so full of his
identity that it breaks forth on every page; and there
is scarce an appropriate remark either in praise or
blame of his own conduct, but he has put himself into
verse. Alas! for the tenor of these remarks! They are,
indeed, his own pitiful apology for such a marred existence and talents so misused and stunted; and they
seem to prove forever how small a part is played by
reason in the conduct of man's affairs. Here was one,
at least, who with unfailing judgment predicted his own
fate; yet his knowledge could not avail him, and with
open eyes he must fulfill his tragic destiny. Ten years

before the end he had written his epitaph; and neither
subsequent events, nor the critical eyes of posterity,
have shown us a word in it to alter. And, lastly, has
he not put in for himself the last unanswerable plea?—

"Then gently scan your brother man,
    Still gentler sister woman;
Though they may gang a kennin wrang,
    To step aside is human:
One point must still be greatly dark—"

One? Alas! I fear every man and woman of us is
"greatly dark" to all their neighbors, from the day of
birth until death removes them, in their greatest virtues
as well as in their saddest faults; and we, who have
been trying to read the character of Burns, may take
home the lesson and be gentle in our thoughts.

WALT WHITMAN

Of late years the name of Walt Whitman has been a good deal bandied about in books and magazines. It has become familiar both in good and ill repute. His works have been largely bespattered with praise by his admirers, and cruelly mauled and mangled by irreverent enemies. Now, whether his poetry is good or bad as poetry, is a matter that may admit of a difference of opinion without alienating those who differ. We could not keep the peace with a man who should put forward claims to taste and yet depreciate the choruses in "Samson Agonistes"; but, I think, we may shake hands with one who sees no more in Walt Whitman's volume, from a literary point of view, than a farrago of incompetent essays in a wrong direction. That may not be at all our own opinion. We may think that, when a work contains many unforgettable phrases, it cannot be altogether devoid of literary merit. We may even see passages of a high poetry here and there among its eccentric contents. But when all is said, Walt Whitman is neither a Milton nor a Shakespeare; to appreciate his works is not a condition necessary to salvation; and I would not disinherit a son upon the question, nor even think much the worse of a critic, for I should always have an idea what he meant.

What Whitman has to say is another affair from

how he says it. It is not possible to acquit any one
of defective intelligence, or else stiff prejudice, who is
not interested by Whitman's matter and the spirit it
represents. Not as a poet, but as what we must call
(for lack of a more exact expression) a prophet, he
occupies a curious and prominent position. Whether he
may greatly influence the future or not, he is a notable
symptom of the present. As a sign of the times, it
would be hard to find his parallel. I should hazard a
large wager, for instance, that he was not unacquainted
with the works of Herbert Spencer; and yet where, in
all the history books, shall we lay our hands on two
more incongruous contemporaries? Mr. Spencer so de-
corous—I had almost said, so dandy—in dissent; and
Whitman, like a large shaggy dog, just unchained,
scouring the beaches of the world and baying at the
moon. And when was an echo more curiously like a
satire, than when Mr. Spencer found his Synthetic Philosophy reverberated from the other shores of the At-
lantic in the "barbaric yawp" of Whitman?

I

Whitman, it cannot be too soon explained, writes
up to a system. He was a theorizer about society before he was a poet. He first perceived something wanting, and then sat down squarely to supply the want.
The reader, running over his works, will find that he
takes nearly as much pleasure in critically expounding
his theory of poetry as in making poems. This is as
far as it can be from the case of the spontaneous village minstrel dear to elegy, who has no theory what-

ever, although sometimes he may have fully as much
poetry as Whitman. The whole of Whitman's work is
deliberate and preconceived. A man born into a society
comparatively new, full of conflicting elements and interests, could not fail, if he had any thoughts at all,
to reflect upon the tendencies around him. He saw
much good and evil on all sides, not yet settled down
into some more or less unjust compromise as in older
nations, but still in the act of settlement. And he
could not but wonder what it would turn out; whether
the compromise would be very just or very much the
reverse, and give great or little scope for healthy human energies. From idle wonder to active speculation
is but a step; and he seems to have been early struck
with the inefficacy of literature and its extreme unsuit-
ability to the conditions. What he calls "Feudal Literature" could have little living action on the tumult of
American democracy; what he calls the "Literature of
Wo," meaning the whole tribe of Werther and Byron,
could have no action for good in any time or place.
Both propositions, if art had none but a direct moral
influence, would be true enough; and as this seems to
be Whitman's view, they were true enough for him.
He conceived the idea of a Literature which was to
inhere in the life of the present; which was to be,
first, human, and next, American; which was to be
brave and cheerful as per contract; to give culture in
a popular and poetical presentment; and, in so doing,
catch and stereotype some democratic ideal of humanity
which should be equally natural to all grades of wealth
and education, and suited, in one of his favorite phrases,
to "the average man." To the formation of some such

literature as this his poems are to be regarded as so
many contributions, one sometimes explaining, sometimes
superseding, the other: and the whole together not so
much a finished work as a body of suggestive hints.
He does not profess to have built the castle, but he
pretends he has traced the lines of the foundation. He
has not made the poetry, but he flatters himself he has
done something toward making the poets.

His notion of the poetic function is ambitious, and
coincides roughly with what Schopenhauer has laid down
as the province of the metaphysician. The poet is to
gather together for men, and set in order, the materials of their existence. He is "The Answerer"; he is
to find some way of speaking about life that shall
satisfy, if only for the moment, man's enduring astonishment at his own position. And besides having an
answer ready, it is he who shall provoke the question.
He must shake people out of their indifference, and
force them to make some election in this world, instead
of sliding dully forward in a dream. Life is a business we are all apt to mismanage; either living reck-
lessly from day to day, or suffering ourselves to be
gulled out of our moments by the inanities of custom.
We should despise a man who gave as little activity
and forethought to the conduct of any other business.
But in this, which is the one thing of all others, since
it contains them all, we cannot see the forest for the
trees. One brief impression obliterates another. There
is something stupefying in the recurrence of unimportant things. And it is only on rare provocations that
we can rise to take an outlook beyond daily concerns,
and comprehend the narrow limits and great possibilities

of our existence. It is the duty of the poet to induce such moments of clear sight. He is the declared enemy of all living by reflex action, of all that is done betwixt sleep and waking, of all the pleasureless pleasurings and imaginary duties in which we coin away our hearts and fritter invaluable years. He has to electrify his readers into an instant unflagging activity, founded on a wide and eager observation of the world, and make them direct their ways by a superior prudence, which has little or nothing in common with the maxims of the copy-book. That many of us lead such lives as they would heartily disown after two hours' serious reflection on the subject is, I am afraid, a true, and, I am sure, a very galling thought. The Enchanted Ground of dead-alive respectability is next, upon the map, to the Beulah of considerate virtue. But there they all slumber and take their rest in the middle of God's beautiful and wonderful universe; the drowsy heads have nodded together in the same position since first their fathers fell asleep; and not even the sound of the last trumpet can wake them to a single active thought. The poet has a hard task before him to stir up such fellows to a sense of their own and other people's principles in life.

And it happens that literature is, in some ways, but an indifferent means to such an end. Language is but a poor bull's-eye lantern wherewith to show off the vast cathedral of the world; and yet a particular thing once said in words is so definite and memorable, that it makes us forget the absence of the many which remain unexpressed; like a bright window in a distant view, which dazzles and confuses our sight of its surroundings. There are not words enough in all Shakespeare to express the merest fraction of a man's experience in an hour. The speed of the eyesight and the hearing, and the continual industry of the mind, produce, in ten minutes, what it would require a laborious volume to shadow forth by comparisons and roundabout approaches. If verbal logic were sufficient, life would be as plain sailing as a piece of Euclid. But, as a matter of fact, we make a travesty of the simplest process of thought when we put it into words; for the words are all colored and forsworn, apply inaccurately, and bring with them, from former uses, ideas of praise and blame that have nothing to do with the question in hand. So we must always see to it nearly, that we judge by the realities of life and not by the partial terms that represent them in man's speech; and at times of choice, we must leave words upon one side, and act upon those brute convictions, unexpressed and perhaps inexpressible, which cannot be flourished in an argument, but which are truly the sum and fruit of our experience. Words are for communication, not for judgment. This is what every thoughtful man knows for himself, for only fools and silly schoolmasters push definitions over far into the domain of conduct; and the majority of women, not learned in these scholastic refinements, live all-of-a-piece and unconsciously, as a tree grows, without caring to put a name upon their acts or motives. Hence, a new difficulty for Whitman's scrupulous and argumentative poet; he must do more than waken up the sleepers to his words; he must persuade them to look over the book and at life with their own eyes.

This side of truth is very present to Whitman; it is this that he means when he tells us that "to glance with an eye confounds the learning of all times." But he is not unready. He is never weary of descanting on the undebatable conviction that is forced upon our minds by the presence of other men, of animals, or of inanimate things. To glance with an eye, were it only at a chair or a park railing, is by far a more persuasive process, and brings us to a far more exact conclusion, than to read the works of all the logicians extant. If both, by a large allowance, may be said to end in certainty, the certainty in the one case transcends the other to an incalculable degree. If people see a lion, they run away; if they only apprehend a deduction, they keep wandering around in an experimental humor. Now, how is the poet to convince like nature, and not like books? Is there no actual piece of nature that he can show the man to his face, as he might show him a tree if they were walking together? Yes, there is one: the man's own thoughts. In fact, if the poet is to speak efficaciously, he must say what is already in his hearer's mind. That, alone, the hearer will believe; that, alone, he will be able to apply intelligently to the facts of life. Any conviction, even if it be a whole system or a whole religion, must pass into the condition of commonplace, or postulate, before it becomes fully operative. Strange excursions and high-flying theories may interest, but they cannot rule behavior. Our faith is not the highest truth that we perceive, but the highest that we have been able to assimilate into the very texture and method of our thinking. It is not, therefore, by flashing before a man's eyes the weapons of dialectic; it is not by induction, deduction, or construction; it is not by forcing him on from one stage of reasoning to another, that the man will be effectually renewed. He cannot be made to believe anything; but he can be made to see that he has always believed it. And this is the practical canon. It is when the reader cries, "Oh, I know!" and is, perhaps, half irritated to see how nearly the author has forestalled his own thoughts, that he is on the way to what is called in theology a Saving Faith.

Here we have the key to Whitman's attitude. To give a certain unity of ideal to the average population of America—to gather their activities about some conception of humanity that shall be central and normal, if only for the moment—the poet must portray that population as it is. Like human law, human poetry is simply declaratory. If any ideal is possible, it must be already in the thoughts of the people; and, by the same reason, in the thoughts of the poet, who is one of them. And hence Whitman's own formula: "The poet is individual—he is complete in himself: the others are as good as he; only he sees it, and they do not." To show them how good they are, the poet must study his fellow-countrymen and himself somewhat like a traveler on the hunt for his book of travels. There is a sense, of course, in which all true books are books of travel; and all genuine poets must run their risk of being charged with the traveler's exaggeration; for to whom are such books more surprising than to those whose own life is faithfully and smartly pictured? But this danger is all upon one side; and you may judiciously flatter the portrait without any likelihood of the sitter's

disowning it for a faithful likeness.   And so Whitman
has reasoned: that by drawing at first hand from himself and his neighbors, accepting without shame the
inconsistencies and brutalities that go to make up man,
and yet treating the whole in a high, magnanimous
spirit, he would make sure of belief, and at the same
time encourage people forward by the means of praise.

II.

We are accustomed nowadays to a great deal of
puling over the circumstances in which we are placed.
The great refinement of many poetical gentlemen has
rendered them practically unfit for the jostling and ugliness of life, and they record their unfitness at considerable length.   The bold and awful poetry of Job's complaint produces too many flimsy imitators; for there is
always something consolatory in grandeur, but the sym-
phony transposed for the piano becomes hysterically sad.
This literature of woe, as Whitman calls it, this *Maladie
de Rene*, as we like to call it in Europe, is in many
ways a most humiliating and sickly phenomenon.   Young
gentlemen with three or four hundred a year of private
means look down from a pinnacle of doleful experience
on all the grown and hearty men who have dared to
say a good word for life since the beginning of the
world.   There is no prophet but the melancholy Jacques,
and the blue devils dance on all our literary wires.

It would be a poor service to spread culture, if this
be its result, among the comparatively innocent and
cheerful ranks of men.   When our little poets have to
be sent to look at the plowman and learn wisdom, we

must be careful how we tamper with our plowmen. Where a man in not the best of circumstances preserves composure of mind, and relishes ale and tobacco, and his wife and children, in the intervals of dull and un-remunerative labor; where a man in this predicament can afford a lesson by the way to what are called his intellectual superiors, there is plainly something to be lost, as well as something to be gained, by teaching him to think differently. It is better to leave him as he is than to teach him whining. It is better that he should go without the cheerful lights of culture, if cheerless doubt and paralyzing sentimentalism are to be the consequence. Let us, by all means, fight against that hide-bound stolidity of sensation and sluggishness of mind which blurs and decolorizes for poor natures the wonderful pageant of consciousness; let us teach people, as much as we can, to enjoy, and they will learn for themselves to sympathize; but let us see to it, above all, that we give these lessons in a brave, viva-cious note, and build the man up in courage while we demolish its substitute, indifference.

Whitman is alive to all this. He sees that, if the poet is to be of any help, he must testify to the livableness of life. His poems, he tells us, are to be "hymns of the praise of things." They are to make for a certain high joy in living, or what he calls him-self "a brave delight fit for freedom's athletes." And he has had no difficulty in introducing his optimism: it fitted readily enough with his system; for the average man is truly a courageous person and truly fond of liv-ing. One of Whitman's remarks upon this head is worth quotation, as he is there perfectly successful, and does precisely what he designs to do throughout: Takes ordinary and even commonplace circumstances; throws them out, by a happy turn of thinking, into significance and something like beauty; and tacks a hopeful moral lesson to the end.

"The passionate tenacity of hunters, woodmen, early risers, cultivators of gardens and orchards and fields, he says, the love of healthy women for the manly form, seafaring persons, drivers of horses, the passion for light and the open air—all is an old unvaried sign of the unfailing perception of beauty, and of a residence of the poetic in outdoor people."

There seems to me something truly original in this choice of trite examples. You will remark how adroitly Whitman begins, hunters and woodmen being confessedly romantic. And one thing more. If he had said "the love of healthy men for the female form," he would have said almost a silliness; for the thing has never been dissembled out of delicacy, and is so obvious as to be a public nuisance. But by reversing it, he tells us something not unlike news; something that sounds quite freshly in words; and, if the reader be a man, gives him a moment of great self-satisfaction and spiritual aggrandizement. In many different authors you may find passages more remarkable for grammar, but few of a more ingenious turn, and none that could be more to the point in our connection. The tenacity of many ordinary people in ordinary pursuits is a sort of standing challenge to everybody else. If one man can grow absorbed in delving his garden, others may grow absorbed and happy over something else. Not to be upsides in this with any groom or gardener, is to be very meanly organized. A man should be ashamed to take his food if he has not alchemy enough in his stomach to turn some of it into intense and enjoyable occupation.

Whitman tries to re-enforce this cheerfulness by keeping up a sort of outdoor atmosphere of sentiment. His book, he tells us, should be read "among the cooling influences of external nature"; and this recommendation, like that other famous one which Hawthorne prefixed to his collected tales, is in itself a character of the work. Every one who has been upon a walking or a boating tour, living in the open air, with the body in constant exercise and the mind in fallow, knows true ease and quiet. The irritating action of the brain is set at rest; we think in a plain, unfeverish temper; little things seem big enough, and great things no longer portentous; and the world is smilingly accepted as it is. This is the spirit that Whitman inculcates and parades. He thinks very ill of the atmosphere of parlors or libraries. Wisdom keeps school outdoors. And he has the art to recommend this attitude of mind by simply pluming himself upon it as a virtue; so that the reader, to keep the advantage over his author which most readers enjoy, is tricked into professing the same view. And this spirit, as it is his chief lesson, is the greatest charm of his work. Thence, in spite of an uneven and emphatic key of expression, something trenchant and straightforward, something simple and surprising, distinguishes his poems. He has sayings that come home to one like the Bible. We fall upon Whitman, after the works of so many men who write better, with a sense of relief from strain, with a sense of touching nature, as when one passes out of the flaring, noisy thoroughfares of a great city into what he himself has called, with unexcelled imaginative justice of language, "the huge and thoughtful night." And his book in consequence, whatever may be the final judgment of its merit, whatever may be its influence on the future, should be in the hands of all parents and guardians as a specific for the distressing malady of being seventeen years old. Green-sick ness yields to his treatment as to a charm of magic; and the youth, after a short course of reading, ceases to carry the universe upon his shoulders.

III

Whitman is not one of those who can be deceived by familiarity. He considers it just as wonderful that there are myriads of stars, as that one man should rise from the dead. He declares "a hair on the back of his hand just as curious as any special revelation." His whole life is to him what it was to Sir Thomas Browne, one perpetual miracle. Everything is strange, everything unaccountable, everything beautiful; from a bug to the moon, from the sight of the eyes to the appetite for food. He makes it his business to see things as if he saw them for the first time, and professes astonishment on principle. But he has no leaning toward mythology; avows his contempt for what he calls "unregenerate poetry"; and does not mean by nature

"The smooth walks, trimmed hedges, butterflies, posies, and nightingales of the English poets, but the whole orb, with its geologic history, the Kosmos, carrying fire and snow, that rolls through the illimitable areas, light as a feather though weighing billions of tons."

Nor is this exhaustive; for in his character of idealist all impressions, all thoughts, trees and people, love and faith, astronomy, history, and religion, enter upon equal terms into his notion of the universe. He is not against religion; not, indeed, against any religion. He wishes to drag with a larger net, to make a more comprehensive synthesis, than any or than all of them put together. In feeling after the central type of man, he must embrace all eccentricities; his cosmology must subsume all cosmologies, and the feelings that gave birth to them; his statement of facts must include all religion and all irreligion, Christ and Buddha, God and the devil. The world as it is, and the whole world as it is, physical, and spiritual, and historical, with its good and bad, with its manifold inconsistencies, is what he wishes to set forth, in strong, picturesque, and popular lineaments, for the understanding of the average man. One of his favorite endeavors is to get the whole matter into a nutshell; to knock the four corners of the universe, one after another, about his readers' ears; to hurry him, in breathless phrases, hither and thither, back and forward, in time and space; to focus all this about his own momentary personality; and then, drawing the ground from under his feet, as if by some cataclysm of nature, to plunge him into the unfathomable abyss sown with enormous suns and systems, and among the inconceivable numbers and magnitudes and velocities of the heavenly bodies. So that he concludes by striking into us some sense of that disproportion of things which Shelley has illuminated by the ironical flash of these eight words: The desire of the moth for the star.

The same truth, but to what a different purpose! Whitman's moth is mightily at his ease about all the planets in heaven, and cannot think too highly of our sublunary tapers. The universe is so large that imagination flags in the effort to conceive it; but here, in the meantime, is the world under our feet, a very warm and habitable corner. "The earth, that is sufficient; I do not want the constellations any nearer," he remarks. And again: "Let your soul stand cool and composed," says he, "before a million universes." It is the language of a transcendental common sense, such as Thoreau held and sometimes uttered. But Whitman, who has a somewhat vulgar inclination for technical talk and the jargon of philosophy, is not content with a few pregnant hints; he must put the dots upon his i's; he must corroborate the songs of Apollo by some of the darkest talk of human metaphysic. He tells his disciples that they must be ready "to confront the growing arrogance of Realism." Each person is, for himself, the keystone and the occasion of this universal edifice. "Nothing, not God," he says, "is greater to one than one's self is;" a statement with an irreligious smack at the first sight; but like most startling sayings, a manifest truism on a second. He will give effect to his own character without apology; he sees "that the elementary laws never apologize." "I reckon," he adds, with quaint colloquial arrogance, "I

reckon I behave no prouder than the level I plant my
house by, after all.'' The level follows the law of its
being; so, unrelentingly, will he; everything, every person, is good in his own place and way; God is the
maker of all, and all are in one design. For he be-
lieves in God, and that with a sort of blasphemous
security. ''No array of terms,'' quoth he, ''no array of
terms can say how much at peace I am about God
and about death.'' There certainly never was a prophet
who carried things with a higher hand; he gives us
less a body of dogmas than a series of proclamations
by the grace of God; and language, you will observe,
positively fails him to express how far he stands above
the highest human doubts and trepidations.

But next in order of truths to a person's sublime
conviction of himself, comes the attraction of one person for another, and all that we mean by the word love:

> ''The dear love of man for his comrade—the
> attraction of friend for friend,
> Of the well-married husband and wife, of
> children and parents,
> Of city for city and land for land.''

The solitude of the most sublime idealist is broken
in upon by other people's faces; he sees a look in their
eyes that corresponds to something in his own heart;
there comes a tone in their voices which convicts him
of a startling weakness for his fellow-creatures. While
he is hymning the *ego* and commercing with God
and the universe, a woman goes below his window;
and at the turn of her skirt, or the color of her eyes,
Icarus is recalled from heaven by the run. Love is so

startlingly real that it takes rank upon an equal footing of reality with the consciousness of personal existence. We are as heartily persuaded of the identity of
those we love as of our own identity. And so sympathy pairs with self-assertion, the two gerents of human life on earth; and Whitman's ideal man must not
only be strong, free, and self-reliant in himself, but his
freedom must be bounded and his strength perfected by
the most intimate, eager, and long-suffering love for
others. To some extent this is taking away with the
left hand what has been so generously given with the
right. Morality has been ceremoniously extruded from
the door only to be brought in again by the window.
We are told, on one page, to do as we please; and
on the next we are sharply upbraided for not having
done as the author pleases. We are first assured that
we are the finest fellows in the world in our own
right; and then it appears that we are only fine fellows in so far as we practice a most quixotic code of
morals. The disciple who saw himself in clear ether a
moment before is plunged down again among the fogs
and complications of duty. And this is all the more
overwhelming because Whitman insists not only on love
between sex and sex, and between friends of the same
sex, but in the field of the less intense political sympathies; and his ideal man must not only be a generous friend but a conscientious voter into the bargain.

His method somewhat lessens the difficulty. He is
not, the reader will remember, to tell us how good we
ought to be, but to remind us how good we are. He
is to encourage us to be free and kind, by proving
that we are free and kind already. He passes our cor-

porate life under review, to show that it is upheld by the very virtues of which he makes himself the advocate. "There is no object so soft," he says somewhere in his big, plain way, "there is no object so soft but it makes a hub for the wheel'd universe." Rightly understood, it is on the softest of all objects, the sympathetic heart, that the wheel of society turns easily and securely as on a perfect axle. There is no room, of course, for doubt or discussion, about conduct, where every one is to follow the law of his being with exact compliance. Whitman hates doubt, deprecates discussion, and discourages to his utmost the craving, carping sensibilities of the conscience. We are to imitate, to use one of his absurd and happy phrases, "the satisfaction and aplomb of animals." If he preaches a sort of ranting Christianity in morals, a fit consequent to the ranting optimism of his cosmology, it is because he declares it to be the original deliverance of the human heart; or at least, for he would be honestly historical in method, of the human heart as at present Christianized. His is a morality without a prohibition; his policy is one of encouragement all round. A man must be a born hero to come up to Whitman's standard in the practice of any of the positive virtues; but of a negative virtue, such as temperance or chastity, he has so little to say, that the reader need not be surprised if he drops a word or two upon the other side. He would lay down nothing that would be a clog; he would prescribe nothing that cannot be done ruddily, in a heat. The great point is to get people under way. To the faithful Whitmanite this would be justified by the belief that God made all, and that all was good; the prophet, in this doctrine, has only to cry "Tally-ho," and mankind will break into a gallop on the road to El Dorado. Perhaps, to another class of minds, it may look like the result of the somewhat cynical reflection that you will not make a kind man out of one who is unkind by any precepts under heaven; tempered by the belief that, in natural circumstances, the large majority is well disposed. Thence it would follow, that if you can only get every one to feel more warmly and act more courageously, the balance of results will be for good.

So far, you see, the doctrine is pretty coherent as a doctrine; as a picture of man's life it is incomplete and misleading, although eminently cheerful. This he is himself the first to acknowledge; for if he is prophetic in anything, it is in his noble disregard of consistency. "Do I contradict myself?" he asks somewhere; and then pat comes the answer, the best answer ever given in print, worthy of a sage, or rather of a woman: "Very well, then, I contradict myself!" with this addition, not so feminine and perhaps not altogether so satisfactory: "I am large—I contain multitudes." Life, as a matter of fact, partakes largely of the nature of tragedy. The gospel according to Whitman, even if it be not so logical, has this advantage over the gospel according to Pangloss, that it does not utterly disregard the existence of temporal evil. Whitman accepts the fact of disease and wretchedness like an honest man; and instead of trying to qualify it in the interest of his optimism, sets himself to spur people up to be helpful. He expresses a conviction, indeed, that all will be made up to the victims in the end;

that "what is untried and afterward" will fail no one,
not even "the old man who has lived without purpose
and feels it with bitterness worse than gall." But this
is not to palliate our sense of what is hard or melancholy in the present. Pangloss, smarting under one of
the worst things that ever was supposed to come from
America, consoled himself with the reflection that it
was the price we have to pay for cochineal. And with
that murderous parody, logical optimism and the praises
of the best of possible words went irrevocably out of
season, and have been no more heard of in the mouths
of reasonable men. Whitman spares us all allusions to
the cochineal; he treats evil and sorrow in a spirit almost as of welcome; as an old sea-dog might have
welcomed the sight of the enemy's topsails off the Span-
ish Main. There, at least, he seems to say, is something obvious to be done. I do not know many better things in literature than the brief pictures—brief
and vivid like things seen by lightning—with which he
tries to stir up the world's heart upon the side of
mercy. He braces us, on the one hand, with examples
of heroic duty and helpfulness; on the other, he touches
us with pitiful instances of people needing help. He
knows how to make the heart beat at a brave story;
to inflame us with just resentment over the hunted
slave; to stop our mouths for shame when he tells of
the drunken prostitute. For all the afflicted, all the
weak, all the wicked, a good word is said in a spirit
which I can only call one of ultra-Christianity; and
however wild, however contradictory, it may be in
parts, this at least may be said for his book, as it
may be said of the Christian Gospels, that no one will

read it, however respectable, but he gets a knock upon his conscience; no one, however fallen, but he finds a kindly and supporting welcome.

IV

Nor has he been content with merely blowing the trumpet for the battle of well-doing; he has given to his precepts the authority of his own brave example. Naturally a grave, believing man, with little or no sense of humor, he has succeeded as well in life as in his printed performances. The spirit that was in him has come forth most eloquently in his actions. Many who have only read his poetry have been tempted to set him down as an ass, or even as a charlatan; but I never met any one who had known him personally who did not profess a solid affection and respect for the man's character. He practices as he professes; he feels deeply that Christian love for all men, that toleration, that cheerful delight in serving others, which he often celebrates in literature with a doubtful measure of success. And perhaps, out of all his writings, the best and the most human and convincing passages are to be found in "these soil'd and creas'd little livraisons, each composed of a sheet or two of paper, folded small to carry in the pocket, and fastened with a pin," which he scribbled during the war by the bedsides of the wounded or in the excitement of great events. They are hardly literature in the formal meaning of the word; he has left his jottings for the most part as he made them; a homely detail, a word from the lips of a dying soldier, a business memorandum, the copy of a letter—short, straightforward to the point, with none of the trappings of composition; but they breathe a profound sentiment, they give us a vivid look at one of the sides of life, and they make us acquainted with a man whom it is an honor to love.

Whitman's intense Americanism, his unlimited belief in the future of These States (as, with reverential capitals, he loves to call them), made the war a period of great trial to his soul. The new virtue, Unionism, of which he is the sole inventor, seemed to have fallen into premature unpopularity. All that he loved, hoped, or hated, hung in the balance. And the game of war was not only momentous to him in its issues; it sublimated his spirit by its heroic displays, and tortured him intimately by the spectacle of its horrors. It was a theater, it was a place of education, it was like a season of religious revival. He watched Lincoln going daily to his work; he studied and fraternized with young soldiery passing to the front; above all, he walked the hospitals, reading the Bible, distributing clean clothes, or apples, or tobacco; a patient, helpful, reverend man, full of kind speeches.

His memoranda of this period are almost bewildering to read. From one point of view they seem those of a district visitor; from another, they look like the formless jottings of an artist in the picturesque. More than one woman, on whom I tried the experiment, immediately claimed the writer for a fellow-woman. More than one literary purist might identify him as a shoddy newspaper correspondent without the necessary faculty of style. And yet the story touches home; and if you are of the weeping order of mankind, you will certainly find your eyes fill with tears, of which you have no reason to be ashamed. There is only one way to characterize a work of this order, and that is to quote. Here is a passage from a letter to a mother, unknown to Whitman, whose son died in hospital:

"Frank, as far as I saw, had everything requisite in surgical treatment, nursing, etc. He had watches much of the time. He was so good and well-behaved, and affectionate, I myself liked him very much. I was in the habit of coming in afternoons and sitting by him, and he liked to have me—liked to put out his arm and lay his hand on my knee—would keep it so a long while. Toward the last he was more restless and flighty at night—often fancied himself with his regiment—by his talk sometimes seem'd as if his feelings were hurt by being blamed by his officers for something he was entirely innocent of—said 'I never in my life was thought capable of such a thing, and never was.' At other times he would fancy himself talking as it seem'd to children or such like, his relatives I suppose, and giving them good advice; would talk to them a long while. All the time he was out of his head not one single bad word, or thought, or idea escaped him. It was remark'd that many a man's conversation in his senses was not half so good as Frank's delirium.

"He was perfectly willing to die—he had become very weak, and had suffer'd a good deal, and was perfectly resign'd, poor boy. I do not know his past life, but I feel as if it must have been good. At any rate what I saw of him here, under the most trying circumstances, with a painful wound, and among strangers, I can say that he behaved so brave, so composed, and so sweet and affectionate, it could not be surpassed. And now, like many other noble and good men, after serving his country as a soldier, he has yielded up his young life at the very outset in her service. Such things are gloomy—yet there is a text, 'God doeth all things well,' the meaning of which, after due time, appears to the soul.

"I thought perhaps a few words, though from a stranger,

about your son, from one who was with him at the last,
might be worth while, for I loved the young man, though I
but saw him immediately to lose him.''

It is easy enough to pick holes in the grammar of
this letter, but what are we to say of its profound
goodness and tenderness? It is written as though he
had the mother's face before his eyes, and saw her
wincing in the flesh at every word. And what, again,
are we to say of its sober truthfulness, not exaggerat-
ing, not running to phrases, not seeking to make a
hero out of what was only an ordinary but good and
brave young man? Literary reticence is not Whitman's
stronghold; and this reticence is not literary, but humane; it is not that of a good artist but that of a
good man. He knew that what the mother wished
to hear about was Frank; and he told her about her
Frank as he was.

V

Something should be said of Whitman's style, for
style is of the essence of thinking. And where a man
is so critically deliberate as our author, and goes solemnly about his poetry for an ulterior end, every indi-
cation is worth notice. He has chosen a rough, un-
rhymed, lyrical verse; sometimes instinct with a fine
processional movement; often so rugged and careless
that it can only be described by saying that he has
not taken the trouble to write prose. I believe myself
that it was selected principally because it was easy to
write, although not without recollections of the march-
ing measures of some of the prose in our English Old
Testament. According to Whitman, on the other hand

"the time has arrived to essentially break down the barriers of form between Prose and Poetry . . . . for the most cogent purposes of those . . . . nland states, and for Texas, and California, and O_ n";—a statement which is among the happiest achievements of American humor. He calls his ver_ "_ ciatives," in easily followed allusion to a musical term. "Easily-written, loose-fingered chords," he cries, "I feel the thrum of your climax and close." Too often, I fear, he is the only one who can perceive the rhythm; and in spite of Mr. Swinburne, a great part of his work considered as verses is poor bald stuff. Considered, not as verse, but as speech, a great part of it is full of strange and admirable merits. The right detail is seized; the right word, bold and trenchant, is thrust into its place. Whitman has small regard to literary decencies, and is totally free from literary timidities. He is neither afraid of being slangy nor of being dull; nor, let me add, of being ridiculous. The result is a most surprising compound of plain grandeur, sentimental affectation, and downright nonsense. It would be useless to follow his detractors and give instances of how bad he can be at his worst; and perhaps if would be not much wiser to give extracted specimens of how happily he can write when he is at his best. These come in to most advantage in their own place; owing something, it may be, to the offset of their curious surroundings. And one thing is certain, that no one can appreciate Whitman's excellences until he has grown accustomed to his faults. Until you are content to pick poetry out of his pages almost as you must pick it out of a Greek play in Bohn's translation, your gravity will be continually upset, your ears perpetually disappointed, and the whole book will be no more to you than a particularly flagrant production by the Poet Close.

A writer of this uncertain quality was, perhaps, unfortunate in taking for thesis the beauty of the world as it now is, not only on the hill-tops but in the factory; not only in the harbor full of stately ships, but in the magazine of the hopelessly prosaic hatter. To show heaven in common things is the work of the rare talent, and is not to be done by the wishing. It is easy to state a theory, but to bring it home to men's minds is the problem of literature, <u>and is only accomplished by rare talent, and in comparatively rare</u> instances. To bid the whole world stand and deliver, with a dogma in one's right hand by way of pistol; to cover reams of paper in a galloping, headstrong vein; to cry louder and louder over everything as it comes up, and make no distinction in one's enthusiasm over the most incomparable matters; to prove one's entire want of sympathy for the jaded, literary palate, by calling, not a spade a spade, but a hatter a hatter, in a lyrical apostrophe;—this, in spite of all the airs of inspiration, is not the way to do it. It may be very wrong, and very wounding to a respectable branch of industry, but the word "hatter" cannot be used seriously in emotional verse; not to understand this, is to have no literary tact; and I would, for his own sake, that this were the only inadmissible expression with which Whitman had bedecked his pages. The book teems with similar comicalities; and, to a reader who is determined to take it from that side only, presents a perfect carnival of fun.

A good deal of this is the result of theory playing its usual vile trick upon the artist. It is because he is a Democrat that Whitman must have in the hatter. If you may say Admiral, he reasons, why may you not say Hatter? One man is as good as another, and it is the business of the "great poet" to show poetry in the life of the one as well as the other. A most incontrovertible sentiment surely, and one which nobody would think of controverting, where—and here is the point—where any beauty has been shown. But how, where that is not the case? where the hatter is simply introduced, as God made him and as his fellow-men have miscalled him, at the crisis of a high-flown rhapsody? And what are we to say, where a man of Whitman's notable capacity for putting things in a bright, picturesque, and novel way, simply gives up the attempt, and indulges, with apparent exultation, in an inventory of trades or implements, with no more color or coherence than so many index-words out of a dictionary? I do not know that we can say anything, but that it is a prodigiously amusing exhibition for a line or so. The worst of it is, that Whitman must have known better. The man is a great critic, and, so far as I can make out, a good one; and how much criticism does it require to know that capitulation is not description, or that fingering on a dumb keyboard, with whatever show of sentiment and execution, is not at all the same thing as discoursing music? I wish I could believe he was quite honest with us; but, indeed, who was ever quite honest who wrote a book for a purpose? It is a flight beyond the reach of human magnanimity.

One other point, where his means failed him, must

be touched upon, however shortly. In his desire to accept all facts loyally and simply, it fell within his programme to speak at some length and with some plainness on what is, for I really do not know what reason, the most delicate of subjects. Seeing in that one of the most serious and interesting parts of life, he was aggrieved that it should be looked upon as ridiculous or shameful. No one speaks of maternity with his tongue in his cheek; and Whitman made a bold push to set the sanctity of fatherhood beside the sanctity of motherhood, and introduce this also among the things that can be spoken of without either a blush or a wink. But the Philistines have been too strong; and, to say truth, Whitman has rather played the fool. We may be thoroughly conscious that his end is improving; that it would be a good thing if a window were opened on these close privacies of life; that on this subject, as on all others, he now and then lets fall a pregnant saying. But we are not satisfied. We feel that he was not the man for so difficult an enterprise. He loses our sympathy in the character of a poet by attracting too much of our attention in that of a Bull in a China Shop. And where, by a little more art, we might have been solemnized ourselves, it is too often Whitman alone who is solemn in the face of an audience somewhat indecorously amused.

VI

Lastly, as most important, after all, to human beings in our disputable state, what is that higher prudence which was to be the aim and issue of these deliberate productions?

Whitman is too clever to slip into a succinct formula. If he could have adequately said his say in a single proverb, it is to be presumed he would not have put himself to the trouble of writing several volumes. It was his programme to state as much as he could of the world with all its contradictions, and leave the upshot with God who planned it. What he has made of the world and the world's meanings is to be found at large in his poems. These altogether give his answers to the problems of belief and conduct; in many ways righteous and high-spirited, in some ways loose and contradictory. And yet there are two passages from the preface to the "Leaves of Grass" which do pretty well condense his teaching on all essential points, and yet preserve a measure of his spirit.

"This is what you shall do," he says in the one, "love the earth, and sun, and animals, despise riches, give alms to every one that asks, stand up for the stupid and crazy, devote your income and labor to others, hate tyrants, argue not concerning God, have patience and indulgence toward the people, take off your hat to nothing known or unknown, or to any man or number of men; go freely with powerful uneducated persons, and with the young, and mothers of families; read these leaves (his own works) in the open air every season of every year of your life; re-examine all you have been told at school or church, or in any book, and dismiss whatever insults your own soul."

"The prudence of the greatest poet," he adds in the other —and the greatest poet is, of course, himself—"knows that the young man who composedly periled his life and lost it, has done exceeding well for himself; while the man who has not periled his life, and retains it to old age in riches and ease, has perhaps achieved nothing for himself worth mentioning; and that only that person has no great prudence to learn, who has learned to prefer real long lived things, and favors body and soul the same, and perceives the indirect surely following the direct, and what evil or good he does leaping onward and waiting to meet him again, and who in his spirit, in any emergency whatever, neither hurries nor avoids death.''

There is much that is Christian in these extracts, startlingly Christian. Any reader who bears in mind Whitman's own advice and "dismisses whatever insults his own soul" will find plenty that is bracing, brightening, and chastening to reward him for a little patience at first. It seems hardly possible that any being should get evil from so healthy a book as the "Leaves of Grass," which is simply comical wherever it falls short of nobility; but if there be any such, who cannot both take and leave, who cannot let a single opportunity pass by without some unworthy and unmanly thought, I should have as great difficulty, and neither more nor less, in recommending the works of Whitman as in lending them Shakespeare, or letting them go abroad outside of the grounds of a private asylum.

HENRY DAVID THOREAU

HIS CHARACTER AND OPINIONS

I

THOREAU'S thin, penetrating, big-nosed face, even in a bad woodcut, conveys some hint of the limitations of his mind and character. With his almost acid sharpness of insight, with his almost animal dexterity in act, there went none of that large, unconscious geniality of the world's heroes. He was not easy, not ample, not urbane, not even kind; his enjoyment was hardly smiling, or the smile was not broad enough to be convincing; he had no waste lands nor kitchen-midden in his nature, but was all improved and sharpened to a point. "He was bred to no profession," says Emerson; "he never married; he lived alone; he never went to church; he never voted; he refused to pay a tax to the State; he ate no flesh, he drank no wine, he never knew the use of tobacco; and, though a naturalist, he used neither trap nor gun. When asked at dinner what dish he preferred, he answered, 'the nearest.'" So many negative superiorities begin to smack a little of the prig. From his later works he was in the habit of cutting out the humorous passages, under the impression that they were beneath the dignity of his moral muse; and there we see the prig stand public and confessed. It was "much easier," says Emerson acutely, much easier for Thoreau to say *no* than *yes;* and that is a characteristic which depicts the man. It is a useful accomplishment to be able to say *no*, but surely it is the essence of amiability to prefer to say *yes* where it is possible. There is something wanting in the man who does not hate himself whenever he is constrained to say no. And there was a great deal wanting in this born dissenter. He was almost shockingly devoid of weaknesses; he had not enough of them to be truly polar with humanity; whether you call him demi-god or demi-man, he was at least not altogether one of us, for he was not touched with a feeling of our infirmities. The world's heroes have room for all positive qualities, even those which are disreputable, in the capacious theater of their dispositions. Such can live many lives; while a Thoreau can live but one, and that only with perpetual foresight.

He was no ascetic, rather an Epicurean of the nobler sort; and he had this one great merit, that he succeeded so far as to be happy. "I love my fate to the core and rind," he wrote once; and even while he lay dying, here is what he dictated (for it seems he was already too feeble to control the pen): "You ask particularly after my health. I *suppose* that I have not many months to live, but of course know nothing about it. I may say that I am enjoying existence as much as ever, and regret nothing." It is not given to all to bear so clear a testimony to the sweetness of their fate, nor to any without courage and wisdom; for this world in itself is but a painful and uneasy place of residence, and lasting happiness, at least to the self-conscious, comes only from within. Now Thoreau's

content and ecstasy in living was, we may say, like a
plant that he had watered and tended with womanish
solicitude; for there is apt to be something unmanly,
something almost dastardly, in a life that does not move
with dash and freedom, and that fears the bracing con
tact of the world. In one word, Thoreau was a skulker.
He did not wish virtue to go out of him among his
fellowmen, but slunk into a corner to hoard it for himself. He left all for the sake of certain virtuous self-
indulgences. It is true that his tastes were noble; that
his ruling passion was to keep himself unspotted from
the world; and that his luxuries were all of the same
healthy order as cold tubs and early rising. But a man
may be both coldly cruel in the pursuit of goodness,
and morbid even in the pursuit of health. I cannot
lay my hands on the passage in which he explains his
abstinence from tea and coffee, but I am sure I have
the meaning correctly. It is this: He thought it bad
economy and worthy of no true virtuoso to spoil the
natural rapture of the morning with such muddy stimu-
lants; let him but see the sun rise, and he was already sufficiently inspirited for the labors of the day.
That may be reason good enough to abstain from tea;
but when we go on to find the same man, on the
same or similar grounds, abstain from nearly everything
that his neighbors innocently and pleasurably use, and
from the rubs and trials of human society itself into
the bargain, we recognize that valetudinarian healthful-
ness which is more delicate than sickness itself. We
need have no respect for a state of artificial training.
True health is to be able to do without it. Shakespeare, we can imagine, might begin the day upon a

quart of ale, and yet enjoy the sunrise to the full as
much as Thoreau, and commemorate his enjoyment in
vastly better verses. A man who must separate himself from his neighbors' habits in order to be happy,
is in much the same case with one who requires to
take opium for the same purpose. What we want to
see is one who can breast into the world, do a man's
work, and still preserve his first and pure enjoyment
of existence.

Thoreau's faculties were of a piece with his moral
shyness; for they were all delicacies. He could guide
himself about the woods on the darkest night by the
touch of his feet. He could pick up at once an exact
dozen of pencils by the feeling, pace distances with accuracy, and gauge cubic contents by the eye. His
smell was so dainty that he could perceive the fetor
of dwelling-houses as he passed them by at night; his
palate so unsophisticated that, like a child, he disliked
the taste of wine—or perhaps, living in America, had
never tasted any that was good; and his knowledge of
nature was so complete and curious that he could have
told the time of year, within a day or so, by the aspect of the plants. In his dealings with animals, he
was the original of Hawthorne's Donatello. He pulled
the woodchuck out of its hole by the tail; the hunted
fox came to him for protection; wild squirrels have
been seen to nestle in his waistcoat; he would thrust
his arm into a pool and bring forth a bright, panting
fish, lying undismayed in the palm of his hand. There
were few things that he could not do. He could make
a house, a boat, a pencil, or a book. He was a sur-
veyor, a scholar, a natural historian. He could run,

walk, climb, skate, swim, and manage a boat. The smallest occasion served to display his physical accomplishment; and a manufacturer, from merely observing his dexterity with the window of a railway carriage, offered him a situation on the spot. "The only fruit of much living," he observes, "is the ability to do some slight thing better." But such was the exactitude of his senses, so alive was he in every fiber, that it seems as if the maxim should be changed in his case, for he could do most things with unusual perfection. And perhaps he had an approving eye to himself when he wrote: "Though the youth at last grows indifferent, the laws of the universe are not indifferent, *but are forever on the side of the most sensitive.*"

II

Thoreau had decided, it would seem, from the very first to lead a life of self-improvement: the needle did not tremble as with richer natures, but pointed steadily north; and as he saw duty and inclination in one, he turned all his strength in that direction. He was met upon the threshold by a common difficulty. In this world, in spite of its many agreeable features, even the most sensitive must undergo some drudgery to live. It is not possible to devote your time to study and meditation without what are quaintly but happily denominated private means; these absent, a man must contrive to earn his bread by some service to the public such as the public cares to pay him for; or, as Thoreau loved to put it, Apollo must serve Admetus. This was to Thoreau even a sourer necessity than it is to most; there was a love of freedom, a strain of the wild man, in his nature, that rebelled with violence against the yoke of custom; and he was so eager to cultivate himself and to be happy in his own society, that he could consent with difficulty even to the interruptions of friendship. *"Such are my engagements to myself that I dare not promise,"* he once wrote in answer to an invitation; and the italics are his own. Marcus Aurelius found time to study virtue, and between whiles to conduct the imperial affairs of Rome; but Thoreau is so busy improving himself that he must think twice about a morning call. And now imagine him condemned for eight hours a day to some uncongenial and unmeaning business! He shrank from the very look of the mechanical in life; all should, if possible, be sweetly spontaneous and swimmingly progressive. Thus he learned to make lead-pencils, and, when he had gained the best certificate and his friends began to congratulate him on his establishment in life, calmly announced that he should never make another. "Why should I?" said he; "I would not do again what I have done once." For when a thing has once been done as well as it wants to be, it is of no further interest to the self-improver. Yet in after years, and when it became needful to support his family, he returned patiently to this mechanical art—a step more than worthy of himself.

The pencils seem to have been Apollo's first experiment in the service of Admetus; but others followed. "I have thoroughly tried school-keeping," he writes, "and found that my expenses were in proportion, or rather out of proportion, to my income; for I was obliged to dress and train, not to say think and be-

lieve, accordingly, and I lost my time into the bargain. As I did not teach for the benefit of my fellow-
men, but simply for a livelihood, this was a failure. I
have tried trade, but I found that it would take ten
years to get under way in that, and that then I should
probably be on my way to the devil." Nothing, indeed, can surpass his scorn for all so-called business.
Upon that subject gall squirts from him at a touch.
"The whole enterprise of this nation is not illustrated
by a thought," he writes; "it is not warmed by a
sentiment; there is nothing in it for which a man
should lay down his life, nor even his gloves." And
again: "If our merchants did not most of them fail,
and the banks too, my faith in the old laws of this
world would be staggered. The statement that ninety-
six in a hundred doing such business surely break down
is perhaps the sweetest fact that statistics have re-
vealed." The wish was probably father to the figures;
but there is something enlivening in a hatred of so
genuine a brand, hot as Corsican revenge, and sneer-
ing like Voltaire.

Pencils, school-keeping, and trade being thus dis-
carded one after another, Thoreau, with a stroke of
strategy, turned the position. He saw his way to get
his board and lodging for practically nothing; and Admetus never got less work out of any servant since
the world began. It was his ambition to be an oriental philosopher; but he was always a very Yankee sort
of oriental. Even in the peculiar attitude in which he
stood to money, his system of personal economics, as
we may call it, he displayed a vast amount of truly
down-East calculation, and he adopted poverty like a

piece of business. Yet his system is based on one or two ideas which, I believe, come naturally to all thoughtful youths, and are only pounded out of them by city uncles. Indeed, something essentially youthful distinguishes all Thoreau's knock-down blows at current opinion. Like the posers of a child, they leave the orthodox in a kind of speechless agony. These know the thing is nonsense. They are sure there must be an answer, yet somehow cannot find it. So it is with his system of economy. He cuts through the subject on so new a plane that the accepted arguments apply no longer; he attacks it in a new dialect where there are no catchwords ready-made for the defender; after you have been boxing for years on a polite, gladiatorial convention, here is an assailant who does not scruple to hit below the belt.

"The cost of a thing," says he, "is *the amount of what I will call life* which is required to be exchanged for it, immediately or in the long run." I have been accustomed to put it to myself, perhaps more clearly, that the price we have to pay for money is paid in liberty. Between these two ways of it, at least, the reader will probably not fail to find a third definition of his own; and it follows, on one or other, that a man may pay too dearly for his livelihood, by giving, in Thoreau's terms, his whole life for it, or, in mine, bartering for it the whole of his available liberty, and becoming a slave till death. There are two questions to be considered—the quality of what we buy, and the price we have to pay for it. Do you want a thousand a year, a two thousand a year, or a ten thousand a year livelihood? and can you afford the one

you want? It is a matter of taste; it is not in the
least degree a question of duty, though commonly supposed so. But there is no authority for that view anywhere. It is nowhere in the Bible. It is true that we
might do a vast amount of good if we were wealthy,
but it is also highly improbable; not many do; and
the art of growing rich is not only quite distinct from
that of doing good, but the practice of the one does
not at all train a man for practicing the other. "Money
might be of great service to me," writes Thoreau;
"but the difficulty now is that I do not improve my
opportunities, and therefore I am not prepared to have
my opportunities increased." It is a mere illusion that,
above a certain income, the personal desires will be
satisfied and leave a wider margin for the generous
impulse. It is as difficult to be generous, or anything
else, except perhaps a member of Parliament, on thirty
thousand as on two hundred a year.

Now Thoreau's tastes were well defined. He loved
to be free, to be master of his times and seasons, to
indulge the mind rather than the body; he preferred
long rambles to rich dinners, his own reflections to the
consideration of society, and an easy, calm, unfettered,
active life among green trees to dull toiling at the coun-
ter of a bank. And such being his inclination he determined to gratify it. A poor man must save off something; he determined to save off his livelihood. "When
a man has attained those things which are necessary to
life," he writes, "there is another alternative than to obtain the superfluities; *he may adventure on life now*,
his vacation from humbler toil having commenced."
Thoreau would get shelter, some kind of covering for

his body, and necessary daily bread; even these he should get as cheaply as possible; and then, his vacation from humbler toil having commenced, devote himself to oriental philosophers, the study of nature, and the work of self-improvement.

Prudence, which bids us all go to the ant for wisdom and hoard against the day of sickness, was not a favorite with Thoreau. He preferred that other, whose name is so much misappropriated: Faith. When he had secured the necessaries of the moment, he would not reckon up possible accidents or torment himself with trouble for the future. He had no toleration for the man "who ventures to live only by the aid of the mutual insurance company, which has promised to bury him decently." He would trust himself a little to the world. "We may safely trust a good deal more than we do," says he. "How much is not done by us! or what if we had been taken sick?" And then, with a stab of satire, he describes contemporary mankind in a phrase: "All the day long on the alert, at night we unwillingly say our prayers and commit ourselves to uncertainties." It is not likely that the public will be much affected by Thoreau, when they blink the direct injunctions of the religion they profess; and yet, whether we will or no, we make the same hazardous ventures; we back our own health and the honesty of our neighbors for all that we are worth; and it is chilling to think how many must lose their wager.

In 1845, twenty-eight years old, an age by which the liveliest have usually declined into some conformity with the world, Thoreau, with a capital of something less than five pounds and a borrowed ax, walked forth into the woods by Walden Pond, and began his new experiment in life. He built himself a dwelling, and returned the ax, he says with characteristic and workman-like pride, sharper than when he borrowed it; he reclaimed a patch, where he cultivated beans, peas, potatoes, and sweet corn; he had his bread to bake, his farm to dig, and for the matter of six weeks in the summer he worked at surveying, carpentry, or some other of his numerous dexterities, for hire. For more than five years, this was all that he required to do for his support, and he had the winter and most of the summer at his entire disposal. For six weeks of occupation, a little cooking and a little gentle hygienic gardening, the man, you may say, had as good as stolen his livelihood. Or we must rather allow that he had done far better; for the thief himself is continually and busily occupied; and even one born to inherit a million will have more calls upon his time than Thoreau. Well might he say, "What old people tell you you cannot do, you try and find you can." And how surprising is his conclusion: "I am convinced that *to maintain one's self on this earth is not a hardship, but a pastime*, if we will live simply and wisely; *as the pursuits of simpler nations are still the sports of the more artificial.*"

When he had enough of that kind of life, he showed the same simplicity in giving it up as in beginning it. There are some who could have done the one, but, vanity forbidding, not the other; and that is perhaps the story of the hermits; but Thoreau made no fetish of his own example, and did what he wanted squarely. And five years is long enough for an experiment and

to prove the success of transcendental Yankeeism. It is
not his frugality which is worthy of note; for, to begin
with, that was inborn, and therefore inimitable by
others who are differently constituted; and again, it
was no new thing, but has often been equaled by poor
Scotch students at the universities. The point is the
sanity of his view of life, and the insight with which
he recognized the position of money, and thought out for
himself the problem of riches and a livelihood. Apart
from his eccentricities, he had perceived, and was act-
ing on, a truth of universal application. For money
enters in two different characters into the scheme of
life. A certain amount, varying with the number and
empire of our desires, is a true necessary to each one
of us in the present order of society; but beyond that
amount, money is a commodity to be bought or not
to be bought, a luxury in which we may either indulge
or stint ourselves, like any other. And there are many
luxuries that we may legitimately prefer to it, such as
a grateful conscience, a country life, or the woman of
our inclination Trite, flat, and obvious as this conclusion
may appear, we have only to look round us in society
to see how scantily it has been recognized; and perhaps even ourselves, after a little reflection, may decide
to spend a trifle less for money, and indulge ourselves
a trifle more in the article of freedom.

III

"To have done anything by which you earned money
merely," says Thoreau, "is to be" (have been, he
means) "idle and worse." There are two passages in
his letters, both, oddly enough, relating to firewood,

which must be brought together to be rightly understood. So taken, they contain between them the marrow of all good sense on the subject of work in its
relation to something broader than mere livelihood. Here
is the first: "I suppose I have burned up a good-sized
tree to-night—and for what? I settled with Mr. Tarbell
for it the other day; but that wasn't the final settlement. I got off cheaply from him. At last one will
say: 'Let us see, how much wood did you burn, sir?'
And I shall shudder to think. that the next question
will be, 'What did you do while you were warm?'"
Even after we have settled with Admetus in the person
of Mr. Tarbell, there comes, you see, a further question.
It is not enough to have earned our livelihood. Either
the earning itself should have been serviceable to mankind, or something else must follow. To live is sometimes very difficult, but it is never meritorious in itself;
and we must have a reason to allege to our own conscience why we should continue to exist upon this
crowded earth. If Thoreau had simply dwelt in his
house at Walden, a lover of trees, birds, and fishes,
and the open air and virtue, a reader of wise books,
an idle, selfish self-improver, he would have managed
to cheat Admetus, but, to cling to metaphor, the devil
would have had him in the end. Those who can avoid
toil altogether and dwell in the Arcadia of private
means, and even those who can, by abstinence, reduce
the necessary amount of it to some six weeks a year,
having the more liberty, have only the higher moral
obligation to be up and doing in the interest of man.

The second passage is this: "There is a far more
important and warming heat, commonly lost, which pre-

cedes the burning of the wood. It is the smoke of industry, which is incense. I had been so thoroughly warmed in body and spirit, that when at length my fuel was housed, I came near selling it to the ashman, as if I had extracted all its heat." Industry is, in itself and when properly chosen, delightful and profitable to the worker; and when your toil has been a pleasure, you have not, as Thoreau says, "earned money merely," but money, health, delight, and moral profit, all in one. "We must heap up a great pile of doing for a small diameter of being," he says in another place; and then exclaims, "How admirably the artist is made to accomplish his self-culture by devotion to his art!" We may escape uncongenial toil, only to devote ourselves to that which is congenial. It is only to transact some higher business that even Apollo dare play the truant from Admetus. We must all work for the sake of work; we must all work, as Thoreau says again, in any "absorbing pursuit—it does not much matter what, so it be honest"; but the most profitable work is that which combines into one continued effort the largest proportion of the powers and desires of a man's nature; that into which he will plunge with ardor, and from which he will desist with reluctance; in which he will know the weariness of fatigue, but not that of satiety; and which will be ever fresh, pleasing, and stimulating to his taste. Such work holds a man together, braced at all points; it does not suffer him to doze or wander; it keeps him actively conscious of himself, yet raised among superior interests; it gives him the profit of industry with the pleasures of a pastime. This is what his art should be to the true artist, and that to a degree un-

known in other and less intimate pursuits. For other
professions stand apart from the human business of life;
but an art has its seat at the center of the artist's
doings and sufferings, deals directly with his experi-
ences, teaches him the lessons of his own fortunes and
mishaps, and becomes a part of his biography. So
says Goethe:

> "Spät erklingt was früh erklang;
> Glück und Unglück wird Gesang."

Now Thoreau's art was literature; and it was one
of which he had conceived most ambitiously. He loved
and believed in good books. He said well, "Life is not
habitually seen from any common platform so truly and
unexaggerated as in the light of literature." But the
literature he loved was of the heroic order. "Books,
not which afford us a cowering enjoyment, but in
which each thought is of unusual daring; such as an
idle man cannot read, and a timid one would not be
entertained by, which even make us dangerous to existing institutions—such I call good books." He did not
think them easy to be read. "The heroic books," he
says, "even if printed in the character of our mother-
tongue, will always be in a language dead to degenerate times; and we must laboriously seek the meaning
of each word and line, conjecturing a larger sense than
common use permits out of what wisdom and valor and
generosity we have." Nor does he suppose that such
books are easily written. "Great prose, of equal eleva-
tion, commands our respect more than great verse,"
says he, "since it implies a more permanent and level
height, a life more pervaded with the grandeur of the

thought. The poet often only makes an irruption, like the Parthian, and is off again, shooting while he retreats; but the prose writer has conquered like a Roman and settled colonies." We may ask ourselves, almost with dismay, whether such works exist at all but in the imagination of the student. For the bulk of the best of books is apt to be made up with ballast; and those in which energy of thought is combined with any stateliness of utterance may be almost counted on the fingers. Looking round in English for a book that should answer Thoreau's two demands of a style like poetry and sense that shall be both original and inspiriting, I come to Milton's "Areopagitica," and can name no other instance for the moment. Two things at least are plain: that if a man will condescend to nothing more commonplace in the way of reading, he must not look to have a large library; and that if he proposes himself to write in a similar vein, he will find his work cut out for him.

Thoreau composed seemingly while he walked, or at least exercise and composition were with him intimately connected; for we are told that "the length of his walk uniformly made the length of his writing." He speaks in one place of "plainness and vigor, the ornaments of style," which is rather too paradoxical to be comprehensively true. In another he remarks: "As for style of writing, if one has anything to say it drops from him simply as a stone falls to the ground." We must conjecture a very large sense indeed for the phrase "if one has anything to say." When truth flows from a man, fittingly clothed in style and without conscious effort, it is because the effort has been

made and the work practically completed before he sat
down to write. It is only out of fullness of thinking
that expression drops perfect like a ripe fruit; and
when Thoreau wrote so nonchalantly at his desk, it
was because he had been vigorously active during his
walk. For neither clearness, compression, nor beauty of
language, come to any living creature till after a busy
and a prolonged acquaintance with the subject on hand.
Easy writers are those who, like Walter Scott, choose
to remain contented with a less degree of perfection
than is legitimately within the compass of their powers.
We hear of Shakespeare and his clean manuscript; but
in face of the evidence of the style itself and of the
various editions of "Hamlet," this merely proves that
Messrs. Hemming and Condell were unacquainted with
the common enough phenomenon called a fair copy. He
who would recast a tragedy already given to the world
must frequently and earnestly have revised details in
the study. Thoreau himself, and in spite of his protes-
tations, is an instance of even extreme research in one
direction; and his effort after heroic utterance is proved
not only by the occasional finish, but by the determined
exaggeration of his style. "I trust you realize what an
exaggerator I am—that I lay myself out to exaggerate," he writes. And again, hinting at the explanation: "Who that has heard a strain of music feared
lest he should speak extravagantly any more forever?"
And yet once more, in his essay on Carlyle, and this
time with his meaning well in hand: "No truth, we
think, was ever expressed but with this sort of emphasis, that for the time there seemed to be no other."
Thus Thoreau was an exaggerative and a parabolical

writer, not because he loved the literature of the East, but from a desire that people should understand and realize what he was writing. He was near the truth upon the general question; but in his own particular method, it appears to me, he wandered. Literature is not less a conventional art than painting or sculpture; and it is the least striking, as it is the most comprehensive of the three. To hear a strain of music, to see a beautiful woman, a river, a great city, or a starry night, is to make a man despair of his Liliputian arts in language. Now, to gain that emphasis which seems denied to us by the very nature of the medium, the proper method of literature is by selection, which is a kind of negative exaggeration. It is the right of the literary artist, as Thoreau was on the point of seeing, to leave out whatever does not suit his purpose. Thus we extract the pure gold; and thus the well-written story of a noble life becomes, by its very omissions, more thrilling to the reader. But to go beyond this, like Thoreau, and to exaggerate directly, is to leave the saner classical tradition, and to put the reader on his guard. And when you write the whole for the half, you do not express your thought more forcibly, but only express a different thought which is not yours.

Thoreau's true subject was the pursuit of self-improvement combined with an unfriendly criticism of life as it goes on in our societies; it is there that he best displays the freshness and surprising trenchancy of his intellect; it is there that his style becomes plain and vigorous, and therefore, according to his own formula, ornamental. Yet he did not care to follow this vein singly, but must drop into it by the way in books of

a different purport. "Walden, or Life in the Woods,"
"A Week on the Concord and Merrimack Rivers,"
"The Maine Woods"—such are the titles he affects.
He was probably reminded by his delicate critical perception that the true business of literature is with narrative; in reasoned narrative, and there alone, that art
enjoys all its advantages, and suffers least from its defects. Dry precept and disembodied disquisition, as they
can only be read with an effort of abstraction, can
never convey a perfectly complete or a perfectly natural impression. Truth, even in literature, must be
clothed with flesh and blood, or it cannot tell its
whole story to the reader. Hence the effect of anec-
dote on simple minds; and hence good biographies and
works of high, imaginative art, are not only far more
entertaining, but far more edifying, than books of theory
or precept. Now Thoreau could not clothe his opinions
in the garment of art, for that was not his talent;
but he sought to gain the same elbow-room for himself, and to afford a similar relief to his readers, by
mingling his thoughts with a record of experience.

Again, he was a lover of nature. The quality which
we should call mystery in a painting, and which belongs so particularly to the aspect of the external world
and to its influence upon our feelings, was one which
he was never weary of attempting to reproduce in his
books. The seeming significance of nature's appearances,
their unchanging strangeness to the senses, and the
thrilling response which they waken in the mind of
man, continued to surprise and stimulate his spirits. It
appeared to him, I think, that if we could only write
near enough to the facts, and yet with no pedestrian

calm, but ardently, we might transfer the glamour of
reality direct upon our pages; and that, if it were once
thus captured and expressed, a new and instructive relation might appear between men's thoughts and the
phenomena of nature. This was the eagle that he pursued all his life long, like a schoolboy with a butterfly
net. Hear him to a friend: "Let me suggest a theme
for you—to state to yourself precisely and completely
what that walk over the mountains amounted to for
you, returning to this essay again and again until you
are satisfied that all that was important in your experience is in it. Don't suppose that you can tell it precisely the first dozen times you try, but at 'em again;
especially when, after a sufficient pause, you suspect
that you are touching the heart or summit of the matter, reiterate your blows there, and account for the
mountain to yourself. Not that the story need be long,
but it will take a long while to make it short." Such
was the method, not consistent for a man whose meanings were to "drop from him as a stone falls to the
ground." Perhaps the most successful work that Thoreau ever accomplished in this direction is to be found
in the passages relating to fish in the "Week." These
are remarkable for a vivid truth of impression and a
happy suitability of language, not frequently surpassed.

Whatever Thoreau tried to do was tried in fair,
square prose, with sentences solidly built, and no help
from bastard rhythms. Moreover, there is a progression
—I cannot call it a progress—in his work toward a
more and more strictly prosaic level, until at last he
sinks into the bathos of the prosy. Emerson mentions
having once remarked to Thoreau: "Who would not

like to write something which all can read, like 'Robinson Crusoe'? and who does not see with regret that
his page is not solid with a right materialistic treatment which delights everybody?" I must say in passing that it is not the right materialistic treatment which
delights the world in "Robinson," but the romantic and
philosophic interest of the fable. The same treatment
does quite the reverse of delighting us when it is applied, in "Colonel Jack," to the management of a planta-
tion. But I cannot help suspecting Thoreau to have
been influenced either by this identical remark or by
some other closely similar in meaning. He began to
fall more and more into a detailed materialistic treatment; he went into the business doggedly, as one who
should make a guide-book; he not only chronicled what
had been important in his own experience, but whatever might have been important in the experience of
anybody else; not only what had affected him, but all
that he saw or heard. His ardor had grown less, or
perhaps it was inconsistent with a right materialistic
treatment to display such emotions as he felt; and, to
complete the eventful change, he chose, from a sense
of moral dignity, to gut these later works of the saving quality of humor. He was not one of those authors
who have learned, in his own words, "to leave out
their dullness." He inflicts his full quantity upon the
reader in such books as "Cape Cod," or "The Yankee
in Canada." Of the latter he confessed that he had
not managed to get much of himself into it. Heaven
knows he had not, nor yet much of Canada, we may
hope. "Nothing," he says somewhere, "can shock a
brave man but dullness." Well, there are few spots

more shocking to the brave than the pages of "The
Yankee in Canada."

There are but three books of his that will be read
with much pleasure: the "Week," "Walden," and the
collected letters. As to his poetry, Emerson's word shall
suffice for us, it is so accurate and so prettily said:
"The thyme and majoram are not yet honey." In this,
as in his prose, he relied greatly on the goodwill of
the reader, and wrote throughout in faith. It was an
exercise of faith to suppose that many would understand the sense of his best work, or that any could be
exhilarated by the dreary chronicling of his worst.
"But," as he says, "the gods do not hear any rude
or discordant sound, as we learn from the echo; and
I know that the nature toward which I launch these
sounds is so rich that it will modulate anew and won-
derfully improve my rudest strain."

IV

"What means the fact," he cries, "that a soul
which has lost all hope for itself can inspire in another listening soul such an infinite confidence in it,
even while it is expressing its despair?" The question
is an echo and an illustration of the words last quoted;
and it forms the key-note of his thoughts on friendship. No one else, to my knowledge, has spoken in so
high and just a spirit of the kindly relations; and I
doubt whether it be a drawback that these lessons
should come from one in many ways so unfitted to be
a teacher in this branch. The very coldness and egoism
of his own intercourse gave him a clearer insight into
the intellectual basis of our warm, mutual tolerations;

and testimony to their worth comes with added force
from one who was solitary and disc   ng, and of
whom a friend remarked, with equal   isdom,
"I love Henry, but I cannot like him

He can hardly be persuaded to ma'   nction
between love and friendship; in such   freezing air, upon the mountain-tops of   had he
taught himself to breathe. He was,   ., too accurate an observer not to have re   at "there
exists already a natural disinterested   liberality"
between men and women; yet, he   friendship
is no respecter of sex." Perhaps on   , sense in
which the words are true; but they   poken in
ignorance; and perhaps we shall have   he matter
most correctly, if we call love a found   n for a
nearer and freer degree of friendship than   be possible without it. For there are delicacies,   ernal between persons of the same sex, which are   elted and
disappear in the warmth of love.

To both, if they are to be right, he   butes the
same nature and condition. "We are n   what we
are," says he, "nor do we treat or esteem   ch other
for such, but for what we are capable of   g." "A
friend is one who incessantly pays us the   ompliment
of expecting all the virtues from us, and who can appreciate them in us." "The friend asks no return but
that his friend will religiously accept and wear and not
disgrace his apotheosis of him." "It is the merit and
preservation of friendship that it takes place on a level
higher than the actual characters of the parties would
seem to warrant." This is to put friendship on a ped-
estal indeed; and yet the root of the matter is there;

and the last sentence, in particular, is like a light in a
dark place, and makes many mysteries plain. We are
different with different friends; yet if we look closely
we shall find that every such relation reposes on some
particular apotheosis of one's self; with each friend, although we could not distinguish it in words from any
other, we have at least one special reputation to preserve: and it is thus that we run, when mortified, to
our friend or the woman that we love, not to hear
ourselves called better, but to be better men in point
of fact. We seek this society to flatter ourselves with
our own good conduct. And hence any falsehood in
the relation, any incomplete or perverted understanding,
will spoil even the pleasure of these visits. Thus says
Thoreau again: "Only lovers know the value of truth."
And yet again: "They ask for words and deeds, when
a true relation is word and deed."

But it follows that since they are neither of them
so good as the other hopes, and each is, in a very
honest manner, playing a part above his powers, such
an intercourse must often be disappointing to both.
"We may bid farewell sooner than complain," says
Thoreau, "for our complaint is too well grounded to
be uttered." "We have not so good a right to hate
any as our friend."

> "It were treason to our love
> And a sin to God above,
> One iota to abate
> Of a pure, impartial hate."

Love is not blind, nor yet forgiving. "Oh, yes, believe me," as the song says, "Love has eyes!" The

nearer the intimacy, the more cuttingly do we feel the unworthiness of those we love; and because you love one, and would die for that love to-morrow, you have not forgiven, and you never will forgive, that friend's misconduct. If you want a person's faults, go to those who love him. They will not tell you, but they know. And herein lies the magnanimous courage of love, that it endures this knowledge without change.

It required a cold, distant personality like that of Thoreau, perhaps, to recognize and certainly to utter this truth; for a more human love makes it a point of honor not to acknowledge those faults of which it is most conscious. But his point of view is both high and dry. He has no illusions; he does not give way to love any more than to hatred, but preserves them both with care like valuable curiosities. A more bald-headed picture of life, if I may so express myself, has seldom been presented. He is an egoist; he does not remember, or does not think it worth while to remark, that, in these near intimacies, we are ninety-nine times disappointed in our beggarly selves for once that we are disappointed in our friend; that it is we who seem most frequently undeserving of the love that unites us; and that it is by our friend's conduct that we are continually rebuked and yet strengthened for a fresh endeavor. Thoreau is dry, priggish, and selfish. It is profit he is after in these intimacies; moral profit, certainly, but still profit to himself. If you will be the sort of friend I want, he remarks naively, "my education cannot dispense with your society." His education! as though a friend were a dictionary. And with all this, not one word about pleasure, or laughter, or kisses, or any quality of flesh and blood. It was not inappropriate, surely, that he had such close relations with the fish. We can understand the friend already quoted, when he cried: "As for taking his arm, I would as soon think of taking the arm of an elm-tree!"

As a matter of fact he experienced ·but a broken enjoyment in his intimacies. He says he has been perpetually on the brink of the sort of intercourse he wanted, and yet never completely attained it. And what else had he to expect when he would not, in a happy phrase of Carlyle's, "nestle down into it"? Truly, so it will be always if you only stroll in upon your friends as you might stroll in to see a cricket match; and even then not simply for the pleasure of the thing, but with some afterthought of self-improvement, as though you had come to the cricket match to bet. It was his theory that people saw each other too frequently, so that their curiosity was not properly whetted, nor had they anything fresh to communicate; but friendship must be something else than a society for mutual improvement—indeed, it must only be that by the way, and to some extent unconsciously; and if Thoreau had been a man instead of a manner of elm-tree, he would have felt that he saw his friends too seldom, and have reaped benefits unknown to his philosophy from a more sustained and easy intercourse. We might remind him of his own words about love: "We should have no reserve; we should give the whole of ourselves to that business. But commonly men have not imagination enough to be thus employed about a human being, but must be coopering a barrel, forsooth." Ay, or reading oriental philosophers. It is not the nature of the rival occupation, it is the fact that you suffer it to be a rival, that renders loving intimacy impossible. Nothing is given for nothing in this world; there can be no true love, even on your own side, without devotion; devotion is the exercise of love, by which it grows; but if you will give enough of that, if you will pay the price in a sufficient "amount of what you call life," why then, indeed, whether with wife or comrade, you may have months and even years of such easy, natural, pleasurable, and yet improving intercourse as shall make time a moment and kindness a delight.

The secret of his retirement lies not in misanthropy, of which he had no tincture, but part in his engrossing design of self-improvement and part in the real deficiencies of social intercourse. He was not so much difficult about his fellow human beings as he could not tolerate the terms of their association. He could take to a man for any genuine qualities, as we see by his admirable sketch of the Canadian woodcutter in "Walden"; but he would not consent, in his own words, to "feebly fabulate and paddle in the social slush." It seemed to him, I think, that society is precisely the reverse of friendship, in that it takes place on a lower level than the characters of any of the parties would warrant us to expect. The society talk of even the most brilliant man is of greatly less account than what you will get from him in (as the French say) a little committee. And Thoreau wanted geniality; he had not enough of the superficial, even at command; he could not swoop into a parlor and, in the naval phrase, "cut out" a human being from that dreary port; nor had he inclination for the task. I suspect he loved books

and nature as well and near as warmly as he loved
his fellow-creatures—a melancholy, lean degeneration of
the human character.

"As for the dispute about solitude and society," he
thus sums up: "Any comparison is impertinent. It is
an idling down on the plain at the base of the mountain instead of climbing steadily to its top. Of course
you will be glad of all the society you can get to go
up with? Will you go to glory with me? is the burden of the song. It is not that we love to be alone,
but that we love to soar, and when we do soar the
company grows thinner and thinner till there is none
at all. It is either the tribune on the plain, a sermon
on the mount, or a very private ecstasy still higher up.
Use all the society that will abet you." But surely it
is no very extravagant opinion that it is better to give
than to receive, to serve than to use our companions;
and above all, where there is no question of service
upon either side, that it is good to enjoy their company like a natural man. It is curious and in some
ways dispiriting that a writer may be always best corrected out of his own mouth; and so, to conclude, here is
another passage from Thoreau which seems aimed directly
at himself: "Do not be too moral; you may cheat yourself out of much life so. . . . *All fables, indeed, have
their morals; but the innocent enjoy the story.*"

V

"The only obligation," says he, "which I have a
right to assume is to do at any time what I think
right." "Why should we ever go abroad, even across

the way, to ask a neighbor's advice?" "There is a
nearer neighbor within, who is incessantly telling us
how we should behave. *But we wait for the neighbor
without to tell us of some false, easier way.*" "The
greater part of what my neighbors call good I believe
in my soul to be bad." To be what we are, and to
become what we are capable of becoming, is the only
end of life. It is "when we fall behind ourselves"
that "we are cursed with duties and the neglect of
duties." "I love the wild," he says, "not less than the
good." And again: "The life of a good man will
hardly improve us more than the life of a freebooter,
for the inevitable laws appear as plainly in the infringement as in the observance, and" (mark this) "*our lives
are sustained by a nearly equal expense of virtue of
some kind.*" Even although he were a prig, it will
be owned he could announce a startling doctrine. "As
for doing good," he writes elsewhere, "that is one of
the professions that are full. Moreover, I have tried it
fairly, and, strange as it may seem, am satisfied that
it does not agree with my constitution. Probably I
should not conscientiously and deliberately forsake my
particular calling to do the good which society demands
of me, to save the universe from annihilation; and I
believe that a like but infinitely greater steadfastness
elsewhere is all that now preserves it. If you should
ever be betrayed into any of these philanthropies, do
not let your left hand know what your right hand
does, for it is not worth knowing." Elsewhere he returns upon the subject, and explains his meaning thus:
"If I ever *did* a man any good in their sense, of
course it was something exceptional and insignificant

compared with the good or evil I am constantly doing by being what I am."

There is a rude nobility, like that of a barbarian king, in this unshaken confidence in himself and indifference to the wants, thoughts, or sufferings of others. In his whole wroks I find no trace of pity. This was partly the result of theory, for he held the world too mysterious to be criticised, and asks conclusively: "What right have I to grieve who have not ceased to wonder?" But it sprang still more from constitutional indifference and superiority; and he grew up healthy, composed, and unconscious from among life's horrors, like a green bay-tree from a field of battle. It was from this lack in himself that he failed to do justice to the spirit of Christ; for while he could glean more meaning from individual precepts than any score of Christians, yet he conceived life in such a different hope, and viewed it with such contrary emotions, that the sense and purport of the doctrine as a whole seems to have passed him by or left him unimpressed. He could understand the idealism of the Christian view, but he was himself so unaffectedly unhuman that he did not recognize the human intention and essence of that teaching. Hence he complained that Christ did not leave us a rule that was proper and sufficient for this world, not having conceived the nature of the rule that was laid down; for things of that character that are sufficiently unacceptable become positively non-existent to the mind. But perhaps we shall best appreciate the defect in Thoreau by seeing it supplied in the case of Whitman. For the one, I feel confident, is the disciple of the other; it is what Thoreau clearly whispered that Whitman so uproariously bawls; it is the same doctrine, but with how immense a difference! the same argument, but used to what a new conclusion! Thoreau had plenty of humor until he tutored himself out of it, and so forfeited that best birth-right of a sensible man; Whitman, in that respect, seems to have been sent into the world naked and unashamed; and yet by a strange consummation, it is the theory of the former that is arid, abstract, and claustral. Of these two philosophies so nearly identical at bottom, the one pursues Self-improvement—a churlish, mangy dog; the other is up with the morning, in the best of health, and following the nymph Happiness, buxom, blithe, and debonair. Happiness, at least, is not solitary; it joys to communicate; it loves others, for it depends on them for its existence; it sanctions and encourages to all delights that are not unkind in themselves; if it lived to a thousand, it would not make excision of a single humorous passage; and while the self-improver dwindles toward the prig, and, if he be not of an excellent constitution, may even grow deformed into an Obermann, the very name and appearance of a happy man breathe of good-nature, and help the rest of us to live.

In the case of Thoreau, so great a show of doctrine demands some outcome in the field of action. If nothing were to be done but build a shanty beside Walden Pond, we have heard altogether too much of these declarations of independence. That the man wrote some books is nothing to the purpose, for the same has been done in a suburban villa. That he kept himself happy is perhaps a sufficient excuse, but it is disappointing to the reader. We may be unjust, but when a man

despises commerce and philanthropy alike, and has
views of good so soaring that he must take himself
apart from mankind for their cultivation, we will not
be content without some striking act. It was not
Thoreau's fault if he were not martyred; had the occasion come, he would have made a noble ending. As it
is, he did once seek to interfere in the world's course;
he made one practical appearance on the stage of affairs;
and a strange one it was, and strangely characteristic of
the nobility and the eccentricity of the man. It was
forced on him by his calm but radical opposition to negro
slavery. "Voting for the right is doing nothing for it,"
he saw; "it is only expressing to men feebly your desire that it should prevail." For his part, he would
not "for an instant recognize that political organization
for *his* government which is the *slave's* government
also." "I do not hesitate to say," he adds, "that those
who call themselves Abolitionists should at once effectually withdraw their support, both in person and prop-
erty, from the government of Massachusetts." That is
what he did: in 1843 he ceased to pay the poll-tax.
The highway-tax he paid, for he said he was as desirous to be a good neighbor as to be a bad subject;
but no more poll-tax to the State of Massachusetts.
Thoreau had now seceded, and was a polity unto himself; or, as he explains it with admirable sense, "In
fact, I quietly declare war with the State after my
fashion, though I will still make what use and get what
advantage of her I can, as is usual in such cases."
He was put in prison; but that was a part of his design. "Under a government which imprisons any un-
justly, the true place for a just man is also a prison

I know this well, that if one thousand, if one hundred, if ten men whom I could name—ay, if *one* HONEST man, in this State of Massachusetts, *ceasing to hold slaves*, were actually to withdraw from this copartnership, and be locked up in the county jail therefor, it would be the abolition of slavery in America. For it matters not how small the beginning may seem to be; what is once well done is done forever." Such was his theory of civil disobedience.

And the upshot? A friend paid the tax for him; continued year by year to pay it in the sequel; and Thoreau was free to walk the woods unmolested. It was a *fiasco*, but to me it does not seem laughable; even those who joined in the laughter at the moment would be insensibly affected by this quaint instance of a good man's horror for injustice. We may compute the worth of that one night's imprisonment as outweighing half a hundred voters at some subsequent election: and if Thoreau had possessed as great a power of persuasion as (let us say) Falstaff, if he had counted a party however small, if his example had been followed by a hundred or by thirty of his fellows, I cannot but believe it would have greatly precipitated the era of freedom and justice. We feel the misdeeds of our country with so little fervor, for we are not witnesses to the suffering they cause; but when we see them wake an active horror in our fellowman, when we see a neighbor prefer to lie in prison rather than be so much as passively implicated in their perpetration, even the dullest of us will begin to realize them with a quicker pulse.

Not far from twenty years later, when Captain John

Brown was taken at Harper's Ferry, Thoreau was the first to come forward in his defense. The committees wrote to him unanimously that his action was premature. "I did not send to you for advice," said he, "but to announce that I was to speak." I have used the word "defense"; in truth he did not seek to defend him, even declared it would be better for the good cause that he should die; but he praised his action as I think Brown would have liked to hear it praised.

Thus this singularly eccentric and independent mind, wedded to a character of so much strength, singleness, and purity, pursued its own path of self-improvement for more than half a century, part gymnosophist, part backwoodsman; and thus did it come twice, though in a subaltern attitude, into the field of political history.

NOTE.—For many facts in the above essay, among which I may mention the incident of the squirrel, I am indebted to "Thoreau: His Life and Aims," by J. A. Page, or, as is well known, Dr. Japp.

YOSHIDA–TORAJIRO

THE name at the head of this page is probably un-known to the English reader, and yet I think it should become a household word like that of Garibaldi or John Brown. Some day soon, we may expect to hear more fully the details of Yoshida's history, and the degree of his influence in the transformation of Japan; even now there must be Englishmen acquainted with the subject, and perhaps the appearance of this sketch may elicit something more complete and exact. I wish to say that I am not, rightly speaking, the author of the present paper: I tell the story on the authority of an intelligent Japanese gentleman, Mr. Taiso Masaki, who told it me with an emotion that does honor to his heart; and though I have taken some pains, and sent my notes to him to be corrected, this can be no more than an imperfect outline.

Yoshida-Torajiro was son to the hereditary military instructor of the house of Choshu. The name you are to pronounce with an equality of accent on the differ-ent syllables, almost as in French, the vowels as in Italian, but the consonants in the English manner—ex-cept the *j*, which has the French sound, or, as it has been cleverly proposed to write it, the sound of *zh*. Yoshida was very learned in Chinese letters, or, as we might say, in the classics, and in his father's subject;

fortification was among his favorite studies, and he was
a poet from his boyhood. He was born to a lively and
intelligent patriotism; the condition of Japan was his
great concern; and while he projected a better future,
he lost no opportunity of improving his knowledge of
her present state. With this end he was continually
traveling in his youth, going on foot and sometimes
with three days' provision on his back, in the brave,
self-helpful manner of all heroes. He kept a full diary
while he was thus upon his journeys, but it is feared
that these notes have been destroyed. If their value
were in any respect such as we have reason to expect
from the man's character, this would be a loss not
easy to exaggerate. It is still wonderful to the Japanese
how far he contrived to push these explorations; a cul-
tured gentleman of that land and period would leave a
complimentary poem wherever he had been hospitably
entertained; and a friend of Mr. Masaki, who was like-
wise a great wanderer, has found such traces of Yoshida's passage in very remote regions of Japan.

Politics is perhaps the only profession for which no
preparation is thought necessary; but Yoshida considered otherwise, and he studied the miseries of his fellow-countrymen with as much attention and research as
though he had been going to write a book instead of
merely to propose a remedy. To a man of his intensity
and singleness, there is no question but that this sur-
vey was melancholy in the extreme. His dissatisfaction
is proved by the eagerness with which he threw himself into the cause of reform; and what would have
discouraged another braced Yoshida for his task. As
he professed the theory of arms, it was first the de

fenses of Japan that occupied his mind. The external
feebleness of that country was then illustrated by the
manners of overriding barbarians, and the visits of big
barbarian war ships: she was a country beleaguered.
Thus the patriotism of Yoshida took a form which
may be said to have defeated itself: he had it upon
him to keep out these all-powerful foreigners, whom it
is now one of his chief merits to have helped to introduce; but a man who follows his own virtuous heart
will be always found in the end to have been fighting
for the best. One thing leads naturally to another in
an awakened mind, and that with an upward progress
from effect to cause. The power and knowledge of
these foreigners were things inseparable; by envying
them their military strength, Yoshida came to envy
them their culture; from the desire to equal them in
the first, sprang his desire to share with them in the
second; and thus he is found treating in the same
book of a new scheme to strengthen the defenses of
Kioto and of the establishment, in the same city, of a
university of foreign teachers. He hoped, perhaps, to
get the good of other lands without their evil; to en-
able Japan to profit by the knowledge of the barba
rians, and still keep her inviolate with her own arts
and virtues. But whatever was the precise nature of
his hope, the means by which it was to be accomplished were both difficult and obvious. Some one with
eyes and understanding must break through the official
cordon, escape into the new world, and study this other
civilization on the spot. And who could be better suited
for the business? It was not without danger, but he
was without fear. It needed preparation and insight;

and what had he done since he was a child but prepare himself with the best culture of Japan, and acquire in his excursions the power and habit of observing?

He was but twenty-two, and already all this was clear in his mind, when news reached Choshu that Commodore Perry was lying near to Yeddo. Here, then, was the patriot's opportunity. Among the Samurai of Choshu, and in particular among the councilors of the Daimio, his general culture, his views, which the enlightened were eager to accept, and, above all, the prophetic charm, the radiant persuasion of the man, had gained him many and sincere disciples. He had thus a strong influence at the provincial Court; and so he obtained leave to quit the district, and, by way of a pretext, a privilege to follow his profession in Yeddo. Thither he hurried, and arrived in time to be too late: Perry had weighed anchor, and his sails had vanished from the waters of Japan. But Yoshida, having put his hand to the plow, was not the man to go back; he had entered upon this business, and, please God, he would carry it through; and so he gave up his professional career and remained in Yeddo to be at hand against the next opportunity. By this behavior he put himself into an attitude toward his superior, the Daimio of Choshu, which I cannot thoroughly explain. Certainly, he became a *Ronyin*, a broken man, a feudal outlaw; certainly he was liable to be arrested if he set foot upon his native province; yet I am cautioned that "he did not really break his allegiance," but only so far separated himself as that the prince could no longer be held accountable for his late vassal's conduct. There is some nicety of feudal custom here that escapes my comprehension.

In Yeddo, with this nondescript political status, and cut off from any means of livelihood, he was joyfully supported by those who sympathized with his design. One was Sákuma-Shozan, hereditary retainer of one of the Shogun's councilors, and from him he got more than money or than money's worth. A steady, respectable man, with an eye to the world's opinion, Sakuma was one of those who, if they cannot do great deeds in their own person, have yet an ardor of admiration for those who can that recommends them to the gratitude of history. They aid and abet greatness more, perhaps, than we imagine. One thinks of them in connection with Nicodemus, who visited our Lord by night. And Sakuma was in a position to help Yoshida more practically than by simple countenance; for he could read Dutch, and was eager to communicate what he knew.

While the young Ronyin thus lay studying in Yeddo, news came of a Russian ship at Nangasaki. No time was to be lost. Sakuma contributed "a long copy of encouraging verses"; and off set Yoshida on foot for Nangasaki. His way lay through his own province of Choshu; but, as the highroad to the south lay apart from the capital, he was able to avoid arrest. He supported himself, like a *trouvère*, by his proficiency in verse. He carried his works along with him, to serve as an introduction. When he reached a town he would inquire for the house of any one celebrated for swordsmanship, or poetry, or some of the other acknowledged forms of culture; and there, on giving a taste of his skill, he would be received and entertained, and leave behind him, when he went away, a compliment in verse. Thus he traveled through the Middle Ages on his voyage of discovery into the nineteenth century. When he reached Nangasaki he was once more too late. The Russians were gone. But he made a profit on his journey in spite of fate, and stayed a while to pick up scraps of knowledge from the Dutch interpreters—a low class of men, but one that had opportunities; and then, still full of purpose, returned to Yeddo on foot, as he had come.

It was not only his youth and courage that supported him under these successive disappointments, but the continual affluence of new disciples. The man had the tenacity of a Bruce or a Columbus, with a pliability that was all his own. He did not fight for what the world would call success; but for "the wages of going on." Check him off in a dozen directions, he would find another outlet and break forth. He missed one vessel after another, and the main work still halted; but so long as he had a single Japanese to enlighten and prepare for the better future, he could still feel that he was working for Japan. Now, he had scarce returned from Nangasaki, when he was sought out by a new inquirer, the most promising of all. This was a common soldier, of the Hemming class, a dyer by birth, who had heard vaguely * of Yoshida's move-

---

* Yoshida, when on his way to Nangasaki, met the soldier and talked with him by the roadside; they then parted, but the soldier was so much struck by the words he heard that, on Yoshida's return, he sought him out and declared his intention of devoting his life to the good cause. I venture, in the absence of the writer, to insert this correction, having been present when the story was told by Mr. Masaki.—F. J. And I, there being none to settle the difference, must reproduce both versions.—R. L. S.

ments, and had become filled with wonder as to their
design. This was a far different inquirer from Sakuma-
Shozan, or the councilors of the Daimio of Choshu.
This was no two-sworded gentleman, but the common
stuff of the country, born in low traditions and unim-
proved by books; and yet that influence, that radiant
persuasion that never failed Yoshida in any circumstance of his short life, enchanted, enthralled, and con-
verted the common soldier, as it had done already with
the elegant and learned. The man instantly burned up
into a true enthusiasm; his mind had been only waiting for a teacher; he grasped in a moment the profit
of these new ideas; he, too, would go to foreign out-
landish parts, and bring back the knowledge that was
to strengthen and renew Japan; and in the meantime,
that he might be the better prepared, Yoshida set himself to teach, and he to learn, the Chinese literature.
It is an episode most honorable to Yoshida, and yet
more honorable still to the soldier, and to the capacity
and virtue of the common people of Japan.

And now, at length, Commodore Perry returned to
Simoda. Friends crowded round Yoshida with help,
counsels, and encouragement. One presented him with
a great sword, three feet long and very heavy, which,
in the exultation of the hour, he swore to carry throughout all his wanderings, and to bring back—a far-trav-
eled weapon—to Japan. A long letter was prepared in
Chinese for the American officers; it was revised and
corrected by Sakuma, and signed by Yoshida, under
the name of Urinaki-Manji, and by the soldier under
that of Ichigi-Koda. Yoshida had supplied himself with
a profusion of materials for writing; his dress was lit-

erally stuffed with paper which was to come back again
enriched with his observations, and make a great and
happy kingdom of Japan.   Thus equipped, this pair of
emigrants set forward on foot from Yeddo, and reached
Simoda about nightfall.   At no period within history can
travel have presented to any European creature the
same face of awe and terror as to these courageous
Japanese.   The descent of Ulysses into hell is a parallel
more near the case than the boldest expedition in the
Polar circles.   For their act was unprecedented; it was
criminal; and it was to take them beyond the pale of
humanity into a land of devils.   It is not to be wondered at if they were thrilled by the thought of their
unusual situation; and perhaps the soldier gave utterance to the sentiment of both when he sang, "in
Chinese singing" (so that we see he had already
profited by his lessons), these two appropriate verses:

> "We do not know where we are to sleep to-night,
>   In a thousand miles of desert where we can see
>   no human smoke."

In a little temple, hard by the seashore, they lay
down to repose; sleep overtook them as they lay; and
when they awoke, "the east was already white" for
their last morning in Japan.   They seized a fisherman's
boat and rowed out—Perry lying far to sea because of
the two tides.   Their very manner of boarding was
significant of determination; for they had no sooner
caught hold upon the ship than they kicked away their
boat to make return impossible.   And now you would
have thought that all was over.   But the Commodore
was already in treaty with the Shogun's Government;

it was one of the stipulations that no Japanese was
to be aided in escaping from Japan; and Yoshida and
his followers were handed over as prisoners to the authorities at Simoda. That night he who had been to
explore the secrets of the barbarian slept, if he might
sleep at all, in a cell too short for lying down at full
length, and too low for standing upright. There are
some disappointments too great for commentary.

Sákuma, implicated by his handwriting, was sent
into his own province in confinement, from which he
was soon released. Yoshida and the soldier suffered a
long and miserable period of captivity, and the latter,
indeed, died, while yet in prison, of a skin disease.
But such a spirit as that of Yoshida-Torajiro is not
easily made or kept a captive; and that which cannot
be broken by misfortune you shall seek in vain to confine in a bastille. He was indefatigably active, writing
reports to Government and treatises for dissemination.
These latter were contraband; and yet he found no
difficulty in their distribution, for he always had the
jailer on his side. It was in vain that they kept
changing him from one prison to another; Government
by that plan only hastened the spread of new ideas;
for Yoshida had only to arrive to make a convert.
Thus, though he himself was laid by the heels, he
confirmed and extended his party in the State.

At last, after many lesser transferences, he was
given over from the prisons of the Shogun to those of
his own superior, the Daimio of Choshu. I conceive it
possible that he may then have served out his time for
the attempt to leave Japan, and was now resigned to
the provincial Government on a lesser count, as a

Ronyin or feudal rebel. But, however that may be,
the change was of great importance to Yoshida; for by
the influence of his admirers in the Daimio's council,
he was allowed the privilege, underhand, of dwelling
in his own house. And there, as well to keep up communication with his fellow-reformers as to pursue his
work of education, he received boys to teach. It must
not be supposed that he was free; he was too marked
a man for that; he was probably assigned to some
small circle, and lived, as we should say, under police
surveillance; but to him, who had done so much from
under lock and key, this would seem a large and
profitable liberty.

It was at this period that Mr. Masaki was brought
into personal contact with Yoshida; and hence, through
the eyes of a boy of thirteen, we get one good look
at the character and habits of the hero. He was ugly
and laughably disfigured with the smallpox; and while
nature had been so niggardly with him from the first,
his personal habits were even sluttish. His clothes were
wretched; when he ate or washed he wiped his hands
upon his sleeves; and as his hair was not tied more
than once in the two months, it was often disgusting
to behold. With such a picture, it is easy to believe
that he never married. A good teacher, gentle in act,
although violent and abusive in speech, his lessons were
apt to go over the heads of his scholars, and to leave
them gaping, or more often laughing. Such was his
passion for study that he even grudged himself natural
repose; and when he grew drowsy over his books he
would, if it was summer, put mosquitoes up his sleeve;
and, if it was winter, take off his shoes and run bare-

foot on the snow. His handwriting was exceptionally villainous; poet though he was, he had no taste for what was elegant; and in a country where to write beautifully was not the mark of a scrivener but an admired accomplishment for gentlemen, he suffered his letters to be jolted out of him by the press of matter and the heat of his convictions. He would not tolerate even the appearance of a bribe; for bribery lay at the root of much that was evil in Japan, as well as in countries nearer home; and once when a merchant brought him his son to educate, and added, as was customary,* a little private sweetner, Yoshida dashed the money in the giver's face, and launched into such an outbreak of indignation as made the matter public in the school. He was still, when Masaki knew him, much weakened by his hardships in prison; and the presentation sword, three feet long, was too heavy for him to wear without distress; yet he would always gird it on when he went to dig in his garden. That is a touch which qualifies the man. A weaker nature would have shrunk from the sight of what only commemorated a failure. But he was of Thoreau's mind, that if you can "make your failure tragical by courage, it will not differ from success." He could look back without confusion to his enthusiastic promise. If events had been contrary, and he found himself unable to carry out that purpose—well, there was but the more reason to be brave and constant in another; if he could not carry the sword into barbarian lands, it should at least be witness to a life spent entirely for Japan.

---

* I understood that the merchant was endeavoring surreptitiously to obtain for his son instruction to which he was not entitled.—F. J.

This is the sight we have of him as he appeared to schoolboys, but not related in the schoolboy spirit. A man so careless of the graces must be out of court with boys and women. And, indeed, as we have all been more or less to school, it will astonish no one that Yoshida was regarded by his scholars as a laughing-stock. The schoolboy has a keen sense of humor. Heroes he learns to understand and to admire in books; but he is not forward to recognize the heroic under the traits of any contemporary man, and least of all in a brawling, dirty, and eccentric teacher. But as the years went by, and the scholars of Yoshida continued in vain to look around them for the abstractly perfect, and began more and more to understand the drift of his instructions, they learned to look back upon their comic schoolmaster as upon the noblest of mankind.

The last act of this brief and full existence was already near at hand. Some of his work was done; for already there had been Dutch teachers admitted into Nangasaki, and the country at large was keen for the new learning. But though the renaissance had begun, it was impeded and dangerously threatened by the power of the Shogun. His minister—the same who was afterward assassinated in the snow in the very midst of his bodyguard—not only held back pupils from going to the Dutchmen, but by spies and detectives, by imprisonment and death, kept thinning out of Japan the most intelligent and active spirits. It is the old story of a power upon its last legs—learning to the bastille, and courage to the block; when there are none left but sheep and donkeys, the State will have been saved. But a man must not think to cope with a Revolution; nor a minister, however fortified with guards, to hold in check a country that had given birth to such men as Yoshida and his soldier-follower. The violence of the ministerial Tarquin only served to direct attention to the illegality of his master's rule; and people began to turn their allegiance from Yeddo and the Shogun to the long-forgotten Mikado in his seclusion at Kioto. At this juncture, whether in consequence or not, the relations between these two rulers became strained; and the Shogun's minister set forth for Kioto to put another affront upon the rightful sovereign. The circumstance was well fitted to precipitate events. It was a piece of religion to defend the Mikado; it was a plain piece of political righteousness to oppose a tyrannical and bloody usurpation. To Yoshida the moment for action seemed to have arrived. He was himself still confined in Choshu. Nothing was free but his intelligence; but with that he sharpened a sword for the Shogun's minister. A party of his followers were to waylay the tyrant at a village on the Yeddo and Kioto road, present him with a petition, and put him to the sword. But Yoshida and his friends were closely observed; and the too great expedition of two of the conspirators, a boy of eighteen and his brother, wakened the suspicion of the authorities, and led to a full discovery of the plot and the arrest of all who were concerned.

In Yeddo, to which he was taken, Yoshida was thrown again into a strict confinement. But he was not left destitute of sympathy in this last hour of trial. In the next cell lay one Kusákabe, a reformer from the southern highlands of Satzuma. They were in prison for different plots indeed, but for the same intention;

they shared the same beliefs and the same aspirations for Japan; many and long were the conversations they held through the prison wall, and dear was the sympathy that soon united them. It fell first to the lot of Kusákabe to pass before the judges; and when sentence had been pronounced he was led toward the place of death below Yoshida's window. To turn the head would have been to implicate his fellow-prisoner; but he threw him a look from his eye, and bade him farewell in a loud voice, with these two Chinese verses:

"It is better to be a crystal and be broken,
Than to remain perfect like a tile upon the housetop."

So Kusákabe, from the highlands of Satzuma, passed out of the theater of this world. His death was like an antique worthy's.

A little after, and Yoshida too must appear before the Court. His last scene was of a piece with his career, and fitly crowned it. He seized on the opportunity of a public audience, confessed and gloried in his design, and, reading his auditors a lesson in the history of their country, told at length the illegality of the Shogun's power and the crimes by which its exercise was sullied. So, having said his say for once, he was led forth and executed, thirty-one years old.

A military engineer, a bold traveler (at least in wish), a poet, a patriot, a schoolmaster, a friend to learning, a martyr to reform—there are not many men, dying at seventy, who have served their country in such various characters. He was not only wise and provident in thought, but surely one of the fieriest of heroes in execution. It is hard to say which is most remarkable—

his capacity for command, which subdued his very jailers; his hot, unflagging zeal; or his stubborn superiority to defeat. He failed in each particular enterprise that he attempted; and yet we have only to look at his country to see how complete has been his general success. His friends and pupils made the majority of leaders in that final Revolution, now some twelve years old; and many of them are, or were until the other day, high placed among the rulers of Japan. And when we see all round us these brisk intelligent students, with their strange foreign air, we should never forget how Yoshida marched afoot from Choshu to Yeddo, and from Yeddo to Nangasaki, and from Nangasaki back again to Yeddo; how he boarded the American ship, his dress stuffed with writing material; nor how he languished in prison, and finally gave his death, as he had formerly given all his life and strength and leisure, to gain for his native land that very benefit which she now enjoys so largely. It is better to be Yoshida and perish, than to be only Sàkuma and yet save hide. Kusákabe, of Satzuma, has said the word: better to be a crystal and be broken.

I must add a word; for I hope the reader will not fail to perceive that this is as much the story of a heroic people as that of a heroic man. It is not enough to remember Yoshida; we must not forget the common soldier, nor Kusákabe, nor the boy of eighteen, Nomura, of Choshu, whose eagerness betrayed the plot. It is exhilarating to have lived in the same days with these great-hearted gentlemen. Only a few miles from us, to speak by the proportion of the universe, while I was droning over my lessons, Yoshida was goading himself to be wakeful with the stings of the mosquito; and while you were grudging a penny income tax, Kusákabe was stepping to death with a noble sentence on his lips.

FRANCOIS VILLON

STUDENT, POET, AND HOUSEBREAKER

PERHAPS one of the most curious revolutions in literary history is the sudden bull's-eye light cast by M. Longnon on the obscure existence of François Villon.* His book is not remarkable merely as a chapter of biography exhumed after four centuries. To readers of the poet it will recall, with a flavor of satire, that characteristic passage in which he bequeaths his spectacles—with a humorous reservation of the case—to the hospital for blind paupers known as the Fifteen-Score. Thus equipped, let the blind paupers go and separate the good from the bad in the cemetery of the Innocents! For his own part the poet can see no distinction. Much have the dead people made of their advantages. What does it matter now that they have lain in state beds and nourished portly bodies upon cakes and cream! Here they all lie, to be trodden in the mud; the large estate and the small, sounding virtue and adroit or powerful vice, in very much the same condition; and a

---

* "Etude Biographique sur François Villon." Paris: H. Menu.

bishop not to be distinguished from a lamplighter with even the strongest spectacles.

Such was Villon's cynical philosophy. Four hundred years after his death, when surely all danger might be considered at an end, a pair of critical spectacles have been applied to his own remains; and though he left behind him a sufficiently ragged reputation from the first, it is only after these four hundred years that his delinquencies have been finally tracked home, and we can assign him to his proper place among the good or wicked. It is a staggering thought, and one that affords a fine figure of the imperishability of men's acts, that the stealth of the private inquiry office can be carried so far back into the dead and dusty past. We are not so soon quit of our concerns as Villon fancied. In the extreme of dissolution, when not so much as a man's name is remembered, when his dust is scattered to the four winds, and perhaps the very grave and the very graveyard where he was laid to rest have been forgotten, desecrated, and buried under populous towns— even in this extreme let an antiquary fall across a sheet of manuscript, and the name will be recalled, the old infamy will pop out into daylight like a toad out of a fissure in the rock, and the shadow of the shade of what was once a man will be heartily pilloried by his descendants. A little while ago and Villon was almost totally forgotten; then he was revived for the sake of his verses; and now he is being revived with a vengeance in the detection of his misdemeanors. How unsubstantial is this projection of a man's existence, which can lie in abeyance for centuries and then be brushed up again and set forth for the consideration of posterity

by a few dips in an antiquary's inkpot! This precarious
tenure of fame goes a long way to justify those (and
they are not few) who prefer cakes and cream in the
immediate present.

A WILD YOUTH

François de Montcorbier, *alias* François des Loges,
alias François Villon, *alias* Michel Mouton, Master of
Arts in the University of Paris, was born in that city
in the summer of 1431. It was a memorable year for
France on other and higher considerations. A great-
hearted girl and a poor-hearted boy made, the one her
last, the other his first appearance on the public stage
of that unhappy country. On the 30th of May the
ashes of Joan of Arc were thrown into the Seine, and
on the 2d of December our Henry Sixth made his Joyous Entry dismally enough into disaffected and depopu-
lating Paris. Sword and fire still ravaged the open
country. On a single April Saturday twelve hundred
persons, besides children, made their escape out of the
starving capital. The hangman, as is not uninteresting
to note in connection with Master Francis, was kept
hard at work in 1431; on the last of April and on
the 4th of May alone, sixty-two bandits swung from
Paris gibbets.* A more confused or troublous time it
would have been difficult to select for a start in life.
Not even a man's nationality was certain; for the people of Paris there was no such thing as a Frenchman.
The English were the English indeed, but the French

---

* "Bourgeois de Paris," ed. Panthéon, pp. 688, 689.

were only the Armagnacs, whom, with Joan of Arc at
their head, they had beaten back from under their ram-
parts not two years before. Such public sentiment as
they had centered about their dear Duke of Burgundy,
and the dear Duke had no more urgent business than
to keep out of their neighborhood. . . . At least,
and whether he liked it or not, our disreputable trouba-
dour was tubbed and swaddled as a subject of the
English crown.

We hear nothing of Villon's father except that he
was poor and of mean extraction. His mother was
given piously, which does not imply very much in an
old Frenchwoman, and quite uneducated. He had an
uncle, a monk in an abbey at Angers, who must have
prospered beyond the family average, and was reported
to be worth five or six hundred crowns. Of this uncle
and his money-box the reader will hear once more. In
1448 Francis became a student of the University of
Paris; in 1450 he took the degree of Bachelor, and in
1452 that of Master of Arts. His *bourse*, or the sum
paid weekly for his board, was of the amount of two
sous. Now two sous was about the price of a pound
of salt butter in the bad times of 1417; it was the
price of half-a-pound in the worse times of 1419; and
in 1444, just four years before Villon joined the University, it seems to have been taken as the average
wage for a day's manual labor.* In short, it cannot
have been a very profuse allowance to keep a sharp-set
lad in breakfast and supper for seven mortal days; and
Villon's share of the cakes and pastry and general good

---

* "Bourgeois," pp. 627, 636, and 725.

cheer, to which he is never weary of referring, must have been slender from the first.

The educational arrangements of the University of Paris were, to our way of thinking, somewhat incomplete. Worldly and monkish elements were presented in a curious confusion, which the youth might disentangle for himself. If he had an opportunity, on the one hand, of acquiring much hair-drawn divinity and a taste for formal disputation, he was put in the way of much gross and flaunting vice upon the other. The lecture room of a scholastic doctor was sometimes under the same roof with establishments of a very different and peculiarly unedifying order. The students had extraordinary privileges, which by all accounts they abused extraordinarily. And while some condemned themselves to an almost sepulchral regularity and seclusion, others fled the schools, swaggered in the street "with their thumbs in their girdle," passed the night in riot, and behaved themselves as the worthy forerunners of Jehan Frollo in the romance of "Notre Dame de Paris." Villon tells us himself that he was among the truants, but we hardly needed his avowal. The burlesque erudition in which he sometimes indulged implies no more than the merest smattering of knowledge; whereas his acquaintance with blackguard haunts and industries could only have been acquired by early and consistent impiety and idleness. He passed his degrees, it is true; but some of us who have been to modern universities will make their own reflections on the value of the test. As for his three pupils, Colin Laurent, Girard Gossouyn, and Jehan Marceau—if they were really his pupils in any serious sense—what can we say but God help them!

And sure enough, by his own description, they turned
out as ragged, rowdy, and ignorant as was to be looked
for from the views and manners of their rare preceptor.

At some time or other, before or during his university career, the poet was adopted by Master Guillaume de Villon, chaplain of Saint Benoît-le-Betourne
near the Sorbonne. From him he borrowed the sur-
name by which he is known to posterity. It was most
likely from his house, called the *Porte Rouge*, and situated in a garden in the cloister of St. Benoît, that
Master Francis heard the bell of the Sorbonne ring
out the Angelus while he was finishing his "Small
Testament" at Christmastide in 1546. Toward this
benefactor he usually gets credit for a respectable display of gratitude. But with his trap and pitfall style
of writing, it is easy to make too sure. His sentiments are about as much to be relied on as those of
a professional beggar; and in this, as in so many other
matters, he comes toward us whining and piping the
eye, and goes off again with a whoop and his finger
to his nose. Thus, he calls Guillaume de Villon his
"more than father," thanks him with a great show of
sincerity for having helped him out of many scrapes,
and bequeaths him his portion of renown. But the portion of renown which belonged to a young thief, distinguished (if, at the period when he wrote this legacy,
he was distinguished at all) for having written some
more or less obscene and scurrilous ballads, must have
been little fitted to gratify the self-respect or increase
the reputation of a benevolent ecclesiastic. The same
remark applies to a subsequent legacy of the poet's library, with specification of one work which was plainly

neither decent nor devout. We are thus left on the horns of a dilemma. If the chaplain was a godly, philanthropic personage, who had tried to graft good principles and good behavior on this wild slip of an adopted son, these jesting legacies would obviously cut him to the heart. The position of an adopted son toward his adoptive father is one full of delicacy; where a man lends his name he looks for great consideration. And this legacy of Villon's portion of renown may be taken as the mere fling of an unregenerate scapegrace who has wit enough to recognize in his own shame the readiest weapon of offense against a prosy benefactor's feelings. The gratitude of Master Francis figures, on this reading, as a frightful *minus* quantity. If, on the other hand, those jests were given and taken in good humor, the whole relation between the pair degenerates into the unedifying complicity of a debauched old chaplain and a witty and dissolute young scholar. At this rate the house with the red door may have rung with the most mundane minstrelsy; and it may have been below its roof that Villon, through a hole in the plaster, studied, as he tells us, the leisures of a rich ecclesiastic.

It was, perhaps, of some moment in the poet's life that he should have inhabited the cloister of Saint Benoît. Three of the most remarkable among his early acquaintances are Catherine de Vausselles, for whom he entertained a short-lived affection and an enduring and most unmanly resentment; Regnier de Montigny, a young blackguard of good birth; and Colin de Cayeux, a fellow with a marked aptitude for picking locks. Now we are on a foundation of mere conjecture, but it is at least curious to find that two of the canons of Saint Benoît answered respectively to the names of Pierre de Vaucel and Etienne de Montigny, and that there was a householder called Nicolas de Cayeux in a street—the Rue des Poirees—in the immediate neighborhood of the cloister. M. Longnon is almost ready to identify Catherine as the niece of Pierre; Regnier as the nephew of Etienne, and Colin as the son of Nicolas. Without going so far, it must be owned that the approximation of names is significant. As we go on to see the part played by each of these persons in the sordid melodrama of the poet's life, we shall come to regard it as even more notable. Is it not Clough who has remarked that, after all, everything lies in juxtaposition? Many a man's destiny has been settled by nothing apparently more grave than a pretty face on the opposite side of the street and a couple of bad companions round the corner.

Catherine de Vausselles (or de Vaucel—the change is within the limits of Villon's license) had plainly delighted in the poet's conversation; near neighbors or not, they were much together; and Villon made no secret of his court, and suffered himself to believe that his feeling was repaid in kind. This may have been an error from the first, or he may have estranged her by subsequent misconduct or temerity. One can easily imagine Villon an impatient wooer. One thing, at least, is sure: that the affair terminated in a manner bitterly humiliating to Master Francis. In presence of his lady-love, perhaps under her window and certainly with her connivance, he was unmercifully thrashed by one Noë le Joly—beaten, as he says himself, like dirty linen on the washing-board. It is characteristic that his malice had notably increased between the time when he wrote the "Small Testament" immediately on the back of the occurrence, and the time when he wrote the "Large Testament" five years after. On the latter occasion nothing is too bad for his "damsel with the twisted nose," as he calls her. She is spared neither hint nor accusation, and he tells his messenger to accost her with the vilest insults. Villon, it is thought, was out of Paris when these amenities escaped his pen; or perhaps the strong arm of Noë le Joly would have been again in requisition. So ends the love story, if love story it may properly be called. Poets are not necessarily fortunate in love; but they usually fall among more romantic circumstances and bear their disappointment with a better grace.

The neighborhood of Regnier de Montigny and Colin de Cayeux was probably more influential on his after life than the contempt of Catherine. For a man who is greedy of all pleasures, and provided with little money and less dignity of character, we may prophesy a safe and speedy voyage downward. Humble or even truckling virtue may walk unspotted in this life. But only those who despise the pleasures can afford to despise the opinion of the world. A man of a strong, heady temperament, like Villon, is very differently tempted. His eyes lay hold on all provocations greedily, and his heart flames up at a look into imperious desire; he is snared and broached-to by anything and everything, from a pretty face to a piece of pastry in a cookshop window; he will drink the rinsing of the wine cup, stay the latest at the tavern party; tap at

the lighted windows, follow the sound of singing, and
beat the whole neighborhood for another reveler, as he
goes reluctantly homeward; and grudge himself every
hour of sleep as a black empty period in which he
cannot follow after pleasure. Such a person is lost if
he have not dignity, or, failing that, at least pride,
which is its shadow and in many ways its substitute.
Master Francis, I fancy, would follow his own eager
instincts without much spiritual struggle. And we soon
find him fallen among thieves in sober, literal earnest,
and counting as acquaintances the most disreputable
people he could lay his hands on: fellows who stole
ducks in Paris Moat; sergeants of the criminal court,
and archers of the watch; blackguards who slept at
night under the butchers' stalls, and for whom the
aforesaid archers peered about carefully with lanters;
Regnier de Montigny, Colin de Cayeux, and their crew,
all bound on a favoring breeze toward the gallows;
the disorderly abbess of Port Royal, who went about
at fair time with soldiers and thieves, and conducted
her abbey on the queerest principles; and most likely
Perette Mauger, the great Paris receiver of stolen goods,
not yet dreaming, poor woman! of the last scene of her
career when Henry Cousin, executor of the high justice, shall bury her, alive and most reluctant, in front
of the new Montigny gibbet.* Nay, our friend soon
began to take a foremost rank in this society. He could
string off verses, which is always an agreeable talent;
and he could make himself useful in many other ways.
The whole ragged army of Bohemia, and whosoever

* "Chronique Scandaleuse," ed. Panthéon, p. 237.

loved good cheer without at all loving to work and
pay for it, are addressed in contemporary verses as the
"Subjects of François Villon." He was a good genius
to all hungry and unscrupulous persons; and became
the hero of a whole legendary cycle of tavern tricks
and cheateries. At best, these were doubtful levities,
rather too thievish for a schoolboy, rather too game-
some for a thief. But he would not linger long in
this equivocal border land. He must soon have com-
plied with his surroundings. He was one who would
go where the cannikin clinked, not caring who should
pay; and from supping in the wolves' den, there is
but a step to hunting with the pack. And here, as
I am on the chapter of his degradation, I shall say
all I mean to say about its darkest expression, and be
done with it for good. Some charitable critics see no
more than a *jeu d'esprit*, a graceful and trifling exercise of the imagination, in the grimy ballad of Fat
Peg ("Grosse Margot"). I am not able to follow these
gentlemen to this polite extreme. Out of all Villon's
works that ballad stands forth in flaring reality, gross
and ghastly, as a thing written in a contraction of
disgust. M. Longnon shows us more and more clearly
at every page that we are to read our poet literally,
that his names are the names of real persons, and the
events he chronicles were actual events. But even if
the tendency of criticism had run the other way, this
ballad would have gone far to prove itself. I can well
understand the reluctance of worthy persons in this matter; for of course it is unpleasant to think of a man of
genius as one who held, in the words of Marina to
Boult—

"A place, for which the pained'st fiend
Of hell would not in reputation change."

But beyond this natural unwillingness, the whole difficulty of the case springs from a highly virtuous ignorance of life. Paris now is not so different from the Paris of then; and the whole of the doings of Bohemia are not written in the sugar-candy pastorals of Murger. It is really not at all surprising that a young man of the fifteenth century, with a knack of making verses, should accept his bread upon disgraceful terms. The race of those who do is not extinct; and some of them to this day write the prettiest verses imaginable. . . . After this, it were impossible for Master Francis to fall lower: to go and steal for himself would be an admirable advance from every point of view, divine or human.

And yet it is not as a thief, but as a homicide, that he makes his first appearance before angry justice. On June 5, 1455, when he was about twenty-four, and had been Master of Arts for a matter of three years, we behold him for the first time quite definitely. Angry justice had, as it were, photographed him in the act of his homicide; and M. Longnon, rummaging among old deeds, has turned up the negative and printed it off for our instruction. Villon had been supping—copiously we may believe—and sat on a stone bench in front of the Church of St. Benoît, in company with a priest called Gilles and a woman of the name of Isabeau. It was nine o'clock, a mighty late hour for the period, and evidently a fine summer's night. Master Francis carried a mantle, like a prudent man, to keep him from the dews (*serain*), and had a sword below it dangling from his girdle. So these three dallied in front of St. Benoît, taking their pleasure (*pour soy esbatre*). Suddenly there arrived upon the scene a priest, Philippe Chermoye or Sermaise, also with sword and cloak, and accompanied by one Master Jehan le Mardi. Sermaise, according to Villon's account, which is all we have to go upon, came up blustering and denying God; as Villon rose to make room for him upon the bench, thrust him rudely back into his place; and finally drew his sword and cut open his lower lip, by what I should imagine was a very clumsy stroke. Up to this point, Villon professes to have been a model of courtesy, even of feebleness: and the brawl, in his version, reads like the fable of the wolf and the lamb. But now the lamb was roused; he drew his sword, stabbed Sermaise in the groin, knocked him on the head with a big stone, and then, leaving him to his fate, went away to have his own lip doctored by a barber of the name of Fouquet. In one version, he says that Gilles, Isabeau, and Le Mardi ran away at the first high words, and that he and Sermaise had it out alone; in another, Le Mardi is represented as returning and wresting Villon's sword from him: the reader may please himself. Sermaise was picked up, lay all that night in the prison of Saint Benoît, where he was examined by an official of the châtelet and expressly pardoned Villon, and died on the following Saturday in the Hotel Dieu.

This, as I have said, was in June. Not before January of the next year could Villon extract a pardon from the king; but while his hand was in, he got two. One is for "François des Loges, alias (*autrement*

dit) de Villon;'' and the other runs in the name of
François de Montcorbier. Nay, it appears there was a
further complication; for in the narrative of the first
of these documents, it is mentioned that he passed himself off upon Fouquet, the barber-surgeon, as one Michel
Mouton. M. Longnon has a theory that this unhappy
accident with Sermaise was the cause of Villon's subsequent irregularities; and that up to that moment he
had been the pink of good behavior. But the matter
has to my eyes a more dubious air. A pardon necessary for Des Loges and another for Montcorbier? and
these two the same person? and one or both of them
known by the *alias* of Villon, however honestly come
by? and lastly, in the heat of the moment, a fourth
name thrown out with an assured countenance? A ship
is not to be trusted that sails under so many colors.
This is not the simple bearing of innocence. No—the
young master was already treading crooked paths; already, he would start and blench at a hand upon his
shoulder, with the look we know so well in the face
of Hogarth's Idle Apprentice; already, in the blue
devils, he would see Henry Cousin, the executor of
high justice, going in dolorous procession toward Montfaucon, and hear the wind and the birds crying around
Paris gibbet.

A GANG OF THIEVES

In spite of the prodigious number of people who
managed to get hanged, the fifteenth century was by
no means a bad time for criminals. A great confusion
of parties and great dust of fighting favored the escape
of private housebreakers and quiet fellows who stole

ducks in Paris Moat. Prisons were leaky; and as we
shall see, a man with a few crowns in his pocket and
perhaps some acquaintance among the officials, could
easily slip out and become once more a free marauder.
There was no want of a sanctuary where he might
harbor until troubles blew by; and accomplices helped
each other with more or less good faith. Clerks, above
all, had remarkable facilities for a criminal way of life;
for they were privileged, except in cases of notorious
incorrigibility, to be plucked from the hands of rude
secular justice and tried by a tribunal of their own.
In 1402, a couple of thieves, both clerks of the University, were condemned to death by the Provost of
Paris. As they were taken to Montfaucon, they kept
crying "high and clearly" for their benefit of clergy,
but were none the less pitilessly hanged and gibbeted.
Indignant Alma Mater interfered before the king; and
the Provost was deprived of all royal offices, and condemned to return the bodies and erect a great stone
cross, on the road from Paris to the gibbet, graven
with the effigies of these two holy martyrs.* We shall
hear more of the benefit of clergy; for after this the
reader will not be surprised to meet with thieves in the
shape of tonsured clerks, or even priests and monks.

To a knot of such learned pilferers our poet certainly
belonged; and by turning over a few more of M. Longnon's negatives, we shall get a clear idea of their character and doings. Montigny and De Cayeux are names
already known; Guy Tabary, Petit-Jehan, Dom Nicolas,
little Thibault, who was both clerk and goldsmith, and

---

* Monstrelet : "Panthéon Littéraire," p. 26.

who made picklocks and melted plate for himself and
his companions—with these the reader has still to become acquainted. Petit-Jehan and De Cayeux were
handy fellows and enjoyed a useful pre eminence in
honor of their doings with the picklock. "*Dictus des
Cahyeus est fortis operator crochetorum,*" says Tabary's interrogation, "*sed dictus Petit-Jehan, ejus so-
cius, est forcius operator.*" But the flower of the
flock was little Thibault; it was reported that no lock
could stand before him; he had a persuasive hand; let
us salute capacity wherever we may find it. Perhaps
the term *gang* is not quite properly applied to the persons whose fortunes we are now about to follow; rather
they were independent malefactors, socially intimate, and
occasionally joining together for some serious operation,
just as modern stockjobbers form a syndicate for an
important loan. Nor were they at all particular to any
branch of misdoing. They did not scrupulously confine
themselves to a single sort of theft, as I hear is common among modern thieves. They were ready for anything, from pitch-and-toss to manslaughter. Montigny,
for instance, had neglected neither of these extremes,
and we find him accused of cheating at games of hazard on the one hand and on the other of the murder
of one Thevenin Pensete in a house by the Cemetery
of St. John. If time had only spared us some particu-
lars, might not this last have furnished us with the
matter of a grisly winter's tale?

At Christmas-time in 1456, readers of Villon will remember that he was engaged on the "Small Testament." About the same period, *circa festum nativi-
tatis Domini*, he took part in a memorable supper at

the Mule Tavern, in front of the Church of St. Mathurin. Tabary, who seems to have been very much
Villon's creature, had ordered the supper in the course
of the afternoon. He was a man who had had troubles
in his time and languished in the Bishop of Paris's
prisons on a suspicion of picking locks; confiding, convivial, not very astute—who had copied out a whole
improper romance with his own right hand. This sup-
per-party was to be his first introduction to De Cayeux
and Petit-Jehan, which was probably a matter of some
concern to the poor man's muddy wits; in the sequel,
at least, he speaks of both with an undisguised respect, based on professional inferiority in the matter
of picklocks. Dom Nicolas, a Picardy monk, was
the fifth and last at table. When supper had been
dispatched and fairly washed down, we may suppose,
with white Baigneux or red Beaune, which were favorite wines among the fellowship, Tabary was solemnly
sworn over to secrecy on the night's performances; and
the party left the Mule and proceeded to an unoccupied
house belonging to Robert de Saint-Simon. This, over
a low wall, they entered without difficulty. All but
Tabary took off their upper garments; a ladder was
found and applied to the high wall which separated
Saint-Simon's house from the court of the College of
Navarre; the four fellows in their shirt-sleeves (as we
might say) clambered over in a twinkling; and Master
Guy Tabary remained alone beside the overcoats. From
the court the burglars made their way into the vestry
of the chapel, where they found a large chest, strengthened with iron bands and closed with four locks. One
of these locks they picked, and then, by levering up

the corner, forced the other three. Inside was a small
coffer, of walnut wood, also barred with iron, but fastened with only three locks, which were all comfortably
picked by way of the keyhole. In the walnut coffer—
a joyous sight by our thieves' lantern—were five hundred crowns of gold. There was some talk of opening
the aumries, where, if they had only known, a booty
eight or nine times greater lay ready to their hand;
but one of the party (I have a humorous suspicion it
was Dom Nicolas, the Picardy monk) hurried them
away. It was ten o'clock when they mounted the ladder; it was about midnight before Tabary beheld them
coming back. To him they gave ten crowns, and promised a share of a two-crown dinner on the morrow;
whereat we may suppose his mouth watered. In course
of time, he got wind of the real amount of their booty
and understood how scurvily he had been used; but he
seems to have borne no malice. How could he, against
such superb operators as Petit-Jehan and De Cayeux;
or a person like Villon, who could have made a new
improper romance out of his own head, instead of
merely copying an old one with mechanical right hand?

The rest of the winter was not uneventful for the
gang. First they made a demonstration against the
Church of St. Mathurin after chalices, and were ignominiously chased away by barking dogs. Then Tabary
fell out with Casin Chollet, one of the fellows who stole
ducks in Paris Moat, who subsequently became a ser-
geant of the Châtelet and distinguished himself by misconduct, followed by imprisonment and public castigation,
during the wars of Louis Eleventh. The quarrel was
not conducted with a proper regard to the king's peace,

and the pair publicly belabored each other until the
police stepped in, and Master Tabary was cast once
more into the prisons of the Bishop. While he still lay
in durance, another job was cleverly executed by the
band in broad daylight, at the Augustine Monastery.
Brother Guillaume Coiffier was beguiled by an accomplice to St. Mathurin to say mass; and during his absence, his chamber was entered and five or six hundred
crowns in money and some silver plate successfully ab-
stracted. A melancholy man was Coiffier on his return!
Eight crowns from this adventure were forwarded by little
Thibault to the incarcerated Tabary; and with these he
bribed the jailer and reappeared in Paris taverns. Some
time before or shortly after this, Villon set out for
Angers, as he had promised in the "Small Testament."
The object of this excursion was not merely to avoid
the presence of his cruel mistress or the strong arm of
Noë le Joly, but to plan a deliberate robbery on his
uncle the monk. As soon as he had properly studied
the ground, the others were to go over in force from
Paris—picklocks and all—and away with my uncle's
strongbox! This throws a comical sidelight on his own
accusation against his relatives, that they had "forgotten
natural duty" and disowned him because he was poor.
A poor relation is a distasteful circumstance at the best,
but a poor relation who plans deliberate robberies against
those of his blood, and trudges hundreds of weary
leagues to put them into execution, is surely a little
on the wrong side of toleration. The uncle at Angers
may have been monstrously undutiful; but the nephew
from Paris was upsides with him.

On the 23d April, that venerable and discreet per-

son, Master Pierre Marchand, Curate and Prior of
Paray-le-Monial, in the diocese of Chartres, arrived in
Paris and put up at the sign of the Three Chandeliers,
in the Rue de la Huchette. Next day, or the day after,
as he was breakfasting at the sign of the Armchair,
he fell into talk with two customers, one of whom
was a priest and the other our friend Tabary. The
idiotic Tabary became mighty confidential as to his past
life. Pierre Marchand, who was an acquaintance of
Guillaume Coiffier's and had sympathized with him over
his loss, pricked up his ears at the mention of picklocks, and led on the transcriber of improper romances
from one thing to another, until they were fast friends.
For picklocks the Prior of Paray professed a keen curiosity; but Tabary, upon some late alarm, had thrown
all his into the Seine. Let that be no difficulty, however, for was there not little Thibault, who could make
them of all shapes and sizes, and to whom Tabary,
smelling an accomplice, would be only too glad to introduce his new acquaintance? On the morrow, accordingly, they met; and Tabary, after having first wet
his whistle at the Prior's expense, led him to Notre
Dame and presented him to four or five "young companions," who were keeping sanctuary in the church.
They were all clerks, recently escaped, like Tabary himself, from the episcopal prisons. Among these we may
notice Thibault, the operator, a little fellow of twenty-
six, wearing long hair behind. The Prior expressed,
through Tabary, his anxiety to become their accomplice
and altogether such as they were (*de leur sorte et de
leurs complices*). Mighty polite they showed themselves,
and made him many fine speeches in return. But for

all that, perhaps because they had longer heads than
Tabary, perhaps because it is less easy to wheedle men
in a body, they kept obstinately to generalities and gave
him no information as to their exploits, past, present,
or to come. I suppose Tabary groaned under this reserve; for no sooner were he and the Prior out of the
church than he fairly emptied his heart to him, gave
him full details of many hanging matters in the past,
and explained the future intentions of the band. The
scheme of the hour was to rob another Augustine monk,
Robert de la Porte, and in this the Prior agreed to
take a hand with simulated greed. Thus, in the course
of two days, he had turned this wineskin of a Tabary
inside out. For a while longer the farce was carried
on; the Prior was introduced to Petit-Jehan, whom he
describes as a little, very smart man of thirty, with a
black beard and a short jacket; an appointment was
made and broken in the de la Porte affair; Tabary
had some breakfast at the Prior's charge and leaked
out more secrets under the influence of wine and friendship; and then all of a sudden, on the 17th of May,
an alarm sprang up, the Prior picked up his skirts and
walked quietly over to the Châtelet to make a deposi-
tion, and the whole band took to their heels and vanished out of Paris and the sight of the police.

Vanish as they like, they all go with a clog about
their feet. Sooner or later, here or there, they will be
caught in the fact, and ignominiously sent home. From
our vantage of four centuries afterward, it is odd and
pitiful to watch the order in which the fugitives are
captured and dragged in.

Montigny was the first. In August of that same

year, he was laid by the hee's on many grievous
counts; sacrilegious robberies, frauds, incorrigibility, and
that bad business about Thevenin Pensete in the house
by the cemetery of St. John. He was reclaimed by the
ecclesiastical authorities as a clerk; but the claim was
rebutted on the score of incorrigibility, and ultimately
fell to the ground; and he was condemned to death by
the Provost of Paris. It was a very rude hour for
Montigny, but hope was not yet over. He was a fellow of some birth; his father had been king's pantler;
his sister, probably married to some one about the
Court, was in the family way, and her health would
be endangered if the execution was proceeded with. So
down comes Charles the Seventh with letters of mercy,
commuting the penalty to a year in a dungeon on
bread and water, and a pilgrimage to the shrine of St.
James in Galicia. Alas! the document was incomplete;
it did not contain the full tale of Montigny's enormities; it did not recite that he had been denied benefit
of clergy, and it said nothing about Thevenin Pensete.
Montigny's hour was at hand. Benefit of clergy, honorable descent from king's pantler, sister in the family
way, royal letters of commutation—all were of no avail.
He had been in prison in Rouen, in Tours, in Bor-
deaux, and four times already in Paris; and out of all
these he had come scatheless; but now he must make a
little excursion as far as Montfaucon with Henry Cousin,
executor of high justice. There let him swing among
the carrion crows.

About a year later, in July 1458, the police laid
hands on Tabary. Before the ecclesiastical commissary
he was twice examined, and, on the latter occasion,

put to the question ordinary and extraordinary. What a dismal change from pleasant suppers at the Mule, where he sat in triumph with expert operators and great wits! He is at the lees of life, poor rogue; and those fingers which once transcribed improper romances are now agonizingly stretched upon the rack. We have no sure knowledge, but we may have a shrewd guess of the conclusion. Tabary, the admirer, would go the same way as those whom he admired.

The last we hear of is Colin de Cayeux. He was caught in autumn 1460, in the great Church of St. Leu d'Esserens, which makes so fine a figure in the pleasant Oise Valley between Creil and Beaumont. He was reclaimed by no less than two bishops; but the Procureur for the Provost held fast by incorrigible Colin. 1460 was an ill-starred year: for justice was making a clean sweep of "poor and indigent persons, thieves, cheats, and lockpickers," in the neighborhood of Paris; * and Colin de Cayeux, with many others, was condemned to death and hanged.†

VILLON AND THE GALLOWS

Villon was still absent on the Angers expedition when the Prior of Paray sent such a bombshell among his accomplices; and the dates of his return and arrest

---

* "Chron. Scand.," ut supra.

† Here and there, principally in the order of events, this article differs from M. Longnon's own reading of his material. The ground on which he defers the execution of Montigny and De Cayeux beyond the date of their trials seems insufficient. There is a law of parsimony for the construction of historical documents; simplicity is the first duty of narration; and hanged they were.

remain undiscoverable. M. Campaux plausibly enough opined for the autumn of 1457, which would make him closely follow on Montigny, and the first of those denounced by the Prior to fall into the toils. We may suppose, at least, that it was not long thereafter; we may suppose him competed for between lay and clerical Courts; and we may suppose him alternately pert and impudent, humble and fawning, in his defense. But at the end of all supposing, we come upon some nuggets of fact. For first, he was put to the question by water. He who had tossed off so many cups of white Baigneux or red Beaune, now drank water through linen folds, until his bowels were flooded and his heart stood still. After so much raising of the elbow, so much outcry of fictitious thirst, here at last was enough drinking for a lifetime. Truly, of our pleasant vices, the gods make whips to scourge us. And secondly he was condemned to be hanged. A man may have been expecting a catastrophe for years, and yet find himself unprepared when it arrives. Certainly, Villon found, in this legitimate issue of his career, a very staggering and grave consideration. Every beast, as he says, clings bitterly to a whole skin. If everything is lost, and even honor, life still remains; nay, and it becomes, like the ewe lamb in Nathan's parable, as dear as all the rest. "Do you fancy," he asks, in a lively ballad, "that I had not enough philosophy under my hood to cry out: 'I appeal'? If I had made any bones about the matter, I should have been planted upright in the fields, by the St. Denis Road"—Montfaucon being on the way to St. Denis. An appeal to Parliament, as we saw in the case of Colin de Cayeux, did not nec-

essarily lead to an acquittal or a commutation; and
while the matter was pending, our poet had ample opportunity to reflect on his position. Hanging is a sharp
argument, and to swing with many others on the gibbet adds a horrible corollary for the imagination. With
the aspect of Montfaucon he was well acquainted; indeed, as the neighborhood appears to have been sacred
to junketing and nocturnal picnics of wild young men
and women, he had probably studied it under all va-
rieties of hour and weather. And now, as he lay in
prison waiting the mortal push, these different aspects
crowded back on his imagination with a new and startling significance; and he wrote a ballad, by way of
epitaph for himself and his companions, which remains
unique in the annals of mankind. It is, in the highest
sense, a piece of his biography:

> "La pluye nous a debuez et lavez,
>   Et le soleil dessechez et noirciz;
>   Pies, corbeaulx, nous ont les yeux cavez,
>   Et arrachez la barbe et les sourcilz.
>   Jamais, nul temps, nous ne sommes rassis;
>   Puis çà, puis là, comme le vent varie,
>   A son plaisir sans cesser nous charie,
>   Plus becquetez d'oiseaulx que dez à couldre.
>   Ne soyez donc de nostre confrairie,
>   Mais priez Dieu que tous nous vueille absouldre."

Here is some genuine thieves' literature after so
much that was spurious; sharp as an etching, written
with a shuddering soul. There is an intensity of consideration in the piece that shows it to be the tran-
script of familiar thoughts. It is the quintessence of
many a doleful nightmare on the straw, when he felt

himself swing helpless in the wind, and saw the birds turn about him, screaming and menacing his eyes.

And, after all, the Parliament changed his sentence into one of banishment; and to Roussillon, in Dauphiny, our poet must carry his woes without delay. Travelers between Lyons and Marseilles may remember a station on the line, some way below Vienne, where the Rhone fleets seaward between vine-clad hills. This was Villon's Siberia. It would be a little warm in summer perhaps, and a little cold in winter in that draughty valley between two great mountain fields; but what with the hills, and the racing river, and the fiery Rhone wines, he was little to be pitied on the conditions of his exile. Villon, in a remarkably bad ballad, written in a breath, heartily thanked and fulsomely belauded the Parliament; the *envoi*, like the proverbial postscript of a lady's letter, containing the pith of his performance in a request for three days' delay to settle his affairs and bid his friends farewell. He was probably not followed out of Paris, like Antoine Fradin, the popular preacher, another exile of a few years later, by weeping multitudes;* but I daresay one or two rogues of his acquaintance would keep him company for a mile or so on the south road, and drink a bottle with him before they turned. For banished people, in those days, seem to have set out on their own responsibility, in their own guard, and at their own expense. It was no joke to make one's way from Paris to Roussillon alone and penniless in the fifteenth century. Villon says he left a rag of his tails on every bush. Indeed, he must have

---

* "Chron. Scand.," p. 338.

had many a weary tramp, many a slender meal, and many a to-do with blustering captains of the Ordonnance. But with one of his light fingers, we may fancy that he took as good as he gave; for every rag of his tail, he would manage to indemnify himself upon the population in the shape of food, or wine, or ringing money; and his route would be traceable across France and Burgundy by housewives and innkeepers lamenting over petty thefts, like the track of a single human locust. A strange figure he must have cut in the eyes of the good country people: this ragged, blackguard city poet, with a smack of the Paris student, and a smack of the Paris street arab, posting along the highways, in rain or sun, among the green fields and vineyards. For himself, he had no taste for rural loveliness; green fields and vineyards would be mighty indifferent to Master Francis; but he would often have his tongue in his cheek at the simplicity of rustic dupes, and often, at city gates, he might stop to contemplate the gibbet with its swinging bodies, and hug himself on his escape.

How long he stayed at Roussillon, how far he became the protege of the Bourbons, to whom that town belonged, or when it was that he took part, under the auspices of Charles of Orleans, in a rhyming tournament to be referred to once again in the pages of the present volume, are matters that still remain in darkness, in spite of M. Longnon's diligent rummaging among archives. When we next find him, in summer 1461, alas! he is once more in durance: this time at Meun-sur-Loire, in the prisons of Thibault d'Aussigny, Bishop of Orleans. He had been lowered in a basket

into a noisome pit, where he lay, all summer, gnaw-
ing hard crusts and railing upon fate. His teeth, he
says, were like the teeth of a rake: a touch of hag-
gard portraiture all the more real for being excessive
and burlesque, and all the more proper to the man for
being a caricature of his own misery. His eyes were
"bandaged with thick walls." It might blow hurricanes
overhead; the lightning might leap in high heaven; but
no word of all this reached him in his noisome pit.
" Il n'entre, ou gist, n'escler ni tourbillon." Above
all, he was fevered with envy and anger at the freedom of others; and his heart flowed over into curses
as he thought of Thibault d'Aussigny, walking the
streets in God's sunlight, and blessing people with extended fingers. So much we find sharply lined in his
own poems. Why he was cast again into prison—how
he had again managed to shave the gallows—this we
know not, nor, from the destruction of authorities, are
we ever likely to learn. But on October 2, 1461, or
some day immediately preceding, the new King, Louis
Eleventh, made his joyous entry into Meun. Now it
was a part of the formality on such occasions for the
new King to liberate certain prisoners; and so the
basket was let down into Villon's pit, and hastily did
Master Francis scramble in, and was most joyfully
hauled up, and shot out, blinking and tottering, but
once more a free man, into the blessed sun and wind.
Now or never is the time for verses! Such a happy
revolution would turn the head of a stocking-weaver,
and set him jingling rhymes. And so—after a voyage
to Paris, where he finds Montigny and De Cayeux clattering their bones upon the gibbet, and his three pupils

roistering in Paris streets, "with their thumbs under
their girdles"—down sits Master Francis to write his
"Large Testament," and perpetuate his name in a sort
of glorious ignominy.

THE "LARGE TESTAMENT"

Of this capital achievement and, with it, of Villon's
style in general, it is here the place to speak. The
"Large Testament" is a hurly-burly of cynical and sentimental reflections about life, jesting legacies to friends
and enemies, and, interspersed among these, many admirable ballades, both serious and absurd. With so free
a design, no thought that occurred to him would need
to be dismissed without expression; and he could draw
at full length the portrait of his own bedeviled soul,
and of the bleak and blackguardly world which was
the theater of his exploits and sufferings. If the reader
can conceive something between the slap-dash inconse-
quence of Byron's "Don Juan" and the racy humorous gravity and brief noble touches that distinguish the
vernacular poems of Burns, he will have formed some
idea of Villon's style. To the latter writer—except in
the ballades, which are quite his own, and can be
paralleled from no other language known to me—he
bears a particular resemblance. In common with Burns
he has a certain rugged compression, a brutal vivacity
of epithet, a homely vigor, a delight in local personali-
ties, and an interest in many sides of life, that are
often despised and passed over by more effete and cul-
tured poets. Both also, in their strong, easy colloquial
way, tend to become difficult and obscure; the obscur-

ity in the case of Villon passing at times into the absolute darkness of cant language. They are perhaps the only two great masters of expression who keep sending their readers to a glossary.

"Shall we not dare to say of a thief," asks Montaigne, "that he has a handsome leg?" It is a far more serious claim that we have to put forward in behalf of Villon. Beside that of his contemporaries, his writing, so full of color, so eloquent, so picturesque, stands out in an almost miraculous isolation. If only one or two of the chroniclers could have taken a leaf out of his book, history would have been a pastime, and the fifteenth century as present to our minds as the age of Charles Second. This gallow's-bird was the one great writer of his age and country, and initiated modern literature for France. Boileau, long ago, in the period of perukes and snuff-boxes, recognized him as the first articulate poet in the language; and if we measure him, not by priority of merit, but living duration of influence, not on a comparison with obscure forerunners, but with great and famous successors, we shall install this ragged and disreputable figure in a far higher niche in glory's temple than was ever dreamed of by the critic. It is, in itself, a memorable fact that, before 1542, in the very dawn of printing, and while modern France was in the making, the works of Villon ran through seven different editions. Out of him flows much of Rabelais; and through Rabelais, directly and indirectly, a deep, permanent, and growing inspiration. Not only his style, but his callous pertinent way of looking upon the sordid and ugly sides of life, becomes every day a more specific feature in the literature of France. And only the other year, a work of some power appeared in Paris, and appeared with infinite scandal, which owed its whole inner significance and much of its outward form to the study of our rhyming thief.

The world to which he introduces us is, as before said, blackguardly and bleak. Paris swarms before us, full of famine, shame, and death; monks and the servants of great lords hold high wassail upon cakes and pastry; the poor man licks his lips before the baker's window; people with patched eyes sprawl all night under the stalls; chuckling Tabary transcribes an improper romance; bare-bosomed lasses and ruffling students swagger in the streets; the drunkard goes stumbling homeward; the graveyard is full of bones; and away on Montfaucon, Colin de Cayeux and Montigny hang draggled in the rain. Is there nothing better to be seen than sordid misery and worthless joys? Only where the poor old mother of the poet kneels in church below painted windows, and makes tremulous supplication to the Mother of God.

In our mixed world, full of green fields and happy lovers, where not long before Joan of Arc had led one of the highest and noblest lives in the whole story of mankind, this was all worth chronicling that our poet could perceive. His eyes were indeed sealed with his own filth. He dwelt all his life in a pit more noisome than the dungeon at Meun. In the moral world, also, there are large phenomena not cognizable out of holes and corners. Loud winds blow, speeding home deep-laden ships and sweeping rubbish from the earth; the lightning leaps and cleans the face of heaven; high purposes and brave passions shake and sublimate men's spirits; and meanwhile, in the narrow dungeon of his soul, Villon is mumbling crusts and picking vermin.

Along with this deadly gloom of outlook, we must take another characteristic of his work: its unrivaled insincerity. I can give no better similitude of this quality than I have given already: that he comes up with a whine, and runs away with a whoop and his finger to his nose. His pathos is that of a professional mendicant who should happen to be a man of genius; his levity that of a bitter street arab, full of bread. On a first reading, the pathetic passages preoccupy the reader, and he is cheated out of an alms in the shape of sympathy. But when the thing is studied the illusion fades away: in the transitions, above all, we can detect the evil, ironical temper of the man; and instead of a flighty work, where many crude but genuine feelings tumble together for the mastery as in the lists of tournament, we are tempted to think of the "Large Testament" as of one long-drawn epical grimace, pulled by a merry-andrew, who has found a certain despicable eminence over human respect and human affections by perching himself astride upon the gallows. Between these two views, at best, all temperate judgments will be found to fall; and rather, as I imagine, toward the last.

There were two things on which he felt with perfect and, in one case, even threatening sincerity.

The first of these was an undisguised envy of those richer than himself. He was forever drawing a parallel, already exemplified from his own words, between the happy life of the well-to-do and the miseries of the poor. Burns, too proud and honest not to work, continued through all reverses to sing of poverty with a light, defiant note. Beranger waited till he was himself beyond the reach of want, before writing the "Old Vagabond" or "Jacques." Samuel Johnson, although he was very sorry to be poor, "was a great arguer for the advantages of poverty" in his ill days. Thus it is that brave men carry their crosses, and smile with the fox burrowing in their vitals. But Villon, who had not the courage to be poor with honesty, now whiningly implores our sympathy, now shows his teeth upon the dung-heap with an ugly snarl. He envies bitterly, envies passionately. Poverty, he protests, drives men to steal, as hunger makes the wolf sally from the forest. The poor, he goes on, will always have a carping word to say, or, if that outlet be denied, nourish rebellious thoughts. It is a calumny on the noble army of the poor. Thousands in a small way of life, ay, and even in the smallest, go through life with tenfold as much honor and dignity and peace of mind, as the rich gluttons whose daintiest and state-beds awakened Villon's covetous temper. And every morning's sun sees thousands who pass whistling to their toil. But Villon was the "mauvais pauvre" defined by Victor Hugo, and, in its English expression, so admirably stereotyped by Dickens. He was the first wicked sansculotte. He is the man of genius with the moleskin cap. He is mighty pathetic and beseeching here in the street, but I would not go down a dark road with him for a large consideration.

The second of the points on which he was genuine and emphatic was common to the Middle Ages; a deep

and somewhat sniveling conviction of the transitory
nature of this life and the pity and horror of death.
Old age and the grave, with some dark and yet half-
skeptical terror of an after-world—these were ideas that
clung about his bones like a disease. An old ape,
as he says, may play all the tricks in its repertory,
and none of them will tickle an audience into good
humor. "Tousjours vieil synge est desplaisant." It
is not the old jester who receives most recognition
at a tavern party, but the young fellow, fresh and
handsome, who knows the new slang, and carries off
his vice with a certain air. Of this, as a tavern jester
himself, he would be pointedly conscious. As for the
women with whom he was best acquainted, his reflections on their old age, in all their harrowing pathos,
shall remain in the original for me. Horace has dis-
graced himself to something the same tune; but what
Horace throws out with an ill-favored laugh, Villon
dwells on with an almost maudlin whimper.

It is in death that he finds his truest inspiration;
in the swift and sorrowful change that overtakes beauty;
in the strange revolution by which great fortunes and
renowns are diminished to a handful of churchyard
dust; and in the utter passing away of what was once
lovable and mighty. It is in this that the mixed texture of his thought enables him to reach such poign-
ant and terrible effects, and to enhance pity with
ridicule, like a man cutting capers to a funeral march.
It is in this, also, that he rises out of himself into the
higher spheres of art. So, in the ballade by which he
is best known, he rings the changes on names that
once stood for beautiful and queenly women, and are

now no more than letters and a legend. "Where are
the snows of yester year?" runs the burden. And so,
in another not so famous, he passes in review the different degrees of bygone men, from the Holy Apostles and
the golden Emperor of the East, down to the heralds,
pursuivants, and trumpeters, who also bore their part
in the world's pageantries and ate greedily at great
folks' tables: all this to the refrain of "So much carry
the winds away!" Probably, there was some melancholy
in his mind for a yet lower grade, and Montigny and
Colin de Cayeux clattering their bones on Paris gibbet.
Alas, and with so pitiful an experience of life, Villon
can offer us nothing but terror and lamentation about
death! No one has ever more skillfully communicated
his own disenchantment; no one ever blown a more
ear-piercing note of sadness. This unrepentant thief can
attain neither to Christian confidence, nor to the spirit
of the bright Greek saying, that whom the gods love
die early. It is a poor heart, and a poorer age, that
cannot accept the conditions of life with some heroic
readiness.

.   .   .   .

The date of the "Large Testament" is the last date
in the poet's biography. After having achieved that admirable and despicable performance, he disappears into
the night from whence he came. How or when he
died, whether decently in bed or trussed up to a gallows, remains a riddle for foolhardy commentators. It
appears his health had suffered in the pit at Méun; he
was thirty years of age and quite bald; with the notch
in his under lip where Sermaise had struck him with
the sword, and what wrinkles the reader may imagine.

In default of portraits, this is all I have been able to
piece together, and perhaps even the baldness should be
taken as a figure of his destitution. A sinister dog,
in all likelihood, but with a look in his eye, and the
loose flexile mouth that goes with wit and an overweening sensual temperament. Certainly the sorriest
figure on the rolls of fame.

CHARLES OF ORLEANS

FOR one who was no great politician, nor (as men
go) especially wise, capable or virtuous, Charles of Orleans is more than usually enviable to all who love
that better sort of fame which consists in being known
not widely, but intimately. "To be content that time
to come should know there was such a man, not caring whether they knew more of him, or to subsist under naked denominations, without deserts or noble acts,"
is, says Sir Thomas Browne, a frigid ambition. It is
to some more specific memory that youth looks forward
in its vigils. Old kings are sometimes disinterred in all
the emphasis of life, the hands untainted by decay, the
beard that had so often wagged in camp or senate still
spread upon the royal bosom; and in busts and pictures, some similitude of the great and beautiful of
former days is handed down. In this way, public
curiosity may be gratified, but hardly any private aspiration after fame. It is not likely that posterity will fall
in love with us, but not impossible that it may respect or

sympathize; and so a man would rather leave behind him the portrait of his spirit than a portrait of his face, *figura animi magis quam corporis*. Of those who have thus survived themselves most completely, left a sort of personal seduction behind them in the world, and retained, after death, the art of making friends, Montaigne and Samuel Johnson certainly stand first. But we have portraits of all sorts of men, from august Cæsar to the king's dwarf; and all sorts of portraits, from a Titian treasured in the Louvre to a profile over the grocer's chimney shelf. And so in a less degree, but no less truly, than the spirit of Montaigne lives on in the delightful Essays, that of Charles of Orleans survives in a few old songs and old account-books; and it is still in the choice of the reader to make this duke's acquaintance, and, if their humors suit, become his friend.

I

His birth—if we are to argue from a man's parents —was above his merit. It is not merely that he was the grandson of one king, the father of another, and the uncle of a third; but something more specious was to be looked for from the son of his father, Louis de Valois, Duke of Orleans, brother to the mad king Charles VI., lover of Queen Isabel, and the leading patron of art and one of the leading politicians in France. And the poet might have inherited yet higher virtues from his mother, Valentina of Milan, a very pathetic figure of the age, the faithful wife of an unfaithful husband, and the friend of a most unhappy king. The father, beautiful, eloquent, and accom-

plished, exercised a strange fascination over his contemporaries; and among those who dip nowadays into
the annals of the time there are not many—and these
few are little to be envied—who can resist the fascination of the mother. All mankind owe her a debt of
gratitude because she brought some comfort into the
life of the poor madman who wore the crown of
France.

Born (May 1391) of such a noble stock, Charles
was to know from the first all favors of nature and
art. His father's gardens were the admiration of his
contemporaries; his castles were situated in the most
agreeable parts of France, and sumptuously adorned.
We have preserved, in an inventory of 1403, the description of tapestried rooms where Charles may have
played in childhood.* "A green room, with the ceiling
full of angels, and the *dossier* of shepherds and shepherdesses seeming (*faisant contenance*) to eat nuts and
cherries. A room of gold, silk and worsted, with a
device of little children in a river, and the sky full of
birds. A room of green tapestry, showing a knight
and lady at chess in a pavilion. Another green room,
with shepherdesses in a trellised garden worked in gold
and silk. A carpet representing cherry-trees, where
there is a fountain, and a lady gathering cherries in
a basin." These were some of the pictures over which
his fancy might busy itself of an afternoon, or at
morning as he lay awake in bed. With our deeper
and more logical sense of life, we can have no idea
how large a space in the attention of mediæval men

---

* Champollion-Figeac's "Louis et Charles d'Orléans," p. 348.

might be occupied by such figured hangings on the
wall. There was something timid and purblind in the
view they had of the world. Morally, they saw nothing outside of traditional axioms; and little of the
physical aspect of things entered vividly into their
mind, beyond what was to be seen on church windows
and the walls and floors of palaces. The reader will
remember how Villon's mother conceived of heaven and
hell and took all her scanty stock of theology from
the stained glass that threw its light upon her as she
prayed. And there is scarcely a detail of external
effect in the chronicles and romances of the time, but
might have been borrowed at second hand from a piece
of tapestry. It was a stage in the history of mankind
which we may see paralleled, to some extent, in the
first infant school, where the representations of lions
and elephants alternate round the wall with moral
verses and trite presentments of the lesser virtues. So
that to live in a house of many pictures was tanta-
mount, for the time, to a liberal education in itself.

At Charles's birth an order of knighthood was in-
augurated in his honor. At nine years old, he was a
squire; at eleven, he had the escort of a chaplain and
a schoolmaster; at twelve, his uncle the king made
him a pension of twelve thousand livres d'or.* He
saw the most brilliant and the most learned persons of
France, in his father's Court; and would not fail to
notice that these brilliant and learned persons were one
and all engaged in rhyming. Indeed, if it is difficult

---

* D'Héricault's admirable "Memoir," prefixed to his edition of
Charles's works, vol. i., p. xi.

to realize the part played by pictures, it is perhaps even more difficult to realize that played by verses in the polite and active history of the age. At the siege of Pontoise, English and French exchanged defiant ballades over the walls.* If a scandal happened, as in the loathsome thirty-third story of the "Cent Nouvelles Nouvelles," all the wits must make rondels and chansonettes, which they would hand from one to another with an unmanly sneer. Ladies carried their favorite's ballades in their girdles.† Margaret of Scotland, all the world knows already, kissed Alain Chartier's lips in honor of the many virtuous thoughts and golden sayings they had uttered; but it is not so well known that this princess was herself the most industrious of poetasters, that she is supposed to have hastened her death by her literary vigils, and sometimes wrote as many as twelve rondels in the day.‡ It was in rhyme, even, that the young Charles should learn his lessons. He might get all manner of instruction in the truly noble art of the chase, not without a smack of ethics by the way, from the compendious didactic poem of Gace de la Bigne. Nay, and it was in rhyme that he should learn rhyming: in the verses of his father's Maître d'Hôtel, Eustache Deschamps, which treated of "l'art de dictier et de faire chançons, ballades, virelais et rondeaux," along with many other matters worth attention, from the courts of Heaven to the misgovernment of France.§ At this rate, all knowledge is to be

---

* Vallet de Viriville, "Charles VII. et son Epoque," ii. 428, note 2.
† See Lecoy de la Marche, "Le Roi René," i. 167.
‡ Vallet, "Charles VII.," ii. 85, 86, note 2.
§ Champollion-Figeac, 193–198.

had in a goody, and the end of it is an old song.
We need not wonder when we hear from Monstrelet
that Charles was a very well educated person. He
could string Latin texts together by the hour, and
make ballades and rondels better than Eustache Deschamps himself. He had seen a mad king who would
not change his clothes, and a drunken emperor who
could not keep his hand from the wine-cup. He had
spoken a great deal with jesters and fiddlers, and with
the profligate lords who helped his father to waste the
revenues of France. He had seen ladies dance on into
broad daylight, and much burning of torches and waste
of dainties and good wine.* And when all is said, it
was no very helpful preparation for the battle of life.
"I believe Louis XI.," writes Comines, "would not
have saved himself, if he had not been very differently brought up from such other lords as I have seen
educated in this country; for these were taught nothing but to play the jackanapes with finery and fine
words." † I am afraid Charles took such lessons to
heart, and conceived of life as a season principally for
junketing and war. His view of the whole duty of
man, so empty, vain, and wearisome to us, was yet
sincerely and consistently held. When he came in his
ripe years to compare the glory of two kingdoms, England and France, it was on three points only—pleasures, valor, and riches—that he cared to measure them;

---

* Champollion-Figeac, 209.

† The student will see that there are facts cited, and expressions
borrowed, in this paragraph, from a period extending over almost the
whole of Charles's life, instead of being confined entirely to his boyhood.
As I do not believe there was any change, so I do not believe there is
any anachronism involved.

and in the very outset of that tract he speaks of the life of the great as passed, "whether in arms, as in assaults, battles, and sieges, or in jousts and tournaments, in high and stately festivities and in funeral solemnities." *

When he was no more than thirteen, his father had him affianced to Isabella, virgin-widow of our Richard II. and daughter of his uncle Charles VI.; and, two years after (June 29, 1406), the cousins were married at Compiegne, he fifteen, she seventeen years of age. It was in every way a most desirable match. The bride brought five hundred thousand francs of dowry. The ceremony was of the utmost magnificence, Louis of Orleans figuring in crimson velvet, adorned with no less than seven hundred and ninety-five pearls, gathered together expressly for this occasion. And no doubt it must have been very gratifying for a young gentleman of fifteen, to play the chief part in a pageant so gayly put upon the stage. Only, the bridegroom might have been a little older; and, as ill-luck would have it, the bride herself was of this way of thinking, and would not be consoled for the loss of her title as queen, or the contemptible age of her new husband. *Pleuroit fort ladite Isabeau;* the said Isabella wept copiously.† It is fairly debatable whether Charles was much to be pitied when, three years later (September 1409), this odd marriage was dissolved by

---

* "The Debate between the Heralds of France and England," translated and admirably edited by Mr. Henry Pyne. For the attribution of this tract to Charles, the reader is referred to Mr. Pyne's conclusive argument.

† Des Ursins.

death. Short as it was, however, this connection left
a lasting stamp upon his mind; and we find that, in
the last decade of his life, and after he had remarried
for perhaps the second time, he had not yet forgotten
or forgiven the violent death of Richard II. "Ce mauvais cas"—that ugly business, he writes, has yet to be
avenged.

The marriage festivity was on the threshold of evil
days. The great rivalry between Louis of Orleans and
John the Fearless, Duke of Burgundy, had been forsworn with the most reverend solemnities. But the
feud was only in abeyance, and John of Burgundy
still conspired in secret. On November 23, 1407—in
that black winter when the frost lasted six and-sixty
days on end—a summons from the king reached Louis
of Orleans at the Hotel Barbette, where he had been
supping with Queen Isabel. It was seven or eight in
the evening, and the inhabitants of the quarter were
abed. He set forth in haste, accompanied by two
squires riding on one horse, a page, and a few var-
lets running with torches. As he rode, he hummed to
himself and trifled with his glove. And so riding, he
was beset by the bravoes of his enemy and slain. My
lord of Burgundy set an ill precedent in this deed, as
he found some years after on the bridge of Montereau;
and even in the meantime he did not profit quietly by
his rival's death. The horror of the other princes seems
to have perturbed himself; he avowed his guilt in the
council, tried to brazen it out, finally lost heart and
fled at full gallop, cutting bridges behind him, toward
Bapaume and Lille. And so there we have the head
of one faction, who had just made himself the most

formidable man in France, engaged in a remarkably
hurried journey, with black care on the pillion. And
meantime, on the other side, the widowed duchess came
to Paris in appropriate mourning, to demand justice for
her husband's death. Charles VI., who was then in a
lucid interval, did probably all that he could, when he
raised up the kneeling suppliant with kisses and smooth
words. Things were at a dead-lock. The criminal might
be in the sorriest fright, but he was still the greatest
of vassals. Justice was easy to ask and not difficult
to promise; how it was to be executed was another
question. No one in France was strong enough to punish John of Burgundy; and perhaps no one, except the
widow, very sincere in wishing to punish him.

She, indeed, was eaten up of zeal; but the intensity of her eagerness wore her out; and she died about
a year after the murder, of grief and indignation, un-
requited love and unsatisfied resentment. It was during the last months of her life that this fiery and generous woman, seeing the soft hearts of her own children,
looked with envy on a certain natural son of her husband's destined to become famous in the sequel as the
Bastard of Orleans, or the brave Dunois. "*You were
stolen from me,*" she said; "it is you who are fit to
avenge your father." These are not the words of ordinary mourning, or of an ordinary woman. It is a
saying over which Balzac would have rubbed his episcopal hands. That the child who was to avenge her
husband had not been born out of her body was a
thing intolerable to Valentina of Milan; and the expression of this singular and tragic jealousy is preserved to us by a rare chance, in such straightforward

and vivid words as we are accustomed to hear only on the stress of actual life, or in the theater. In history —where we see things as in a glass darkly, and the fashion of former times is brought before us, deplorably adulterated and defaced, fitted to very vague and pompous words, and strained through many men's minds of everything personal or precise — this speech of the widowed duchess startles a reader, somewhat as the footprint startled Robinson Crusoe. A human voice breaks in upon the silence of the study, and the student is aware of a fellow-creature in his world of documents. With such a clew in hand, one may imagine how this wounded lioness would spur and exasperate the resentment of her children, and what would be the last words of counsel and command she left behind her.

With these instancies of his dying mother—almost a voice from the tomb—still tingling in his ears, the position of young Charles of Orleans, when he was left at the head of that great house, was curiously similar to that of Shakespeare's Hamlet. The times were out of joint; here was a murdered father to avenge on a powerful murderer; and here, in both cases, a lad of inactive disposition born to set these matters right. Valentina's commendation of Dunois involved a judgment on Charles, and that judgment was exactly correct. Whoever might be, Charles was not the man to avenge his father. Like Hamlet, this son of a dear father murdered was sincerely grieved at heart. Like Hamlet, too, he could unpack his heart with words, and wrote a most eloquent letter to the king, complaining that what was denied to him would not be denied "to the lowest born and poorest man on earth."

Even in his private hours he strove to preserve a lively
recollection of his injury, and keep up the native hue
of resolution. He had gems engraved with appropriate
legends, hortatory or threatening: *"Dieu le scet,"* God
knows it; or *"Souvenez-vous de—"* Remember! * It is
only toward the end that the two stories begin to
differ; and in some points the historical version is the
more tragic. Hamlet only stabbed a silly old councilor
behind the arras; Charles of Orleans trampled France
for five years under the hoofs of his banditti. The
miscarriage of Hamlet's vengeance was confined, at
widest, to the palace; the ruin wrought by Charles of
Orleans was as broad as France.

Yet the first act of the young duke is worthy of
honorable mention. Prodigal Louis had made enormous
debts; and there is a story extant, to illustrate how
lightly he himself regarded these commercial obligations.
It appears that Louis, after a narrow escape he made
in a thunder-storm, had a smart access of penitence,
and announced he would pay his debts on the following Sunday. More than eight hundred creditors presented themselves, but by that time the devil was well
again, and they were shown the door with more
gayety than politeness. A time when such cynical dishonesty was possible for a man of culture is not, it
will be granted, a fortunate epoch for creditors. When
the original debtor was so lax, we may imagine how
an heir would deal with the incumbrances of his inheritance. On the death of Philip the Forward, father
of that John the Fearless whom we have seen at work,

---

* Michelet, iv. App. 179, p., 337.

the widow went through the ceremony of a public re-
nunciation of goods; taking off her purse and girdle,
she left them on the grave, and thus, by one notable
act, canceled her husband's debts and defamed his
honor. The conduct of young Charles of Orleans was
very different. To meet the joint liabilities of his
father and mother (for Valentina also was lavish), he
had to sell or pledge a quantity of jewels; and yet
he would not take advantage of a pretext, even legally
valid, to diminish the amount. Thus, one Godefroi
Lefevre, having disbursed many odd sums for the late
duke, and received or kept no vouchers, Charles ordered that he should be believed upon his oath.* To
a modern mind this seems as honorable to his father's
memory as if John the Fearless had been hanged as
high as Haman. And as things fell out, except a re-
cantation from the University of Paris, which had justified the murder out of party feeling, and various
other purely paper reparations, this was about the outside of what Charles was to effect in that direction.
He lived five years, and grew up from sixteen to
twenty-one, in the midst of the most horrible civil war,
or series of civil wars, that ever devastated France;
and from first to last his wars were ill-starred, or else
his victories useless. Two years after the murder (March
1409), John the Fearless having the upper hand for the
moment, a shameful and useless reconciliation took
place, by the king's command, in the church of Our
Lady at Chartres. The advocate the Duke of Burgundy stated that Louis of Orleans had been killed

---

* Champollion-Figeac, pp. 279-282.

"for the good of the king's person and realm." Charles
and his brothers, with tears of shame, under protest,
pour ne pas desobeir au roi, forgave their father's mur·
derer and swore peace upon the missal. It was, as I
say, a shameful and useless ceremony; the very greffier,
entering it in his register, wrote in the margin, "Pax,
pax, inquit Propheta, et non est pax."* Charles was soon
after allied with the abominable Bernard d'Armagnac,
even betrothed or married to a daughter of his, called
by a name that sounds like a contradiction in terms,
Bonne d'Armagnac. From that time forth, throughout
all this monstrous period—a very nightmare in the history of France—he is no more than a stalking-horse
for the ambitious Gascon. Sometimes the smoke lifts,
and you can see him for the twinkling of an eye, a
very pale figure; at one moment there is a rumor he
will be crowned king; at another, when the uproar
has subsided, he will be heard still crying out for jus·
tice; and the next (1412), he is showing himself to the
applauding populace on the same horse with John of
Burgundy. But these are exceptional seasons, and, for
the most part, he merely rides at the Gascon's bridle
over devastated France. His very party go, not by
the name of Orleans, but by the name of Armagnac.
Paris is in the hands of the butchers: the peasants
have taken to the woods. Alliances are made and
broken as if in a country dance; the English called
in, now by this one, now by the other. Poor people
sing in church, with white faces and lamentable music:
"Domine Jesu, parce populo tuo, dirige in viam pacis

---

* Michelet, iv., pp. 123-124.

principes." And the end and upshot of the whole
affair for Charles of Orleans is another peace with
John the Fearless. France is once more tranquil, with
the tranquillity of ruin; he may ride home again to
Blois, and look, with what countenance he may, on
those gems he had got engraved in the early days of
his resentment, "*Souvenez-vous de—*" Remember! He
has killed Polonius, to be sure; but the king is never
a penny the worse.

II

From the battle of Agincourt (Oct. 1415) dates the
second period of Charles's life. The English reader will
remember the name of Orleans in the play of "Henry
V."; and it is at least odd that we can trace a resemblance between the puppet and the original. The
interjection, "I have heard a sonnet begin so to one's
mistress" (Act. iii., scene 7), may very well indicate
one who was already an expert in that sort of trifle;
and the game of proverbs he plays with the Constable
in the same scene would be quite in character for a
man who spent many years of his life capping verses
with his courtiers. Certainly, Charles was in the great
battle with five hundred lances (say, three thousand
men), and there he was made prisoner as he led the
van. According to one story, some ragged English
archer shot him down; and some diligent English
Pistol, hunting ransoms on the field of battle, extracted him from under a heap of bodies and retailed
him to our King Henry. He was the most important
capture of the day, and used with all consideration.
On the way to Calais, Henry sent him a present of

bread and wine (and bread, you will remember, was
an article of luxury in the English camp), but Charles
would neither eat nor drink. Thereupon, Henry came
to visit him in his quarters. "Noble cousin," said he,
"how are you?" Charles replied that he was well.
"Why, then, do you neither eat nor drink?" And
then with some asperity, as I imagine, the young duke
told him that "truly he had no inclination for food."
And our Henry improved the occasion with something
of a snuffle, assuring his prisoner that God had fought
against the French on account of their manifold sins
and transgressions. Upon this there supervened the
agonies of a rough sea passage; and many French
lords, Charles, certainly, among the number, declared
they would rather endure such another defeat than such
another sore trial on shipboard. Charles, indeed, never
forgot his sufferings. Long afterward, he declared his
hatred to a seafaring life, and willingly yielded to England the empire of the seas, "because there is danger
and loss of life, and God knows what pity when it
storms; and sea-sickness is for many people hard to
bear; and the rough life that must be led is little suitable for the nobility:" * which, of all babyish utterances that ever fell from any public man, may surely
bear the bell. Scarcely disembarked, he followed his
victor, with such wry face as we may fancy, through
the streets of holiday London. And then the doors
closed upon his last day of garish life for more than
a quarter of a century. After a boyhood passed in the
dissipations of a luxurious court or in the camp of

* " Debate between the Heralds."

war, his ears still stunned and his cheeks still burning
from his enemies' jubilations; out of all this ringing
of English bells and singing of English anthems, from ·
among all these shouting citizens in scarlet cloaks, and
beautiful virgins attired in white, he passed into the
silence and solitude of a political prison.*

His captivity was not without alleviations. He was
allowed to go hawking, and he found England an admirable country for the sport; he was a favorite with
English ladies, and admired their beauty; and he did
not lack for money, wine, or books; he was honorably
imprisoned in the strongholds of great nobles, in Windsor Castle and the Tower of London. But when all is
said, he was a prisoner for five-and-twenty years. For
five-and-twenty years he could not go where he would,
or do what he liked, or speak with any but his jailers. We may talk very wisely of alleviations; there is
only one alleviation for which the man would thank
you: he would thank you to open the door. With
what regret Scottish James I. bethought him (in the
next room perhaps to Charles) of the time when he
rose "as early as the day." What would he not have
given to wet his boots once more with morning dew,
and follow his vagrant fancy among the meadows? The
only alleviation to the misery of constraint lies in the
disposition of the prisoner. To each one this place of
discipline brings his own lesson. It stirs Latude or
Baron Trenck into heroic action; it is a hermitage for
pious and conformable spirits. Beranger tells us he
found prison life, with its regular hours and long even-

---

* Sir H. Nicholas, "Agincourt."

ings, both pleasant and profitable. The "Pilgrim's Progress" and "Don Quixote" were begun in prison. It was after they were become (to use the words of one of them), "Oh, worst imprisonment — the dungeon of themselves!" that Homer and Milton worked so hard and so well for the profit of mankind. In the year 1415 Henry V. had two distinguished prisoners, French Charles of Orleans and Scottish James I., who whiled away the hours of their captivity with rhyming. Indeed, there can be no better pastime for a lonely man than the mechanical exercise of verse. Such intricate forms as Charles had been used to from childhood, the ballade with its scanty rhymes; the rondel, with the recurrence first of the whole, then of half the burden, in thirteen verses, seem to have been invented for the prison and the sick bed. The common Scotch saying, on the sight of anything operose and finical, "he must have had little to do that made that!" might be put as epigraph on all the song books of old France. Making such sorts of verse belongs to the same class of pleasures as guessing acrostics or "burying proverbs." It is almost purely formal, almost purely verbal. It must be done gently and gingerly. It keeps the mind occupied a long time, and never so intently as to be distressing; for anything like strain is against the very nature of the craft. Sometimes things go easily, the refrains fall into their place as if of their own accord, and it becomes something of the nature of an intellectual tennis; you must make your poem as the rhymes will go, just as you must strike your ball as your adversary played it. So that these forms are suitable rather for those who wish to make verses, than for those who wish to express opinions. Sometimes, on the other hand, difficulties arise: rival verses come into a man's head, and fugitive words elude his memory. Then it is that he enjoys at the same time the deliberate pleasures of a connoisseur comparing wines, and the ardor of the chase. He may have been sitting all day long in prison with folded hands; but when he goes to bed, the retrospect will seem animated and eventful.

Besides confirming himself as an habitual maker of verses, Charles acquired some new opinions during his captivity. He was perpetually reminded of the change that had befallen him. He found the climate of England cold and "prejudicial to the human frame"; he had a great contempt for English fruit and English beer; even the coal fires were unpleasing in his eyes.* He was rooted up from among his friends and customs and the places that had known him. And so in this strange land he began to learn the love of his own. Sad people all the world over are like to be moved when the wind is in some particular quarter. So Burns preferred when it was in the west, and blew to him from his mistress; so the girl in the ballade, looking south to Yarrow, thought it might carry a kiss betwixt her and her gallant; and so we find Charles singing of the "pleasant wind that comes from France." † One day, at "Dover-on-the-Sea," he looked across the straits, and saw the sandhills about Calais. And it happened to him, he tells us in a ballade, to remember his happiness over there in the past; and he was both sad

---

* "Debate between the Heralds."   † Works (ed. d'Héricault), i. 43.

and merry at the recollection, and could not have his
fill of gazing on the shores of France.* Although
guilty of unpatriotic acts, he had never been exactly
unpatriotic in feeling. But his sojourn in England
gave, for the time at least, some consistency to what
had been a very weak and ineffectual prejudice. He
must have been under the influence of more than usually solemn considerations, when he proceeded to turn
Henry's puritanical homily after Agincourt into a ballade, and reproach France, and himself by implication,
with pride, gluttony, idleness, unbridled covetousness,
and sensuality.† For the moment, he must really have
been thinking more of France than of Charles of
Orleans.

And another lesson he learned. He who was only
to be released in case of peace, begins to think upon
the disadvantages of war. "Pray for peace," is his
refrain: a strange enough subject for the ally of Bernard d'Armagnac.‡ But this lesson was plain and practical; it had one side in particular that was specially
attractive for Charles; and he did not hesitate to explain it in so many words. "Everybody," he writes—
I translate roughly—"everybody should be much inclined to peace, for everybody has a deal to gain by
it." §

Charles made laudable endeavors to acquire English,
and even learned to write a rondel in that tongue of
quite average mediocrity.‖ He was for some time bil-

---

* Works (ed. d'Héricault), 143.   † "Ibid." i. 190.
‡ "Ibid." 144.   § "Ibid." 158.
‖ M. Champollion-Figeac gives many in his editions of Charles's
works, most (as I should think) of very doubtful authenticity, or worse.

leted on the unhappy Suffolk, who received fourteen
shillings and fourpence a day for his expenses; and
from the fact that Suffolk afterward visited Charles in
France while he was negotiating the marriage of Henry
VI., as well as the terms of that nobleman's impeach-
ment, we may believe there was some not unkindly
intercourse between the prisoner and his jailer: a fact
of considerable interest when we remember that Suffolk's
wife was the granddaughter of the poet Geoffrey
Chaucer.* Apart from this, and a mere catalogue of
dates and places, only one thing seems evident in the
story of Charles's captivity. It seems evident that, as
these five-and-twenty years drew on, he became less
and less resigned. Circumstances were against the growth
of such a feeling. One after another of his fellow-
prisoners was ransomed and went home. More than
once he was himself permitted to visit France; where
he worked on abortive treaties and showed himself
more eager for his own deliverance than for the profit
of his native land. Resignation may follow after a
reasonable time upon despair; but if a man is persecuted by a series of brief and irritating hopes, his
mind no more attains to a settled frame of resolution,
than his eye would grow familiar with a night of
thunder and lightning. Years after, when he was
speaking at the trial of that Duke of Alençon, who
began life so hopefully as the boyish favorite of Joan
of Arc, he sought to prove that captivity was a harder
punishment than death. "For I have had experience

---

* Rymer, x. 564. D'Héricault's "Memoir," p. xli. Gairdner's "Paston
Letters," i. 27, 99.

myself," he said; "and in my prison of England, for
the weariness, danger, and displeasure in which I then
lay, I have many a time wished I had been slain at
the battle where they took me." * This is a flourish,
if you will, but it is something more. His spirit would
sometimes rise up in a fine anger against the petty desires and contrarieties of life. He would compare his
own condition with the quiet and dignified estate of
the dead; and aspire to lie among his comrades on the
field of Agincourt, as the Psalmist prayed to have the
wings of a dove and dwell in the uttermost parts of
the sea. But such high thoughts came to Charles only
in a flash.

John the Fearless had been murdered in his turn
on the bridge of Montereau so far back as 1419. His
son, Philip the Good—partly to extinguish the feud,
partly that he might do a popular action, and partly,
in view of his ambitious schemes, to detach another
great vassal from the throne of France—had taken up
the cause of Charles of Orleans, and negotiated dili-
gently for his release. In 1433 a Burgundian embassy
was admitted to an interview with the captive duke,
in the presence of Suffolk. Charles shook hands most
affectionately with the embassadors. They asked after
his health. "I am well enough in body," he replied,
"but far from well in mind. I am dying of grief at
having to pass the best days of my life in prison, with
none to sympathize." The talk falling on the chances
of peace, Charles referred to Suffolk if he were not
sincere and constant in his endeavors to bring it about.

---

* Champollion-Figeac, 377.

"If peace depended on me," he said, "I should procure it gladly, were it to cost me my life seven days after." We may take this as showing what a large price he set, not so much on peace, as on seven days of freedom. Seven days!—he would make them seven years in the employment. Finally, he assured the embassadors of his good will to Philip of Burgundy; squeezed one of them by the hand and nipped him twice in the arm to signify things unspeakable before Suffolk; and two days after sent them Suffolk's barber, one Jean Carnet, a native of Lille, to testify more freely of his sentiments. "As I speak French," said this emissary, "the Duke of Orleans is more familiar with me than with any other of the household; and I can bear witness he never said anything against Duke Philip." * It will be remembered that this person, with whom he was so anxious to stand well, was no other than his hereditary enemy, the son of his father's murderer. But the honest fellow bore no malice, indeed not he. He began exchanging ballades with Philip, whom he apostrophizes as his companion, his cousin, and his brother. He assures him that, soul and body, he is altogether Burgundian; and protests that he has given his heart in pledge to him. Regarded as the history of a vendetta, it must be owned that Charles's life has points of some originality. And yet there is an engaging frankness about these ballades which disarms criticism.† You see Charles throwing himself headforemost into the trap; you hear Burgundy, in his answers, begin to inspire him with his own prejudices,

---

* Dom Plancher, iv. 178–179.   † Works, i. 157–163.

and draw melancholy pictures of the misgovernment of
France. But Charles's own spirits are so high and so
amiable, and he is so thoroughly convinced his cousin
is a fine fellow, that one's scruples are carried away
in the torrent of his happiness and gratitude. And his
would be a sordid spirit who would not clap hands at
the consummation (Nov. 1440); when Charles, after
having sworn on the Sacrament that he would never
again bear arms against England, and pledged himself
body and soul to the unpatriotic faction in his own
country, set out from London with a light heart and
a damaged integrity.

In the magnificent copy of Charles's poems, given
by our Henry VII. to Elizabeth of York on the occasion of their marriage, a large illumination figures at
the head of one of the pages, which, in chronological
perspective, is almost a history of his imprisonment. It
gives a view of London with all its spires, the river
passing through the old bridge and busy with boats.
One side of the White Tower has been taken out, and
we can see, as under a sort of shrine, the paved room
where the duke sits writing. He occupies a high-backed
bench in front of a great chimney; red and black ink
are before him; and the upper end of the apartment
is guarded by many halberdiers, with the red cross of
England on their breast. On the next side of the
tower he appears again, leaning out of window and
gazing on the river; doubtless there blows just then
"a pleasant wind from out the land of France," and
some ship comes up the river: "the ship of good
news." At the door we find him yet again; this time
embracing a messenger, while a groom stands by hold-

ing two saddled horses. And yet further to the left, a cavalcade defiles out of the tower; the duke is on his way at last toward "the sunshine of France."

III

During the five-and-twenty years of his captivity, Charles had not lost in the esteem of his fellow countrymen. For so young a man, the head of so great a house, and so numerous a party, to be taken prisoner as he rode in the vanguard of France, and stereotyped for all men in this heroic attitude, was to taste untimeously the honors of the grave. Of him, as of the dead, it would be ungenerous to speak evil; what little energy he had displayed would be remembered with piety, when all that he had done amiss was courteously forgotten. As English folk looked for Arthur; as Danes awaited the coming of Ogier; as Somersetshire peasants or sergeants of the Old Guard expected the return of Monmouth or Napoleon; the countrymen of Charles of Orleans looked over the straits toward his English prison with desire and confidence. Events had so fallen out while he was rhyming ballades that he had become the type of all that was most truly patriotic. The remnants of his old party had been the chief defenders of the unity of France. His enemies of Burgundy had been notoriously favorers and furtherers of English domination. People forgot that his brother still lay by the heels for an unpatriotic treaty with England, because Charles himself had been taken prisoner patriotically fighting against it. That Henry V. had left special orders against his liberation served to increase the wistful pity with which he was regarded. And when, in defiance of all contemporary virtue, and against express pledges, the English carried war into their prisoner's fief, not only France, but all thinking men in Christendom, were roused to indignation against the oppressors, and sympathy with the victim. It was little wonder if he came to bulk somewhat largely in the imagination of the best of those at home. Charles le Boutteillier, when (as the story goes) he slew Clarence at Beauge, was only seeking an exchange for Charles of Orleans.* It was one of Joan of Arc's declared intentions to deliver the captive duke. If there was no other way, she meant to cross the seas and bring him home by force. And she professed before her judges a sure knowledge that Charles of Orleans was beloved of God.†

Alas! it was not at all as a deliverer that Charles returned to France. He was nearly fifty years old. Many changes had been accomplished since, at twenty-three, he was taken on the field of Agincourt. But of all these he was profoundly ignorant, or had only heard of them in the discolored reports of Philip of Burgundy. He had the ideas of a former generation, and sought to correct them by the scandal of a factious party. With such qualifications he came back eager for the domination, the pleasures, and the display that befitted his princely birth. A long disuse of all political activity combined with the flatteries of his new friends to fill him with an overweening conceit of his own capac-

---

* Vallet's "Charles VII.," i. 251.
† "Procès de Jeanne d'Arc," i. 133–155.

ity and influence. If aught had gone wrong in his absence, it seemed quite natural men should look to him for its redress. Was not King Arthur come again?

The Duke of Burgundy received him with politic honors. He took his guest by his foible for pageantry, all the easier as it was a foible of his own; and Charles walked right out of prison into much the same atmosphere of trumpeting and bell-ringing as he had left behind when he went in. Fifteen days after his deliverance he was married to Mary of Cleves, at St. Omer. The marriage was celebrated with the usual pomp of the Burgundian court; there were joustings, and illuminations, and animals that spouted wine; and many nobles dined together, *comme en brigade*, and were served abundantly with many rich and curious dishes.* It must have reminded Charles not a little of his first marriage at Compiegne; only then he was two years the junior of his bride, and this time he was five-and-thirty years her senior. It will be a fine question which marriage promises more: for a boy of fifteen to lead off with a lass of seventeen, or a man of fifty to make a match of it with a child of fifteen. But there was something bitter in both. The lamentations of Isabella will not have been forgotten. As for Mary, she took up with one Jaquet de la Lain, a sort of muscular Methody of the period, with a huge appetite for tournaments, and a habit of confessing himself the last thing before he went to bed.† With such a hero,

---

* Monstrelet.
† Vallet's "Charles VII.," iii. chap. i. But see the chronicle that bears Jaquet's name: a lean and dreary book.

the young duchess's amours were most ¹'' y innocent;
and in all other ways she was a suitable partner for
the duke, and well fitted to enter into his pleasures.

When the festivities at St. Omer had come to an
end, Charles and his wife set forth by Ghent and
Tournay. The towns gave him offerings of money as
he passed through, to help in the payment of his ran-
som. From all sides, ladies and gentlemen thronged to
offer him their services; some gave him their sons for
pages, some archers for a bodyguard; and by the time
he reached Tournay, he had a following of three hundred horse. Everywhere he was received as though he
had been the King of France.* If he did not come to
imagine himself something of the sort, he certainly forgot the existence of any one with a better claim to
the title. He conducted himself on the hypothesis that
Charles VII. was another Charles VI. He signed with
enthusiasm that treaty of Arras, which left France almost at the discretion of Burgundy. On December 18
he was still no further than Bruges, where he entered
into a private treaty with Philip; and it was not until
January 14, ten weeks after he disembarked in France,
and attended by a ruck of Burgundian gentlemen, that
he arrived in Paris and offered to present himself before Charles VII. The king sent word that he might
come, if he would, with a small retinue, but not with
his present following; and the duke, who was mightily
on his high horse after all the ovations he had received,
took the king's attitude amiss, and turned aside into
Touraine, to receive more welcome and more presents,
and be convoyed by torchlight into faithful cities.

---

* Monstrelet.

And so you see, here was King Arthur home again, and matters nowise mended in consequence. The best we can say is, that this last stage of Charles's public life was of no long duration. His confidence was soon knocked out of him in the contact with others. He began to find he was an earthen vessel among many vessels of brass; he began to be shrewdly aware that he was no King Arthur. In 1442, at Limoges, he made himself the spokesman of the malcontent nobility. The king showed himself humiliatingly indifferent to his counsels, and humiliatingly generous toward his necessities. And there, with some blushes, he may be said to have taken farewell of the political stage. A feeble attempt on the county of Asti is scarce worth the name of exception. Thenceforward let Ambition wile whom she may into the turmoil of events, our duke will walk cannily in his well ordered garden, or sit by the fire to touch the slender reed.*

IV

If it were given each of us to transplant his life wherever he pleased in time or space, with all the ages and all the countries of the world to choose from, there would be quite an instructive diversity of taste. A certain sedentary majority would prefer to remain where they were. Many would choose the Renaissance; many some stately and simple period of Grecian life; and still more elect to pass a few years wandering among the villages of Palestine with an inspired conductor. For some of our quaintly vicious contemporaries, we

---

* D'Héricault's " Memoir," xl. xli.   Vallet, " Charles VI.," ii. 435.

have the decline of the Roman Empire and the reign
of Henry III. of France. But there are others not
quite so vicious, who yet cannot look upon the world
with perfect gravity, who have never taken the cate-
gorical imperative to wife, and have more taste for
what is comfortable than for what is magnanimous and
high; and I can imagine some of these casting their
lot in the Court of Blois during the last twenty years
of the life of Charles of Orleans.

The duke and duchess, their staff of officers and
ladies, and the high-born and learned persons who were
attracted to Blois on a visit, formed a society for kill-
ing time and perfecting each other in various elegant
accomplishments, such as we might imagine for an
ideal watering-place in the Delectable Mountains. The
company hunted and went on pleasure - parties; they
played chess, tables, and many other games. What
we now call the history of the period passed, I imagine, over the heads of these good people much as it
passes over our own. News reached them, indeed, of
great and joyful import. William Peel received eight
livres and five sous from the duchess, when he brought
the first tidings that Rouen was recaptured from the
English.* A little later and the duke sang, in a truly
patriotic vein, the deliverance of Guyenne and Normandy.† They were liberal of rhymes and largesse,
and welcomed the prosperity of their country much as
they welcomed the coming of spring, and with no
more thought of collaborating toward the event. Religion was not forgotten in the Court of Blois. Pilgrim-

---

* Champollion-Figeac, 368. † Works, i., 115.

ages were agreeable and picturesque excursions. In
those days a well-served chapel was something like a
good vinery in our own, an opportunity for display and
the source of mild enjoyments. There was probably
something of his rooted delight in pageantry, as well
as a good deal of gentle piety, in the feelings with
which Charles gave dinner every Friday to thirteen
poor people, served them himself, and washed their feet
with his own hands.* Solemn affairs would interest
Charles and his courtiers from their trivial side. The
duke perhaps cared less for the deliverance of Guyenne
and Normandy than for his own verses on the occasion; just as Dr. Russell's correspondence in "The
Times" was among the most material parts of the Cri-
mean War for that talented correspondent. And I think
it scarcely cynical to suppose that religion as well as
patriotism was principally cultivated as a means of fill-
ing up the day.

It was not only messengers fiery red with haste
and charged with the destiny of nations, who were
made welcome at the gates of Blois. If any man of
accomplishment came that way, he was sure of an audience, and something for his pocket. The courtiers
would have received Ben Jonson like Drummond of
Hawthornden, and a good pugilist like Captain Barclay.
They were catholic, as none but the entirely idle can
be catholic. It might be Pierre, called Dieu d'amours,
the juggler; or it might be three high English min-
strels; or the two men, players of ghitterns, from the
kingdom of Scotland, who sang the destruction of the

---

* D'Héricault's "Memoir," xlv.

Turks; or again Jehan Rognelet, player of instruments
of music, who played and danced with his wife and
two children; they would each be called into the castle
to give a taste of his proficiency before my lord the
duke.* Sometimes the performance was of a more personal interest, and produced much the same sensations
as are felt on an English green on the arrival of a
professional cricketer, or round an English billiard table
during a match between Roberts and Cooke. This was
when Jehan Negre, the Lombard, came to Blois and
played chess against all these chess-players, and won
much money from my lord and his intimates; or when
Baudet Harenc, of Chalons, made ballades before all
these ballade-makers.†

It will not surprise the reader to learn they were
all makers of ballades and rondels. To write verses for
May day seems to have been as much a matter of
course, as to ride out with the cavalcade that went to
gather hawthorn. The choice of Valentines was a standing challenge, and the courtiers pelted each other with
humorous and sentimental verses as in a literary carnival. If an indecorous adventure befell our friend
Maistre Estienne le Gout, my lord the duke would
turn it into the funniest of rondels, all the rhymes being the names of the cases of nouns or the moods of
verbs; and Maistre Estienne would make reply in similar fashion, seeking to prune the story of its more humiliating episodes. If Fredet was too long away from
Court, a rondel went to upbraid him; and it was in
a rondel that Fredet would excuse himself. Sometimes

---

*Champollion-Figeac, 381, 361, 381.   † "Ibid." 359, 361.

two or three, or as many as a dozen, would set to
work on the same refrain, the same idea, or in the
same macaronic jargon. Some of the poetasters were
heavy enough; others were not wanting in address;
and the duchess herself was among those who most
excelled. On one occasion eleven competitors made a
ballade on the idea,

"I die of thirst beside the fountain's edge"
(Je meurs de soif empres de la fontaine).

These eleven ballades still exist; and one of them ar-
rests the attention rather from the name of the author
than from any special merit in itself. It purports to
be the work of François Villon; and so far as a foreigner can judge (which is indeed a small way), it
may very well be his. Nay, and if any one thing is
more probable than another, in the great *tabula rasa*,
or unknown land, which we are fain to call the biography of Villon, it seems probable enough that he may
have gone upon a visit to Charles of Orleans. Where
Master Baudet Harenc, of Chalons, found a sympathetic, or perhaps a derisive audience (for who can tell
nowadays the degree of Baudet's excellence in his art?),
favor would not be wanting for the greatest ballade-
maker of all time. Great as would seem the incongruity, it may have pleased Charles to own a sort of
kinship with ragged singers, and whimsically regard
himself as one of the confraternity of poets. And he
would have other grounds of intimacy with Villon. A
room looking upon Windsor gardens is a different matter from Villon's dungeon at Meun; yet each in his
own degree had been tried in prison. Each in his own

way, also, loved the good things of this life and the
service of the Muses. But the same gulf that separated Burns from his Edinburgh patrons would separate
the singer of Bohemia from the rhyming duke. And
it is hard to imagine that Villon's training among
thieves, loose women, and vagabond students, had fitted
him to move in a society of any dignity and courtli-
ness. Ballades are very admirable things; and a poet
is doubtless a most interesting visitor. But among the
courtiers of Charles there would be considerable regard
for the proprieties of etiquette; and even a duke will
sometimes have an eye to his teaspoons. Moreover, as
a poet, I can conceive he may have disappointed expectation. It need surprise nobody if Villon's ballade
on the theme,

"I die of thirst beside the fountain's edge,"

was but a poor performance. He would make better
verses on the lee-side of a flagon at the sign of the
Pomme du Pin, than in a cushioned settle in the halls
of Blois.

Charles liked change of place. He was often, not so
much traveling as making a progress; now to join the
king for some great tournament; now to visit King Rene,
at Tarascon, where he had a study of his own and saw
all manner of interesting things—oriental curios, King
Rene painting birds, and, what particularly pleased him,
Triboulet, the dwarf jester, whose skull-cap was no big-
ger than an orange.* Sometimes the journeys were set
about on horseback in a large party, with the *fourriers*

---

* Lecoy de la Marche, " Roi René," ii. 155, 177.

sent forward to prepare a lodging at the next stage.
We find almost Gargantuan details of the provision
made by these officers against the duke's arrival, of
eggs and butter and bread, cheese and peas and chick-
ens, pike and bream and barbel, and wine both white
and red.* Sometimes he went by water in a barge,
playing chess or tables with a friend in the pavilion,
or watching other vessels as they went before the wind.†
Children ran along the bank, as they do to this day
on the Crinan Canal; and when Charles threw in
money, they would dive and bring it up.‡ As he
looked on at their exploits, I wonder whether that
room of gold and silk and worsted came back into his
memory, with the device of little children in a river,
and the sky full of birds?

He was a bit of a book-fancier, and had vied with
his brother Angouleme in bringing back the library of
their grandfather Charles V., when Bedford put it up
for sale in London.§ The duchess had a library of her
own; and we hear of her borrowing romances from
ladies in attendance on the blue-stocking Margaret of
Scotland.‖ Not only were books collected, but new
books were written at the court of Blois. The widow
of one Jean Fougere, a bookbinder, seems to have
done a number of odd commissions for the bibliophilous

---

* Champollion-Figeac, chaps. v. and vi.

† " Ibid." 364; Works, i. 172.

‡ Champollion-Figeac, 364: " Jeter de l'argent aux petis enfans qui
estoient au long de Bourbon, pour les faire nonner en l'eau et aller
querre l'argent au fond."

§ " Ibid." 387.

‖ " Nouvelle Biographie Didot," art. " Marie de Clèves." Vallet,
" Charles VII.," iii. 85, note 1.

count. She it was who received three vellum-skins to
bind the duchess's Book of Hours, and who was employed to prepare parchment for the use of the duke's
scribes. And she it was who bound in vermilion leather
the great manuscript of Charles's own poems, which
was presented to him by his secretary, Anthony Astesan, with the text in one column, and Astesan's
Latin version in the other.*

Such tastes, with the coming of years, would doubtless take the place of many others. We find in
Charles's verse much semi-ironical regret for other
days, and resignation to growing infirmities. He who
had been "nourished in the schools of love," now sees
nothing either to please or displease him. Old age has
imprisoned him within doors, where he means to take
his ease, and let younger fellows bestir themselves in
life. He had written (in earlier days, we may presume) a bright and defiant little poem in praise of solitude. If they would but leave him alone with his own
thoughts and happy recollections, he declared it was
beyond the power of melancholy to affect him. But
now, when his animal strength has so much declined
that he sings the discomforts of winter instead of the
inspirations of spring, and he has no longer any appetite for life, he confesses he is wretched when alone,
and, to keep his mind from grievous thoughts, he must
have many people around him, laughing, talking, and
singing.†

While Charles was thus falling into years, the order
of things, of which he was the outcome and ornament,

---

* Champollion-Figeac, 383, 384–386.   † Works, ii. 57, 258.

was growing old along with him. The semi-royalty of
the princes of the blood was already a thing of the
past; and when Charles VII. was gathered to his
fathers, a new king reigned in France, who seemed
every way the opposite of royal. Louis XI. had aims
that were incomprehensible, and virtues that were inconceivable to his contemporaries. But his contemporaries were able enough to appreciate his sordid exte-
rior, and his cruel and treacherous spirit. To the whole
nobility of France he was a fatal and unreasonable
phenomenon. All such courts as that of Charles at
Blois, or his friend Rene's in Provence, would soon be
made impossible; interference was the order of the
day; hunting was already abolished; and who should
say what was to go next? Louis, in fact, must have
appeared to Charles primarily in the light of a kill-
joy. I take it, when missionaries land in South Sea
Islands and lay strange embargo on the simplest things
in life, the islanders will not be much more puzzled
and irritated than Charles of Orleans at the policy of
the Eleventh Louis. There was one thing, I seem to
apprehend, that had always particularly moved him;
and that was, any proposal to punish a person of his
acquaintance. No matter what treason he may have
made or meddled with, an Alençon or an Armagnac
was sure to find Charles reappear from private life,
and do his best to get him pardoned. He knew them
quite well. He had made rondels with them. They
were charming people in every way. There must certainly be some mistake. Had not he himself made
anti-national treaties almost before he was out of his
nonage? And for the matter of that, had not every one

else done the like? Such are some of the thoughts by
which he might explain to himself his aversion to such
extremities; but it was on a deeper basis that the feeling probably reposed. A man of his temper could not
fail to be impressed at the thought of disastrous revolutions in the fortunes of those he knew. He would
feel painfully the tragic contrast, when those who had
everything to make life valuable were deprived of life
itself. And it was shocking to the clemency of his
spirit, that sinners should be hurried before their Judge
without a fitting interval for penitence and satisfaction.
It was this feeling which brought him at last, a poor,
purblind blue-bottle of the later autumn, into collision
with "the universal spider," Louis XI. He took up
the defense of the Duke of Brittany at Tours. But
Louis was then in no humor to hear Charles's texts
and Latin sentiments; he had his back to the wall,
the future of France was at stake; and if all the old
men in the world had crossed his path, they would
have had the rough side of his tongue like Charles of
Orleans. I have found nowhere what he said, but it
seems it was monstrously to the point, and so rudely
conceived that the old duke never recovered the indig-
nity. He got home as far as Amboise, sickened, and
died two days after (Jan. 4, 1465), in the seventy-
fourth year of his age. And so a whiff of pungent
prose stopped the issue of melodious rondels to the end
of time.

V

The futility of Charles's public life was of a piece
throughout. He never succeeded in any single purpose

he set before him; for his deliverance from England, after twenty-five years of failure and at the cost of dignity and consistency, it would be ridiculously hyperbolical to treat as a success. During the first part of his life he was the stalking horse of Bernard d'Armagnac; during the second, he was the passive instrument of English diplomatists; and before he was well entered on the third, he hastened to become the dupe and cat's-paw of Burgundian treason. On each of these occasions, a strong and not dishonorable personal motive determined his behavior. In 1407 and the following years, he had his father's murder uppermost in his mind. During his English captivity, that thought was displaced by a more immediate desire for his own liberation. In 1440 a sentiment of gratitude to Philip of Burgundy blinded him to all else, and led him to break with the tradition of his party and his own former life. He was born a great vassal, and he conducted himself like a private gentleman. He began life in a showy and brilliant enough fashion, by the light of a petty personal chivalry. He was not without some tincture of patriotism; but it was resolvable into two parts: a preference for life among his fellow-countrymen, and a barren point of honor. In England, he could comfort himself by the reflection that "he had been taken while loyally doing his devoir," without any misgiving as to his conduct in the previous years, when he had prepared the disaster of Agincourt by wasteful feud. This unconsciousness of the larger interests is perhaps most happily exampled out of his own mouth. When Alencon stood accused of betraying Normandy into the hands of the English, Charles made a speech in his defense, from which I have already quoted more than once. Alencon, he said, had professed a great love and trust toward him; "yet did he give no great proof thereof, when he sought to betray Normandy; whereby he would have made me lose an estate of ten thousand livres a year, and might have occasioned the destruction of the kingdom and of all us Frenchmen." These are the words of one, mark you, against whom Gloucester warned the English Council because of his "great subtility and cautelous disposition." It is not hard to excuse the impatience of Louis XI., if such stuff was foisted on him by way of political deliberation.

This incapacity to see things with any greatness, this obscure and narrow view, was fundamentally characteristic of the man as well as of the epoch. It is not even so striking in his public life, where he failed, as in his poems, where he notably succeeded. For wherever we might expect a poet to be unintelligent, it certainly would not be in his poetry. And Charles is unintelligent even there. Of all authors whom a modern may still read and read over again with pleasure, he has perhaps the least to say. His poems seem to bear testimony rather to the fashion of rhyming, which distinguished the age, than to any special vocation in the man himself. Some of them are drawing-room exercises, and the rest seem made by habit. Great writers are struck with something in nature or society, with which they become pregnant and longing; they are possessed with an idea, and cannot be at peace until they have put it outside of them in some distinct embodiment. But with Charles literature was an object rather than a mean; he was one who loved bandying words for its own sake; the rigidity of intricate metrical forms stood him in lieu of precise thought; instead of communicating truth, he observed the laws of a game; and when he had no one to challenge at chess or rackets, he made verses in a wager against himself. From the very idleness of the man's mind, and not from intensity of feeling, it happens that all his poems are more or less autobiographical. But they form an autobiography singularly bald and uneventful. Little is therein recorded beside sentiments. Thoughts, in any true sense, he had none to record. And if we can gather that he had been a prisoner in England, that he had lived in the Orleannese, and that he hunted and went in parties of pleasure, I believe it is about as much definite experience as is to be found in all these five hundred pages of autobiographical verse. Doubtless, we find here and there a complaint on the progress of the infirmities of age. Doubtless, he feels the great change of the year, and distinguishes winter from spring; winter as the time of snow and the fireside; spring as the return of grass and flowers, the time of St. Valentine's day and a beating heart. And he feels love after a fashion. Again and again, we learn that Charles of Orleans is in love, and hear him ring the changes through the whole gamut of dainty and tender sentiment. But there is never a spark of passion; and heaven alone knows whether there was any real woman in the matter, or the whole thing was an exercise in fancy. If these poems were indeed inspired by some living mistress, one would think he had never seen, never heard, and never touched her. There

is nothing in any one of these so numerous love-songs
to indicate who or what the lady was. Was she dark
or fair, passionate or gentle like himself, witty or simple? Was it always one woman? or are there a dozen
here immortalized in cold indistinction? The old English translator mentions gray eyes in his version of one
of the amorous rondels; so far as I remember, he
was driven by some emergency of the verse; but in
the absence of all sharp lines of character and anything specific, we feel for the moment a sort of surprise, as though the epithet were singularly happy and
unusual, or as though we had made our escape from
cloudland into something tangible and sure. The measure of Charles's indifference to all that now preoccupies
and excites a poet, is best given by a positive example. If, besides the coming of spring, any one external circumstance may be said to have struck his
imagination, it was the dispatch of *fourriers*, while on
a journey, to prepare the night's lodging. This seems
to be his favorite image; it reappears like the upas-
tree in the early work of Coleridge: we may judge
with what childish eyes he looked upon the world, if
one of the sights which most impressed him was that
of a man going to order dinner.

Although they are not inspired by any deeper motive than the common run of contemporaneous drawing-room verses, those of Charles of Orleans are executed with inimitable lightness and delicacy of touch.
They deal with floating and colorless sentiments, and
the writer is never greatly moved, but he seems always genuine. He makes no attempt to set off thin
conceptions with a multiplicity of phrases. His ballades

are generally thin and scanty of import; for the ballade presented too large a canvas, and he was preoccupied by technical requirements. But in the rondel he
has put himself before all competitors by a happy knack
and a prevailing distinction of manner. He is very
much more of a duke in his verses than in his absurd
and inconsequential career as a statesman; and how he
shows himself a duke is precisely by the absence of all
pretension, turgidity, or emphasis. He turns verses, as
he would have come into the king's presence, with a
quiet accomplishment of grace.

Theodore de Banville, the youngest poet of a famous
generation now nearly extinct, and himself a sure and
finished artist, knocked off, in his happiest vein, a few
experiments in imitation of Charles of Orleans. I would
recommend these modern rondels to all who care about
the old duke, not only because they are delightful in
themselves, but because they serve as a contrast to
throw into relief the peculiarities of their model. When
de Banville revives a forgotten form of verse—and he
has already had the honor of reviving the ballade—he
does it in the spirit of a workman choosing a good
tool wherever he can find one, and not at all in that
of the dilettante, who seeks to renew bygone forms of
thought and make historic forgeries. With the ballade
this seemed natural enough; for in connection with ballades the mind recurs to Villon, and Villon was almost
more of a modern than de Banville himself. But in
the case of the rondel, a comparison is challenged with
Charles of Orleans, and the difference between two
ages and two literatures is illustrated in a few poems
of thirteen lines. Something, certainly, has been re-

tained of the old movement; the refrain falls in time
like a well-played bass; and the very brevity of the
thing, by hampering and restraining the greater fecund-
ity of the modern mind, assists the imitation. But de
Banville's poems are full of form and color; they
smack racily of modern life, and own small kindred
with the verse of other days, when it seems as if men
walked by twilight, seeing little, and that with dis-
tracted eyes, and instead of blood, some thin and spec-
tral fluid circulated in their veins. They might gird
themselves for battle, make love, eat and drink, and
acquit themselves manfully in all the external parts of
life; but of the life that is within, and those processes
by which we render ourselves an intelligent account of
what we feel and do, and so represent experience that
we for the first time make it ours, they had only a
loose and troubled possession. They beheld or took part
in great events, but there was no answerable commo-
tion in their reflective being; and they passed throughout turbulent epochs in a sort of ghostly quiet and abstraction. Feeling seems to have been strangely dispro-
portioned to the occasion, and words were laughably
trivial and scanty to set forth the feeling even such as
it was. Juvenal des Ursins chronicles calamity after
calamity, with but one comment for them all: that "it
was great pity." Perhaps, after too much of our florid
literature, we find an adventitious charm in what is so
different; and while the big drums are beaten every
day by perspiring editors over the loss of a cock-boat
or the rejection of a clause, and nothing is heard that
is not proclaimed with sound of trumpet, it is not wonderful if we retire with pleasure into old books, and

listen to authors who speak small and clear, as if in a private conversation. Truly this is so with Charles of Orleans. We are pleased to find a small man without the buskin, and obvious sentiments stated without affectation. If the sentiments are obvious, there is all the more chance we may have experienced the like. As we turn over the leaves, we may find ourselves in sympathy with some one or other of these staid joys and smiling sorrows. If we do we shall be strangely pleased, for there is a genuine pathos in these simple words, and the lines go with a lilt, and sing themselves to music of their own.

SAMUEL PEPYS

In two books a fresh light has recently been thrown on the character and position of Samuel Pepys. Mr. Mynors Bright has given us a new transcription of the Diary, increasing it in bulk by near a third, correcting many errors, and completing our knowledge of the man in some curious and important points. We can only regret that he has taken liberties with the author and the public. It is no part of the duties of the editor of an established classic to decide what may or may not be "tedious to the reader." The book is either an historical document or not, and in condemning Lord Braybrooke Mr. Bright condemns himself. As for the time-honored phrase, "unfit for publication," without being cynical, we may regard it as the sign of a precaution more or less commercial; and we may think, without being sordid, that when we purchase six huge and distressingly expensive volumes, we are entitled to be treated rather more like scholars and rather less like children. But Mr. Bright may rest assured: while we complain, we are still grateful. Mr. Wheatley, to divide our obligation, brings together, clearly and with no lost words, a body of illustrative material. Sometimes we might ask a little more; never, I think, less. And as a matter of fact, a great part of Mr. Wheatley's volume might be transferred, by a good editor of Pepys, to the margin of the text, for it is precisely what the reader wants.

In the light of these two books, at least, we have now to read our author. Between them they contain all we can expect to learn for, it may be, many years. Now, if ever, we should be able to form some notion of that unparalleled figure in the annals of mankind—unparalleled for three good reasons: first, because he was a man known to his contemporaries in a halo of almost historical pomp, and to his remote descendants with an indecent familiarity, like a tap-room comrade; second, because he has outstripped all competitors in the art or virtue of a conscious honesty about one's self; and, third, because, being in many ways a very ordinary person, he has yet placed himself before the public eye with such a fullness and such an intimacy of detail as might be envied by a genius like Montaigne. Not then for his own sake only, but as a character in a unique position, endowed with a unique talent, and shedding a unique light upon the lives of the mass of mankind, he is surely worthy of prolonged and patient study.

THE DIARY

That there should be such a book as Pepys's Diary is incomparably strange. Pepys, in a corrupt and idle period, played the man in public employments, toiling hard and keeping his honor bright. Much of the little good that is set down to James the Second comes by right to Pepys; and if it were little for a king, it is much for a subordinate. To his clear, capable head was owing somewhat of the greatness of England on the seas. In the exploits of Hawke, Rodney, or Nelson, this dead Mr. Pepys of the Navy Office had some considerable share. He stood well by his business in the appalling plague of 1666. He was loved and respected by some of the best and wisest men in England. He was President of the Royal Society; and when he came to die, people said of his conduct in that solemn hour —thinking it needless to say more—that it was answerable to the greatness of his life. Thus he walked in dignity, guards of soldiers sometimes attending him in his walks, subalterns bowing before his periwig; and when he uttered his thoughts they were suitable to his state and services. On February 8, 1668, we find him writing to Evelyn, his mind bitterly occupied with the late Dutch war, and some thoughts of the different story of the repulse of the Great Armada: "Sir, you will not wonder at the backwardness of my thanks for the present you made me, so many days since, of the Prospect of the Medway, while the Hollander rode master in it, when I have told you that the sight of it hath led me to such reflections on my particular interest, by my employment, in the reproach due to that miscarriage, as have given me little less disquiet than he is fancied to have who found his face in Michelangelo's hell. The same should serve me also in excuse for my silence in celebrating your mastery shown in the design and draught, did not indignation rather than courtship urge me so far to commend them, as to wish the furniture of our House of Lords changed from the story of '88 to that of '67 (of Evelyn's designing), till the pravity of this were reformed to the temper of that age, wherein God Almighty found his blessings more operative than, I fear, he doth in ours his judgments."

This is a letter honorable to the writer, where the meaning rather than the words is eloquent. Such was the account he gave of himself to his contemporaries; such thoughts he chose to utter, and in such language: giving himself out for a grave and patriotic public servant. We turn to the same date in the Diary by which he is known, after two centuries, to his descendants. The entry begins in the same key with the letter, blaming the "madness of the House of Commons" and "the base proceedings, just the epitome of all our public proceedings in this age, of the House of Lords;" and then, without the least transition, this is how our diarist proceeds: "To the Strand, to my bookseller's, and there bought an idle, roguish French book, 'L'escholle des Filles,' which I have bought in plain binding, avoiding the buying of it better bound, because I resolve, as soon as I have read it, to burn it, that it may not stand in the list of books, nor among them, to disgrace them, if it should be found." Even in our day, when responsibility is so much more clearly apprehended, the man who wrote the letter would be notable; but what about the man, I do not say who bought a roguish book, but who was ashamed of doing so, yet did it, and recorded both the doing and the shame in the pages of his daily journal?

We all, whether we write or speak, must somewhat drape ourselves when we address our fellows; at a given moment we apprehend our character and acts by some particular side; we are merry with one, grave with another, as befits the nature and demands of the relation. Pepys's letter to Evelyn would have little in common with that other one to Mrs. Knipp which he signed by the pseudonym of "Dapper Dicky"; yet each would be suitable to the character of his correspondent. There is no untruth in this, for man, being a Protean animal, swiftly shares and changes with his company and surroundings; and these changes are the better part of his education in the world. To strike a posture once for all, and to march through life like a drum-major, is to be highly disagreeable to others and a fool for one's self into the bargain. To Evelyn and to Knipp we understand the double facing; but to whom was he posing in the Diary, and what, in the name of astonishment, was the nature of the pose? Had he suppressed all mention of the book, or had he bought it, gloried in the act, and cheerfully recorded his glorification, in either case we should have made him out. But no; he is full of precautions to conceal the "disgrace" of the purchase, and yet speeds to chronicle the whole affair in pen and ink. It is a sort of anomaly

in human action, which we can exactly parallel from
another part of the Diary.

Mrs. Pepys had written a paper of her too just
complaints against her husband, and written it in plain
and very pungent English. Pepys, in an agony lest
the world should come to see it, brutally seizes and
destroys the tell-tale document; and then—you disbe-
lieve your eyes—down goes the whole story with un-
sparing truth and in the cruelest detail. It seems he
has no design but to appear respectable, and here he
keeps a private book to prove he was not. You are
at first faintly reminded of some of the vagaries of the
morbid religious diarist; but at a moment's thought
the resemblance disappears. The design of Pepys is not
at all to edify; it is not from repentance that he chronicles his peccadilloes, for he tells us when he does repent, and, to be just to him, there often follows some
improvement. Again, the sins of the religious diarist
are of a very formal pattern, and are told with an
elaborate whine. But in Pepys you come upon good,
substantive misdemeanors; beams in his eye of which
he alone remains unconscious; healthy outbreaks of the
animal nature, and laughable subterfuges to himself
that always command belief and often engage the sympathies.

Pepys was a young man for his age, came slowly
to himself in the world, sowed his wild oats late, took
late to industry, and preserved till nearly forty the
headlong gusto of a boy. So, to come rightly at the
spirit in which the Diary was written, we must recall
a class of sentiments which with most of us are over
and done before the age of twelve. In our tender years

we still preserve a freshness of surprise at our prolonged existence; events make an impression out of all
proportion to their consequence; we are unspeakably
touched by our own past adventures, and look forward
to our future personality with sentimental interest. It
was something of this, I think, that clung to Pepys.
Although not sentimental in the abstract, he was
sweetly sentimental about himself. His own past clung
about his heart, an evergreen. He was the slave of
an association. He could not pass by Islington, where
his father used to carry him to cakes and ale, but he
must light at the "King's Head" and eat and drink
"for remembrance of the old house sake." He counted
it good fortune to lie a night at Epsom to renew his
old walks, "where Mrs. Hely and I did use to walk
and talk, with whom I had the first sentiments of love
and pleasure in a woman's company, discourse and taking her by the hand, she being a pretty woman." He
goes about weighing up the "Assurance," which lay
near Woolwich under water, and cries in a parenthesis,
"Poor ship, that I have been twice merry in, in Captain Holland's time;" and after revisiting the "Nase-
by," now changed into the "Charles," he confesses
"it was a great pleasure to myself to see the ship that
I began my good fortune in." The stone that he was
cut for he preserved in a case; and to the Turners he
kept alive such gratitude for their assistance that for
years, and after he had begun to mount himself into
higher zones, he continued to have that family to dinner on the anniversary of the operation. Not Hazlitt
nor Rousseau had a more romantic passion for their
past, although at times they might express it more ro-

mantically; and if Pepys shared with them this child-ish fondness, did not Rousseau, who left behind him the "Confessions," or Hazlitt, who wrote the "Liber Amoris," and loaded his essays with loving personal detail, share with Pepys in his unwearied egotism? For the two things go hand in hand; or, to be more ex-act, it is the first that makes the second either pos-sible or pleasing.

But, to be quite in sympathy with Pepys, we must return once more to the experience of children. I can remember to have written, in the fly-leaf of more than one book, the date and the place where I then was— if, for instance, I was ill in bed or sitting in a cer-tain garden; these were jottings for my future self; if I should chance on such a note in after years, I thought it would cause me a particular thrill to rec-ognize myself across the intervening distance. Indeed, I might come upon them now, and not be moved one tittle—which shows that I have comparatively failed in life, and grown older than Samuel Pepys. For in the Diary we can find more than one such note of perfect childish egotism; as when he explains that his candle is going out, "which makes me write thus slobber-ingly"; or as in this incredible particularity, "To my study, where I only wrote thus much of this day's passages to this*, and so out again;" or lastly, as here, with more of circumstance: "I stayed up till the bellman came by with his bell under my window, *as I was writing of this very line*, and cried, 'Past one of the clock, and a cold, frosty, windy morning.'" Such passages are not to be misunderstood. The ap-peal to Samuel Pepys years hence is unmistakable. He

desires that dear, though unknown, gentleman keenly
to realize his predecessor; to remember why a passage
was uncleanly written; to recall (let us fancy, with a
sigh) the tones of the bellman, the chill of the early,
windy morning, and the very line his own romantic
self was scribing at the moment. The man, you will
perceive, was making reminiscences—a sort of pleasure
by ricochet, which comforts many in distress, and turns
some others into sentimental libertines: and the whole
book, if you will but look at it in that way, is seen
to be a work of art to Pepys's own address.

Here, then, we have the key to that remarkable attitude preserved by him throughout his Diary, to that
unflinching—I had almost said, that unintelligent—sincerity which makes it a miracle among human books.
He was not unconscious of his errors—far from it; he
was often startled into shame, often reformed, often
made and broke his vows of change. But whether he
did ill or well, he was still his own unequaled self;
still that entrancing *ego* of whom alone he cared to
write; and still sure of his own affectionate indulgence, when the parts should be changed, and the
writer come to read what he had written. Whatever
he did, or said, or thought, or suffered, it was still a
trait of Pepys, a character of his career; and as, to
himself, he was more interesting than Moses or than
Alexander, so all should be faithfully set down. I have
called his Diary a work of art. Now when the artist
has found something, word or deed, exactly proper to
a favorite character in play or novel, he will neither
suppress nor diminish it, though the remark be silly or
the act mean. The hesitation of Hamlet, the credulity

of Othello, the baseness of Emma Bovary, or the irregularities of Mr. Swiveller, caused neither disappointment nor disgust to their creators. And so with Pepys
and his adored protagonist: adored not blindly, but with
trenchant insight and enduring, human toleration. I
have gone over and over the greater part of the Diary;
and the points where, to the most suspicious scrutiny,
he has seemed not perfectly sincere, are so few, so
doubtful, and so petty, that I am ashamed to name
them. It may be said that we all of us write such a
diary in airy characters upon our brain; but I fear
there is a distinction to be made; I fear that as we
render to our consciousness an account of our daily
fortunes and behavior, we too often weave a tissue of
romantic compliments and dull excuses; and even if
Pepys were the ass and coward that men call him, we
must take rank as sillier and more cowardly than he.
The bald truth about one's self, what we are all too
timid to admit when we are not too dull to see it,
that was what he saw clearly and set down unspar-
ingly.

It is improbable that the Diary can have been carried on in the same single spirit in which it was begun. Pepys was not such an ass, but he must have
perceived, as he went on, the extraordinary nature of
the work he was producing. He was a great reader,
and he knew what other books were like. It must, at
least, have crossed his mind that some one might ultimately decipher the manuscript, and he himself, with
all his pains and pleasures, be resuscitated in some
later day; and the thought, although discouraged, must
have warmed his heart. He was not such an ass, be-

sides, but he must have been conscious of the deadly explosives, the gun-cotton and the giant powder, he was hoarding in his drawer. Let some contemporary light upon the Journal, and Pepys was plunged forever in social and political disgrace. We can trace the growth of his terrors by two facts. In 1660, while the Diary was still in its youth, he tells about it, as a matter of course, to a lieutenant in the navy; but in 1669, when it was already near an end, he could have bitten his ongue out, as the saying is, because he had let slip his secret to one so grave and friendly as Sir William Coventry. And from two other facts I think we may infer that he had entertained, even if he had not acquiesced in, the thought of a far-distant publicity. The first is of capital importance: the Diary was not destroyed. The second—that he took unusual precautions to confound the cipher in "roguish" passages— proves, beyond question, that he was thinking of some other reader besides himself. Perhaps while his friends were admiring the "greatness of his behavior" at the approach of death, he may have had a twinkling hope of immortality. *Mens cujusque is est quisque,* said his chosen motto; and, as he had stamped his mind with every crook and foible in the pages of the Diary, he might feel that what he left behind him was indeed himself. There is perhaps no other instance so remarkable of the desire of man for publicity and an enduring name. The greatness of his life was open, yet he longed to communicate its smallness also; and, while contemporaries bowed before him, he must buttonhole posterity with the news that his periwig was once alive with nits. But this thought, although I cannot doubt

he had it, was neither his first nor his deepest; it
did not color one word that he wrote; and the Diary,
for as long as he kept it, remained what it was when
he began, a private pleasure for himself. It was his
bosom secret; it added a zest to all his pleasures; he
lived in and for it, and might well write these solemn
words, when he closed that confidant forever: "And so
I betake myself to that course which is almost as
much as to see myself go into the grave; for which,
and all the discomforts that will accompany my being
blind, the good God prepare me."

A LIBERAL GENIUS

Pepys spent part of a certain winter Sunday, when
he had taken physic, composing "a song in praise of
a liberal genius (such as I take my own to be) to all
studies and pleasures." The song was unsuccessful, but
the Diary is, in a sense, the very song that he was
seeking; and his portrait by Hales, so admirably reproduced in Mynors Bright's edition, is a confirmation
of the Diary. Hales, it would appear, had known his
business; and though he put his sitter to a deal of
trouble, almost breaking his neck "to have the portrait
full of shadows," and draping him in an Indian gown
hired expressly for the purpose, he was preoccupied
about no merely picturesque effects, but to portray the
essence of the man. Whether we read the picture by
the Diary or the Diary by the picture, we shall at
least agree that Hales was among the number of those
who can "surprise the manners in the face." Here we
have a mouth pouting, moist with desires; eyes greedy,

protuberant, and yet apt for weeping too; a nose great alike in character and dimensions; and altogether a most fleshly, melting countenance. The face is attractive by its promise of reciprocity. I have used the word *greedy*, but the reader must not suppose that he can change it for that closely kindred one of *hungry*, for there is here no aspiration, no waiting for better things, but an animal joy in all that comes. It could never be the face of an artist; it is the face of a *viveur*—kindly, pleased and pleasing, protected from excess and upheld in contentment by the shifting versatility of his desires. For a single desire is more rightly to be called a lust; but there is health in a variety, where one may balance and control another.

The whole world, town or country, was to Pepys a garden of Armida. Wherever he went, his steps were winged with the most eager expectation; whatever he did, it was done with the most lively pleasure. An insatiable curiosity in all the shows of the world and all the secrets of knowledge, filled him brimful of the longing to travel, and supported him in the toils of study. Rome was the dream of his life; he was never happier than when he read or talked of the Eternal City. When he was in Holland, he was "with child" to see any strange thing. Meeting some friends and singing with them in a palace near the Hague, his pen fails him to express his passion of delight, "the more so because in a heaven of pleasure and in a strange country." He must go to see all famous executions. He must needs visit the body of a murdered man, defaced "with a broad wound," he says, "that makes my hand now shake to write of it." He learned

to dance, and was "like to make a dancer." He
learned to sing, and walked about Gray's Inn Fields
"humming to myself (which is now my constant practice) the trillo." He learned to play the lute, the
flute, the flageolet, and the theorbo, and it was not
the fault of his intention if he did not learn the harp-
sichord or the spinet. He learned to compose songs,
and burned to give forth "a scheme and theory of
music not yet ever made in the world." When he
heard "a fellow whistle like a bird exceeding well,"
he promised to return another day and give an angel
for a lesson in the art. Once, he writes, "I took the
Bezan back with me, and with a brave gale and tide
reached up that night to the Hope, taking great pleasure in learning the seamen's manner of singing when
they sound the depths." If he found himself rusty in
his Latin grammar, he must fall to it like a schoolboy. He was a member of Harrington's Club till its
dissolution, and of the Royal Society before it had received the name. Boyle's "Hydrostatics" was "of infinite delight" to him, walking in Barnes Elms. We
find him comparing Bible concordances, a captious judge
of sermons, deep in Descartes and Aristotle. We find
him, in a single year, studying timber and the meas-
urement of timber; tar and oil, hemp, and the process
of preparing cordage; mathematics and accounting; the
hull and the rigging of ships from a model; and "looking and improving himself of the (naval) stores with"
—hark to the fellow!—"great delight." His familiar
spirit of delight was not the same with Shelley's; but
how true it was to him through life! He is only copying something, and behold, he "takes great pleasure to

rule the lines, and have the capital words wrote with red ink;" he has only had his coal-cellar emptied and cleaned, and behold, "it do please him exceedingly." A hog's harslett is "a piece of meat he loves." He cannot ride home in my Lord Sandwich's coach, but he must exclaim, with breathless gusto, "his noble, rich coach." When he is bound for a supper party, he anticipates a "glut of pleasure." When he has a new watch, "to see my childishness," says he, "I could not forbear carrying it in my hand and seeing what o'clock it was an hundred times." To go to Vauxhall, he says, and "to hear the nightingales and other birds, hear fiddles, and there a harp and here a Jew's trump, and here laughing, and there fine people walking, is mighty divertizing." And the nightingales, I take it, were particularly dear to him; and it was again "with great pleasure" that he paused to hear them as he walked to Woolwich, while the fog was rising and the April sun broke through.

He must always be doing something agreeable, and, by preference, two agreeable things at once. In his house he had a box of carpenter's tools, two dogs, an eagle, a canary, and a blackbird that whistled tunes, lest, even in that full life, he should chance upon an empty moment. If he had to wait for a dish of poached eggs, he must put in the time by playing on the flageolet; if a sermon were dull, he must read in the book of Tobit or divert his mind with sly advances on the nearest women. When he walked, it must be with a book in his pocket to beguile the way in case the nightingales were silent; and even along the streets of London, with so many pretty faces to be spied for and dignitaries to be saluted, his trail was marked by little debts "for wine, pictures, etc.," the true headmark of a life intolerant of any joyless passage. He had a kind of idealism in pleasure; like the princess in the fairy story, he was conscious of a rose-leaf out of place. Dearly as he loved to talk, he could not enjoy nor shine in a conversation when he thought himself unsuitably dressed. Dearly as he loved eating, he "knew not how to eat alone"; pleasure for him must heighten pleasure; and the eye and ear must be flattered like the palate ere he avow himself content. He had no zest in a good dinner when it fell to be eaten "in a bad street and in a periwig-maker's house"; and a collation was spoiled for him by indifferent music. His body was indefatigable, doing him yeoman's service in this breathless chase of pleasures. On April 11, 1662, he mentions that he went to bed "weary, *which I seldom am*"; and already over thirty, he would sit up all night cheerfully to see a comet. But it is never pleasure that exhausts the pleasure-seeker; for in that career, as in all others, it is failure that kills. The man who enjoys so wholly and bears so impatiently the slightest widowhood from joy, is just the man to lose a night's rest over some paltry question of his right to fiddle on the leads, or to be "vexed to the blood" by a solecism in his wife's attire; and we find in consequence that he was always peevish when he was hungry, and that his head "aked mightily" after a dispute. But nothing could divert him from his aim in life; his remedy in care was the same as his delight in prosperity; it was with pleasure, and with pleasure only, that he sought to drive out sorrow; and, whether he was jealous of his wife or skulking from a bailiff, he would equally take refuge in the theater. There, if the house be full and the company noble, if the songs be tunable, the actors perfect, and the play diverting, this odd hero of the secret Diary, this private self-adorer, will speedily be healed of his distresses.

Equally pleased with a watch, a coach, a piece of meat, a tune upon the fiddle, or a fact in hydrostatics, Pepys was pleased yet more by the beauty, the worth, the mirth, or the mere scenic attitude in life of his fellow-creatures. He shows himself throughout a sterling humanist. Indeed, he who loves himself, not in idle vanity, but with a plenitude of knowledge, is the best equipped of all to love his neighbors. And perhaps it is in this sense that charity may be most properly said to begin at home. It does not matter what quality a person has: Pepys can appreciate and love him for it. He "fills his eyes" with the beauty of Lady Castlemaine; indeed, he may be said to dote upon the thought of her for years; if a woman be good looking and not painted, he will walk miles to have another sight of her; and even when a lady by a mischance spat upon his clothes, he was immediately consoled when he had observed that she was pretty. But, on the other hand, he is delighted to see Mrs. Pett upon her knees, and speaks thus of his Aunt James: "a poor, religious, well-meaning, good soul, talking of nothing but God Almighty, and that with so much innocence that mightily pleased me." He is taken with Pen's merriment and loose songs, but not less taken with the sterling worth of Coventry. He is

jolly with a drunken sailor, but listens with interest
and patience, as he rides the Essex roads, to the story
of a Quaker's spiritual trials and convictions. He lends
a critical ear to the discourse of kings and royal dukes.
He spends an evening at Vauxhall with "Killigrew and
young Newport—loose company," says he, "but worth
a man's being in for once, to know the nature of it,
and their manner of talk and lives." And when a
rag-boy lights him home, he examines him about his
business and other ways of livelihood for destitute children. This is almost half-way to the beginning of philanthropy; had it only been the fashion, as it is at
present, Pepys had perhaps been a man famous for
good deeds. And it is through this quality that he
rises, at times, superior to his surprising egotism; his
interest in the love affairs of others is, indeed, impersonal; he is filled with concern for my Lady Castlemaine, whom he only knows by sight, shares in her
very jealousies, joys with her in her successes; and it
is not untrue, however strange it seems in his abrupt
presentment, that he loved his maid Jane because she
was in love with his man Tom.

Let us hear him, for once, at length: "So the
women and W. Hewer and I walked upon the Downes,
where a flock of sheep was; and the most pleasant and
innocent sight that ever I saw in my life. We found
a shepherd and his little boy reading, far from any
houses or sight of people, the Bible to him; so I made
the boy read to me, which he did with the forced tone
that children do usually read, that was mighty pretty;
and then I did give him something, and went to the
father, and talked with him. He did content himself

mightily in my liking his boy's reading, and did bless God for him, the most like one of the old patriarchs that ever I saw in my life, and it brought those thoughts of the old age of the world in my mind for two or three days after. We took notice of his woolen knit stockings of two colors mixed, and of his shoes shod with iron, both at the toe and heels, and with great nails in the soles of his feet, which was mighty pretty; and taking notice of them, 'Why,' says the poor man, 'the downes, you see, are full of stones, and we are faine to shoe ourselves thus; and these,' says he, 'will make the stones fly till they ring before me.' I did give the poor man something, for which he was mighty thankful, and I tried to cast stones with his horne crooke. He values his dog mightily, that would turn a sheep any way which he would have him, when he goes to fold them; told me there was about eighteen score sheep in his flock, and that he hath four shillings a week the year round for keeping of them; and Mrs. Turner, in the common fields here, did gather one of the prettiest nosegays that ever I saw in my life."

And so the story rambles on to the end of that day's pleasuring; with cups of milk, and glowworms, and people walking at sundown with their wives and children, and all the way home Pepys still dreaming "of the old age of the world" and the early innocence of man. This was how he walked through life, his eyes and ears wide open, and his hand, you will observe, not shut; and thus he observed the lives, the speech, and the manners of his fellow-men, with prose fidelity of detail and yet a lingering glamour of romance.

It was "two or three days after" that he extended
this passage in the pages of his Journal, and the style
has thus the benefit of some reflection. It is generally
supposed that, as a writer, Pepys must rank at the
bottom of the scale of merit. But a style which is
indefatigably lively, telling, and picturesque through six
large volumes of everyday experience, which deals with
the whole matter of a life, and yet is rarely wearisome, which condescends to the most fastidious particu-
lars, and yet sweeps all away in the forthright current
of the narrative—such a style may be ungrammatical,
it may be inelegant, it may be one tissue of mistakes,
but it can never be devoid of merit. The first and the
true function of the writer has been thoroughly per-
formed throughout; and though the manner of his utterance may be childishly awkward, the matter has been
transformed and assimilated by his unfeigned interest
and delight. The gusto of the man speaks out fierily
after all these years. For the difference between Pepys
and Shelley, to return to that half-whimsical approximation, is one of quality but not one of degree; in his
sphere, Pepys felt as keenly, and his is the true prose
of poetry—prose because the spirit of the man was narrow and earthly, but poetry because he was delightedly
alive. Hence, in such a passage as this about the Epsom shepherd, the result upon the reader's mind is entire conviction and unmingled pleasure. So, you feel,
the thing fell out, not otherwise; and you would no
more change it than you would change a sublimity of
Shakespeare's, a homely touch of Bunyan's, or a favored
reminiscence of your own.

There never was a man nearer being an artist, who

yet was not one. The tang was in the family; while he was writing the Journal for our enjoyment in his comely house in Navy Gardens, no fewer than two of his cousins were tramping the fens, kit under arm, to make music to the country girls. But he himself, though he could play so many instruments and pass judgment in so many fields of art, remained an amateur. It is not given to any one so keenly to enjoy, without some greater power to understand. That he did not like Shakespeare as an artist for the stage may be a fault, but it is not without either parallel or excuse. He certainly admired him as a poet; he was the first beyond mere actors on the rolls of that innumerable army who have got "To be or not to be" by heart. Nor was he content with that; it haunted his mind; he quoted it to himself in the pages of the Diary, and, rushing in where angels fear to tread, he set it to music. Nothing, indeed, is more notable than the heroic quality of the verses that our little sensualist in a periwig chose out to marry with his own mortal strains. Some gust from brave Elizabethan times must have warmed his spirit, as he sat tuning his sublime theorbo. "To be or not to be. Whether 'tis nobler"—"Beauty retire, thou dost my pity move"—"It is decreed, nor shall thy fate, O Rome";—open and dignified in the sound, various and majestic in the sentiment, it was no inapt, as it was certainly no timid, spirit that selected such a range of themes. Of "Gaze not on Swans," I know no more than these four words; yet that also seems to promise well. It was, however, on a probable suspicion, the work of his master, Mr. Berkenshaw—as the drawings that figure at the breaking

up of a young ladies' seminary are the work of the
professor attached to the establishment. Mr. Berkenshaw
was not altogether happy in his pupil. The amateur
cannot usually rise into the artist, some leaven of the
world still clogging him; and we find Pepys behaving
like a pickthank to the man who taught him composition. In relation to the stage, which he so warmly
loved and understood, he was not only more hearty,
but more generous to others. Thus he encounters
Colonel Reames, "a man," says he, "who understands
and loves a play as well as I, and I love him for it."
And again, when he and his wife had seen a most
ridiculous insipid piece, "Glad we were," he writes,
"that Betterton had no part in it." It is by such a
zeal and loyalty to those who labor for his delight that
the amateur grows worthy of the artist. And it should
be kept in mind that, not only in art, but in morals,
Pepys rejoiced to recognize his betters. There was not
one speck of envy in the whole human-hearted egotist.

RESPECTABILITY

When writers inveigh against respectability, in the
present degraded meaning of the word, they are usually
suspected of a taste for clay pipes and beer cellars;
and their performances are thought to hail from the
"Owl's Nest" of the comedy. They have something
more, however, in their eye than the dullness of a round
million dinner parties that sit down yearly in old England. For to do anything because others do it, and
not because the thing is good, or kind, or honest in
its own right, is to resign all moral control and cap-

taincy upon yourself, and go post-haste to the devil with the greater number. We smile over the ascendency of priests; but I had rather follow a priest than what they call the leaders of society. No life can better than that of Pepys illustrate the dangers of this respectable theory of living. For what can be more untoward than the occurrence, at a critical period and while the habits are still pliable, of such a sweeping transformation as the return of Charles the Second? Round went the whole fleet of England on the other tack; and while a few tall pintas, Milton or Pen, still sailed a lonely course by the stars and their own private compass, the cock-boat, Pepys, must go about with the majority among "the stupid starers and the loud huzzas."

The respectable are not led so much by any desire of applause as by a positive need for countenance. The weaker and the tamer the man, the more will he require this support; and any positive quality relieves him, by just so much, of this dependence. In a dozen ways, Pepys was quite strong enough to please himself without regard for others; but his positive qualities were not co-extensive with the field of conduct; and in many parts of life he followed, with gleeful precision, in the footprints of the contemporary Mrs. Grundy. In morals, particularly, he lived by the countenance of others; felt a slight from another more keenly than a meanness in himself; and then first repented when he was found out. You could talk of religion or morality to such a man; and by the artist side of him, by his lively sympathy and apprehension, he could rise, as it were dramatically, to the significance of what you said. All that matter in religion which has been nicknamed

other-worldliness was strictly in his gamut; but a rule
of life that should make a man rudely virtuous, following right in good report and ill report, was foolishness
and a stumbling-block to Pepys. He was much thrown
across the Friends; and nothing can be more instructive
than his attitude toward these most interesting people
of that age. I have mentioned how he conversed with
one as he rode; when he saw some brought from a
meeting under arrest, "I would to God," said he, "they
would either conform, or be more wise and not be
catched"; and to a Quaker in his own office he extended a timid though effectual protection. Meanwhile
there was growing up next door to him that beautiful
nature, William Pen. It is odd that Pepys condemned
him for a fop; odd, though natural enough when you
see Pen's portrait, that Pepys was jealous of him with
his wife. But the cream of the story is when Pen
publishes his "Sandy Foundation Shaken," and Pepys
has it read aloud by his wife. "I find it," he says,
"so well writ as, I think, it is too good for him ever to
have writ it; and it is a serious sort of book, and *not
fit for everybody to read.*" Nothing is more galling
to the merely respectable than to be brought in contact
with religious ardor. Pepys had his own foundation,
sandy enough, but dear to him from practical considerations, and he would read the book with true uneasiness
of spirit; for conceive the blow if, by some plaguy
accident, this Pen were to convert him! It was a
different kind of doctrine that he judged profitable for
himself and others. "A good sermon of Mr. Gifford's
at our church, upon 'Seek ye first the kingdom of
heaven.' A very excellent and persuasive, good and

moral sermon. He showed, like a wise man, that
righteousness is a surer moral way of being rich than
sin and villainy." It is thus that respectable people
desire to have their Greathearts address them, telling,
in mild accents, how you may make the best of both
worlds, and be a moral hero without courage, kindness, or troublesome reflection; and thus the Gospel,
cleared of Eastern metaphor, becomes a manual of
worldly prudence, and a handybook for Pepys and the
successful merchant.

The respectability of Pepys was deeply grained. He
has no idea of truth except for the Diary. He has no
care that a thing shall be, if it but appear; gives out
that he has inherited a good estate, when he has seemingly got nothing but a lawsuit; and is pleased to be
thought liberal when he knows he has been mean. He
is conscientiously ostentatious. I say conscientiously, with
reason. He could never have been taken for a fop, like
Pen, but arrayed himself in a manner nicely suitable
to his position. For long he hesitated to assume the
famous periwig; for a public man should travel gravely
with the fashions, not foppishly before, nor dowdily behind, the central movement of his age. For long he
durst not keep a carriage; that, in his circumstances,
would have been improper; but a time comes, with the
growth of his fortune, when the impropriety has shifted
to the other side, and he is "ashamed to be seen in a
hackney." Pepys talked about being "a Quaker or some
very melancholy thing"; for my part, I can imagine
nothing so melancholy, because nothing half so silly, as
to be concerned about such problems. But so respectability and the duties of society haunt and burden their

poor devotees; and what seems at first the very prim-
rose path of life, proves difficult and thorny like the
rest. And the time comes to Pepys, as to all the
merely respectable, when he must not only order his
pleasures, but even clip his virtuous movements, to the
public pattern of the age. There was some juggling
among officials to avoid direct taxation; and Pepys, with
a noble impulse, growing ashamed of this dishonesty,
designed to charge himself with £1,000; but finding
none to set him an example, "nobody of our ablest
merchants" with this moderate liking for clean hands,
he judged it "not decent"; he feared it would "be
thought vain glory"; and, rather than appear singular,
cheerfully remained a thief. One able merchant's countenance, and Pepys had dared to do an honest act!
Had he found one brave spirit, properly recognized by
society, he might have gone far as a disciple. Mrs.
Turner, it is true, can fill him full of sordid scandal,
and make him believe, against the testimony of his
senses, that Pen's venison pasty stank like the devil;
but, on the other hand, Sir William Coventry can raise
him by a word into another being. Pepys, when he is
with Coventry, talks in the vein of an old Roman.
What does he care for office or emolument? "Thank
God, I have enough of my own," says he, "to buy
me a good book and a good fiddle, and I have a good
wife." And again, we find this pair projecting an old
age when an ungrateful country shall have dismissed
them from the field of public service; Coventry living
retired in a fine house, and Pepys dropping in, "it may
be, to read a chapter of Seneca."

Under this influence, the only good one in his life.

Pepys continued zealous and, for the period, pure in his employment. He would not be "bribed to be unjust," he says, though he was "not so squeamish as to refuse a present after," suppose the king to have received no wrong. His new arrangement for the victualing of Tangier, he tells us with honest complacency, will save the king a thousand and gain Pepys three hundred pounds a year—a statement which exactly fixes the degree of the age's enlightenment. But for his industry and capacity no praise can be too high. It was an unending struggle for the man to stick to his business in such a garden of Armida as he found this life; and the story of his oaths, so often broken, so courageously renewed, is worthy rather of admiration than the contempt it has received.

Elsewhere, and beyond the sphere of Coventry's influence, we find him losing scruples and daily complying further with the age. When he began the Journal, he was a trifle prim and puritanic; merry enough, to be sure, over his private cups, and still remembering Magdalene ale and his acquaintance with Mrs. Ainsworth of Cambridge. But youth is a hot season with all; when a man smells April and May he is apt at times to stumble; and in spite of a disordered practice, Pepys's theory, the better things that he approved and followed after, we may even say were strict. Where there was "tag, rag, and bobtail, dancing, singing, and drinking," he felt "ashamed, and went away"; and when he slept in church, he prayed God forgive him. In but a little while we find him with some ladies keeping each other awake "from spite," as though not to sleep in church were an obvious hardship; and yet

later he calmly passes the time of service, looking about
him, with a perspective glass, on all the pretty women.
His favorite ejaculation, "Lord!" occurs but once that
I have observed in 1660, never in '61, twice in '62,
and at least five times in '63; after which the "Lords"
may be said to pullulate like herrings, with here and
there a solitary "damned," as it were a whale among
the shoal.   He and his wife, once filled with dudgeon
by some innocent freedoms at a marriage, are soon
content to go pleasuring with my Lord Brouncker's
mistress, who was not even, by his own account, the
most discreet of mistresses. Tag, rag, and bobtail, danc·
ing, singing, and drinking, become his natural element;
actors and actresses and drunken, roaring courtiers are
to be found in his society; until the man grew so involved with Saturnalian manners and companions that
he was shot almost unconsciously into the grand domestic crash of 1668.⌡

That was the legitimate issue and punishment of
years of staggering walk and conversation. The man
who has smoked his pipe for half a century in a
powder magazine finds himself at last the author and
the victim of a hideous disaster. So with our pleasant-
minded Pepys and his peccadilloes. All of a sudden,
as he still trips dexterously enough among the dangers
of a double-faced career, thinking no great evil, humming to himself the trillo, Fate takes the further conduct of that matter from his hands, and brings him
face to face with the consequences of his acts. For a
man still, after so many years, the lover, although not
the constant lover, of his wife—for a man, besides, who
was so greatly careful of appearances—the revelation

of his infidelities was a crushing blow. The tears that
he shed, the indignities that he endured, are not to be
measured. (A vulgar woman, and now justly incensed,
Mrs. Pepys spared him no detail of suffering. She was
violent, threatening him with the tongs; she was careless of his honor, driving him to insult the mistress
whom she had driven him to betray and to discard;
worst of all, she was hopelessly inconsequent, in word
and thought and deed, now lulling him with reconciliations, and anon flaming forth again with the original
anger. Pepys had not used his wife well; he had
wearied her with jealousies, even while himself unfaithful; he had grudged her clothes and pleasures, while
lavishing both upon himself; he had abused her in
words; he had bent his fist at her in anger; he had
once blacked her eye; and it is one of the oddest par-
ticulars in that odd Diary of his, that, while the injury is referred to once in passing, there is no hint as
to the occasion or the manner of the blow. But now,
when he is in the wrong, nothing can exceed the long-
suffering affection of this impatient husband. While he
was still sinning and still undiscovered, he seems not
to have known a touch of penitence stronger than what
might lead him to take his wife to the theater, or for
an airing, or to give her a new dress, by way of com-
pensation. Once found out, however, and he seems to
himself to have lost all claim to decent usage. It is
perhaps the strongest instance of his externality. His
wife may do what she pleases, and though he may
groan, it will never occur to him to blame her; he
has no weapon left but tears and the most abject submission.) We should perhaps have respected him more

had he not given way so utterly—above all, had he refused to write, under his wife's dictation, an insulting letter to his unhappy fellow culprit, Miss Willet; but somehow I believe we like him better as he was.

The death of his wife, following so shortly after, must have stamped the impression of this episode upon his mind. For the remaining years of his long life we have no Diary to help us, and we have seen already how little stress is to be laid upon the tenor of his correspondence; but what with the recollection of the catastrophe of his married life, what with the natural influence of his advancing years and reputation, it seems not unlikely that the period of gallantry was at an end for Pepys; and it is beyond a doubt that he sat down at last to an honored and agreeable old age among his books and music, the correspondent of Sir Isaac Newton, and, in one instance at least, the poetical counselor of Dryden. Through all this period, that Diary which contained the secret memoirs of his life, with all its inconsistencies and escapades, had been religiously preserved; nor, when he came to die, does he appear to have provided for its destruction. So we may conceive him faithful to the end to all his dear and early memories; still mindful of Mrs. Hely in the woods at Epsom; still lighting at Islington for a cup of kindness to the dead; still, if he heard again that air that once so much disturbed him, thrilling at the recollection of the love that bound him to his wife.

JOHN KNOX AND HIS RELATIONS TO WOMEN

I.—THE CONTROVERSY ABOUT FEMALE RULE

WHEN first the idea became widely spread among men that the Word of God, instead of being truly the foundation of all existing institutions, was rather a stone which the builders had rejected, it was but natural that the consequent havoc among received opinions should be accompanied by the generation of many new and lively hopes for the future. Somewhat as in the early days of the French Revolution, men must have looked for an immediate and universal improvement in their condition. Christianity, up to that time, had been somewhat of a failure politically. The reason was now obvious, the capital flaw was detected, the sickness of the body politic traced at last to its efficient cause. It was only necessary to put the Bible thoroughly into practice, to set themselves strenuously to realize in life the Holy Commonwealth, and all abuses and iniquities would surely pass away. Thus, in a pageant played at Geneva in the year 1523, the world was represented as a sick man at the end of his wits for help, to whom his doctor recommends Lutheran specifics.[*]

The Reformers themselves had set their affections in

---

[*] Gaberel's "Eglise de Genève," i. 88.

a different world, and professed to look for the finished
result of their endeavors on the other side of death.
They took no interest in politics as such; they even
condemned political action as Antichristian: notably,
Luther in the case of the Peasants' War. And yet,
as the purely religious question was inseparably complicated with political difficulties, and they had to make
opposition, from day to day, against principalities and
powers, they were led, one after another, and again
and again, to leave the sphere which was more strictly
their own, and meddle, for good and evil, with the
affairs of State. Not much was to be expected from
interference in such a spirit. Whenever a minister
found himself galled or hindered, he would be inclined
to suppose some contravention of the Bible. Whenever
Christian liberty was restrained (and Christian liberty
for each individual would be about coextensive with
what he wished to do), it was obvious that the State
was Antichristian. The great thing, and the one thing,
was to push the Gospel and the Reformers' own inter-
pretation of it. Whatever helped was good; whatever
hindered was evil; and if this simple classification proved
inapplicable over the whole field, it was no business of
his to stop and reconcile incongruities. He had more
pressing concerns on hand; he had to save souls; he
had to be about his Father's business. This short-sighted
view resulted in a doctrine that was actually Jesuitical
in application. They had no serious ideas upon politics, and they were ready, nay, they seemed almost
bound, to adopt and support whichever insured for the
moment the greatest benefit to the souls of their fellowmen. They were dishonest in all sincerity. Thus

Labitte, in the introduction to a book* in which he exposes the hypocritical democracy of the Catholics under the League, steps aside for a moment to stigmatize the hypocritical democracy of the Protestants. And nowhere was this expediency in political questions more apparent than about the question of female sovereignty. So much was this the case that one James Thomasius, of Leipsic, wrote a little paper † about the religious partialities of those who took part in the controversy, in which some of these learned disputants cut a very sorry figure.

Now Knox has been from the first a man well hated; and it is somewhat characteristic of his luck that he figures here in the very forefront of the list of partial scribes who trimmed their doctrine with the wind in all good conscience, and were political weathercocks out of conviction. Not only has Thomasius mentioned him, but Bayle has taken the hint from Thomasius, and dedicated a long note to the matter at the end of his article on the Scotch Reformer. This is a little less than fair. If any one among the evangelists of that period showed more serious political sense than another, it was assuredly Knox; and even in this very matter of female rule, although I do not suppose any one nowadays will feel inclined to indorse his sentiments, I confess I can make great allowance for his conduct. The controversy, besides, has an interest of its own, in view of later controversies.

John Knox, from 1556 to 1559, was resident in Geneva, as minister, jointly with Goodman, of a little

---

* " La Démocratie chez les Prédicateurs de la Ligue."

† " Historia affectuum se immiscentium controversiæ de gynæcocratia." It is in his collected prefaces, Leipsic, 1683.

church of English refugees. He and his congregation
were banished from England by one woman, Mary Tudor, and proscribed in Scotland by another, the Regent
Mary of Guise. The coincidence was tempting: here
were many abuses centering about one abuse; here was
Christ's Gospel persecuted in the two kingdoms by one
anomalous power. He had not far to go to find the
idea that female government was anomalous. It was
an age, indeed, in which women, capable and incapable, played a conspicuous part upon the stage of European history; and yet their rule, whatever may have
been the opinion of here and there a wise man or en-
thusiast, was regarded as an anomaly by the great
bulk of their contemporaries. It was defended as an
anomaly. It, and all that accompanied and sanctioned
it, was set aside as a single exception; and no one
thought of reasoning down from queens and extending
their privileges to ordinary women. Great ladies, as
we know, had the privilege of entering into monasteries
and cloisters, otherwise forbidden to their sex. As with
one thing, so with another. Thus, Margaret of Navarre wrote books with great acclamation, and no one,
seemingly, saw fit to call her conduct in question; but
Mademoiselle de Gournay, Montaigne's adopted daughter,
was in a controversy with the world as to whether a
woman might be an author without incongruity. Thus,
too, we have Theodore Agrippa d'Aubigne writing to
his daughters about the learned women of his century,
and cautioning them, in conclusion, that the study of
letters was unsuited to ladies of a middling station,
and should be reserved for princesses.* And once more,

---

* " Œuvres de d'Aubigné," i. 449.

if we desire to see the same principle carried to ludicrous extreme, we shall find that Reverend Father in God the Abbot of Brantôme, claiming, on the authority of some lord of his acquaintance, a privilege, or rather a duty, of free love for great princesses, and carefully excluding other ladies from the same gallant dispensation.* One sees the spirit in which these immunities were granted; and how they were but the natural consequence of that awe for courts and kings that made the last writer tell us, with simple wonder, how Catherine de Medici would "laugh her fill just like another" over the humors of pantaloons and zanies. And such servility was, of all things, what would touch most nearly the republican spirit of Knox. It was not difficult for him to set aside this weak scruple of loyalty. The lantern of his analysis did not always shine with a very serviceable light; but he had the virtue, at least, to carry it into many places of fictitious holiness, and was not abashed by the tinsel divinity that hedged kings and queens from his contemporaries. And so he could put the proposition in the form already mentioned: there was Christ's Gospel persecuted in the two kingdoms by one anomalous power; plainly, then, the "regiment of women" was Antichristian. Early in 1558 he communicated this discovery to the world, by publishing at Geneva his notorious book —"The First Blast of the Trumpet against the Monstrous Regiment of Women."†

As a whole, it is a dull performance; but the pref-

---

* "Dames Illustres," pp. 358–360.
† Works of John Knox, iv. 349.

ace, as is usual with Knox, is both interesting and
morally fine. Knox was not one of those who are
humble in the hour of triumph; he was aggressive
even when things were at their worst. He had a grim
reliance in himself, or rather in his mission; if he were
not sure that he was a great man, he was at least
sure that he was one set apart to do great things.
And he judged simply that whatever passed in his
mind, whatever moved him to flee from persecution instead of constantly facing it out, or, as here, to publish and withhold his name from the title-page of a
critical work, would not fail to be of interest, perhaps
of benefit, to the world. There may be something
more finely sensitive in the modern humor, that tends
more and more to withdraw a man's personality from
the lessons he inculcates or the cause that he has
espoused; but there is a loss herewith of wholesome
responsibility; and when we find in the works of Knox,
as in the Epistles of Paul, the man himself standing
nakedly forward, courting and anticipating criticism,
putting his character, as it were, in pledge for the
sincerity of his doctrine, we had best waive the question of delicacy, and make our acknowledgments for a
lesson of courage, not unnecessary in these days of
anonymous criticism, and much light, otherwise unat-
tainable, on the spirit in which great movements were
initiated and carried forward. Knox's personal revelations are always interesting; and, in the case of the
"First Blast," as I have said, there is no exception to
the rule. He begins by stating the solemn responsibility of all who are watchmen over God's flock; and all
are watchmen (he goes on to explain, with that fine

breadth of spirit that characterizes him even when, as here, he shows himself most narrow), all are watch-men "whose eyes God doth open, and whose conscience he pricketh to admonish the ungodly." And with the full consciousness of this great duty before him, he sets himself to answer the scruples of timorous or worldly-minded people. How can a man repent, he asks, unless the nature of his transgression is made plain to him? "And therefore I say," he continues, "that of necessity it is that this monstriferous empire of women (which among all enormities that this day do abound upon the face of the whole earth, is most detestable and damnable) be openly and plainly declared to the world, to the end that some may repent and be saved." To those who think the doctrine useless, because it cannot be expected to amend those princes whom it would dispossess if once accepted, he makes answer in a strain that shows him at his greatest. After having instanced how the rumor of Christ's censures found its way to Herod in his own court, "even so," he continues, "may the sound of our weak trumpet, by the support of some wind (blow it from the south, or blow it from the north, it is of no matter), come to the ears of the chief offenders. *But whether it do or not, yet dare we not cease to blow as God will give strength. For we are debtors to more than to princes, to wit, to the great multitude of our brethren*, of whom, no doubt, a great number have heretofore offended by error and ignorance."

It is for the multitude, then, he writes; he does not greatly hope that his trumpet will be audible in palaces, or that crowned women will submissively dis-

crown themselves at his appeal; what he does hope, in
plain English, is to encourage and justify rebellion; and
we shall see, before we have done, that he can put
his purpose into words as roundly as I can put it for
him.   This he sees to be a matter of much hazard;
he is not "altogether so brutish and insensible, but that
he has laid his account what the finishing of the work
may cost."   He knows that he will find many adver-
saries, since "to the most part of men, lawful and
godly appeareth whatsoever antiquity hath received."
He looks for opposition, "not only of the ignorant multitude, but of the wise, politic, and quiet spirits of the
earth."   He will be called foolish, curious, despiteful,
and a sower of sedition; and one day, perhaps, for all
he is now nameless, he may be attainted of treason.
Yet he has "determined to obey God, notwithstanding
that the world shall rage thereat."   Finally, he makes
some excuse for the anonymous appearance of this first
installment: it is his purpose thrice to blow the trumpet
in this matter, if God so permit; twice he intends to
do it without name; but at the last blast to take the
odium upon himself, that all others may be purged.

Thus he ends the preface, and enters upon his argument with a secondary title: "The First Blast to awake
Women degenerate."   We are in the land of assertion
without delay.   That a woman should bear rule, superiority, dominion or empire over any realm, nation, or
city, he tells us, is repugnant to nature, contumely to
God, and a subversion of good order.   Women are
weak, frail, impatient, feeble, and foolish.   God has
denied to woman wisdom to consider, or providence to
foresee, what is profitable to a commonwealth.   Women

have been ever lightly esteemed; they have been denied the tutory of their own sons, and subjected to
the unquestionable sway of their husbands; and surely
it is irrational to give the greater where the less has
been withheld, and suffer a woman to reign supreme
over a great kingdom who would be allowed no authority by her own fireside. He appeals to the Bible;
but though he makes much of the first transgression
and certain strong texts in Genesis and Paul's Epistles,
he does not appeal with entire success. The cases of
Deborah and Huldah can be brought into no sort of
harmony with his thesis. Indeed, I may say that,
logically, he left his bones there; and that it is but
the phantom of an argument that he parades thenceforward to the end. Well was it for Knox that he
succeeded no better; it is under this very ambiguity
about Deborah that we shall find him fain to creep for
shelter before he is done with the regiment of women.
After having thus exhausted Scripture, and formulated
its teaching in the somewhat blasphemous maxim that
the man is placed above the woman, even as God
above the angels, he goes on triumphantly to adduce
the testimonies of Tertullian, Augustine, Ambrose, Basil,
Chrysostom, and the Pandects; and having gathered
this little cloud of witnesses about him, like pursuivants
about a herald, he solemnly proclaims all reigning
women to be traitoresses and rebels against God; dis-
charges all men thenceforward from holding any office
under such monstrous regiment, and calls upon all the
lieges with one consent to *"study to repress the inordinate pride and tyranny"* of queens. If this is
not treasonable teaching, one would be glad to know

what is; and yet, as if he feared he had not made
the case plain enough against himself, he goes on to
deduce the startling corollary that all oaths of allegiance must be incontinently broken. If it was sin thus
to have sworn even in ignorance, it were obstinate sin
to continue to respect them after fuller knowledge.
Then comes the peroration, in which he cries aloud
against the cruelties of that cursed Jezebel of England
—that horrible monster Jezebel of England; and after
having predicted sudden destruction to her rule and to
the rule of all crowned women, and warned all men
that if they presume to defend the same when any
"noble heart" shall be raised up to vindicate the liberty of his country, they shall not fail to perish themselves in the ruin, he concludes with a last rhetorical
flourish: "And therefore let all men be advertised, for
THE TRUMPET HATH ONCE BLOWN."

The capitals are his own. In writing, he probably
felt the want of some such reverberation of the pulpit
under strong hands as he was wont to emphasize his
spoken utterances withal; there would seem to him a
want of passion in the orderly lines of type; and I
suppose we may take the capitals as a mere substitute
for the great voice with which he would have given it
forth, had we heard it from his own lips. Indeed, as it
is, in this little strain of rhetoric about the trumpet,
this current allusion to the fall of Jericho, that alone
distinguishes his bitter and hasty production, he was
probably right, according to all artistic canon, thus to
support and accentuate in conclusion the sustained
metaphor of a hostile proclamation. It is curious, by
the way, to note how favorite an image the trumpet

was with the Reformer. He returns to it again and again; it is the Alpha and Omega of his rhetoric; it is to him what a ship is to the stage sailor; and one would almost fancy he had begun the world as a trumpeter's apprentice. The partiality is surely characteristic. All his life long he was blowing summonses before various Jerichos, some of which fell duly, but not all. Wherever he appears in history his speech is loud, angry, and hostile; there is no peace in his life, and little tenderness; he is always sounding hopefully to the front for some rough enterprise. And as his voice had something of the trumpet's hardness, it had something also of the trumpet's warlike inspiration. So Randolph, possibly fresh from the sound of the Reformer's preaching, writes of him to Cecil: "Where your honor exhorteth us to stoutness, I assure you the voice of one man is able, in an hour, to put more life in us than six hundred trumpets continually blustering in our ears." *

Thus was the proclamation made. Nor was it long in wakening all the echoes of Europe. What success might have attended it, had the question decided been a purely abstract question, it is difficult to say. As it was, it was to stand or fall, not by logic, but by political needs and sympathies. Thus, in France, his doctrine was to have some future, because Protestants suffered there under the feeble and treacherous regency of Catherine de Medici; and thus it was to have no future anywhere else, because the Protestant interest was bound up with the prosperity of Queen Elizabeth.

---

* M'Crie's "Life of Knox," ii. 41.

This stumbling-block lay at the very threshold of the matter; and Knox, in the text of the "First Blast," had set everybody the wrong example and gone to the ground himself. He finds occasion to regret "the blood of innocent Lady Jane Dudley." But Lady Jane Dudley, or Lady Jane Gray, as we call her, was a would-be traitoress and rebel against God, to use his own expressions. If, therefore, political and religious sympathy led Knox himself into so grave a partiality, what was he to expect from his disciples? If the trumpet gave so ambiguous a sound, who could heartily prepare himself for the battle? The question whether Lady Jane Dudley was an innocent martyr, or a traitoress against God, whose inordinate pride and tyranny had been effectually repressed, was thus left altogether in the wind; and it was not, perhaps, wonderful if many of Knox's readers concluded that all right and wrong in the matter turned upon the degree of the sovereign's orthodoxy and possible helpfulness to the Reformation. He should have been the more careful of such an ambiguity of meaning, as he must have known well the lukewarm indifference and dishonesty of his fellow-reformers in political matters. He had already, in 1556 or 1575, talked the matter over with his great master, Calvin, in "a private conversation"; and the interview* must have been truly distasteful to both parties. Calvin, indeed, went a far way with him in theory, and owned that the "government of women was a deviation from the original and proper order of nature, to be ranked, no less than slavery, among the punishments

---

* Described by Calvin in a letter to Cecil, Knox's Works, vol. iv.

consequent upon the fall of man." But, in practice, their two roads separated. For the Man of Geneva saw difficulties in the way of the Scripture proof in the cases of Deborah and Huldah, and in the prophecy of Isaiah that queens should be the nursing mothers of the Church. And as the Bible was not decisive, he thought the subject should be let alone, because, "by custom and public consent. and long practice, it has been established that realms and principalities may descend to females by hereditary right, and it would not be lawful to unsettle governments which are ordained by the peculiar providence of God." I imagine Knox's ears must have burned during this interview. Think of him listening dutifully to all this—how it would not do to meddle with anointed kings—how there was a peculiar providence in these great affairs; and then think of his own peroration, and the "noble heart" whom he looks for "to vindicate the liberty of his country"; or his answer to Queen Mary, when she asked him who he was, to interfere in the affairs of Scotland: "Madam, a subject born within the same!" Indeed, the two doctors who differed at this private conversation represented, at the moment, two principles of enormous import in the subsequent history of Europe. In Calvin we have represented that passive obedience, that toleration of injustice and absurdity, that holding back of the hand from political affairs as from something unclean, which lost France, if we are to believe M. Michelet, for the Reformation; a spirit necessarily fatal in the long run to the existence of any sect that may profess it; a suicidal doctrine that survives among us to this day in narrow views of personal duty, and the low political morality of many virtuous men. In Knox, on the other hand, we see foreshadowed the whole Puritan Revolution and the scaffold of Charles I.

There is little doubt in my mind that this interview was what caused Knox to print his book without a name.* It was a dangerous thing to contradict the Man of Geneva, and doubly so, surely, when one had had the advantage of correction from him in a private conversation; and Knox had his little flock of English refugees to consider. If they had fallen into bad odor at Geneva, where else was there left to flee to? It was printed, as I said, in 1558; and, by a singular *mal-à-propos*, in that same year Mary died, and Elizabeth succeeded to the throne of England. And just as the accession of Catholic Queen Mary had condemned female rule in the eyes of Knox, the accession of Protestant Queen Elizabeth justified it in the eyes of his colleagues. Female rule ceases to be an anomaly, not because Elizabeth can "reply to eight embassadors in one day in their different languages," but because she represents for the moment the political future of the Reformation. The exiles troop back to England with songs of praise in their mouths. The bright occidental star, of which we have all read in the Preface to the Bible, has risen over the darkness of Europe. There is a thrill of hope through the persecuted Churches of the Continent. Calvin writes to Cecil, washing his hands of Knox and his political heresies. The sale of the "First Blast" is prohibited in Geneva; and along with it the bold book

---

* It was anonymously published, but no one seems to have been in doubt about its authorship; he might as well have set his name to it, for all the good he got by holding it back.

of Knox's colleague, Goodman—a book dear to Milton—
where female rule was briefly characterized as a "monster in nature and disorder among men."* Any who
may ever have doubted, or been for a moment led
away by Knox or Goodman, or their own wicked
imaginations, are now more than convinced. They have
seen the occidental star. Aylmer, with his eye set
greedily on a possible bishopric, and "the better to obtain the favor of the new Queen,"† sharpens his pen
to confound Knox by logic. What need? He has been
confounded by facts. "Thus what had been to the
refugees of Geneva as the very word of God, no sooner
were they back in England than, behold! it was the
word of the devil."‡

Now, what of the real sentiments of these loyal
subjects of Elizabeth? They professed a holy horror for
Knox's position: let us see if their own would please
a modern audience any better, or was, in substance,
greatly different.

John Aylmer, afterward Bishop of London, published
an answer to Knox, under the title of "An Harbor for
Faithful and true Subjects against the late Blown Blast,
concerning the government of Women."§ And certainly
he was a thought more acute, a thought less precipitate
and simple, than his adversary. He is not to be led
away by such captious terms as *natural* and *unnatural*.
It is obvious to him that a woman's disability to rule
is not natural in the same sense in which it is natural

---

* Knox's Works, iv. 358.   † Strype's " Aylmer," p. 16.

‡ It may interest the reader to know that these (so says Thomasius)
are the " ipsissima verba Schlusselburgii."

§ I am indebted for a sight of this book to the kindness of Mr. David
Laing, the editor of Knox's Works.

for a stone to fall or fire to burn. He is doubtful, on the whole, whether this disability be natural at all; nay, when he is laying it down that a woman should not be a priest, he shows some elementary conception of what many of us now hold to be the truth of the matter. "The bringing-up of women," he says, "is commonly such" that they cannot have the necessary qualifications, "for they are not brought up in learning in schools, nor trained in disputation." And even so, he can ask, "Are there not in England women, think you, that for learning and wisdom could tell their household and neighbors as good a tale as any Sir John there?" For all that, his advocacy is weak. If women's rule is not unnatural in a sense preclusive of its very existence, it is neither so convenient nor so profitable as the government of men. He holds England to be specially suitable for the government of women, because there the governor is more limited and restrained by the other members of the constitution than in other places; and this argument has kept his book from being altogether forgotten. It is only in hereditary monarchies that he will offer any defense of the anomaly. "If rulers were to be chosen by lot or suffrage, he would not that any women should stand in the election, but men only." The law of succession of crowns was a law to him, in the same sense as the law of evolution is a law to Mr. Herbert Spencer; and the one and the other counsels his readers, in a spirit suggestively alike, not to kick against the pricks or seek to be more wise than He who made them.* If God has put a female child

---

* "Social Statics," p. 64, etc.

into the direct line of inheritance, it is God's affair.
His strength will be perfected in her weakness. He
makes the Creator address the objectors in this not
very flattering vein: "I, that could make Daniel, a
sucking babe, to judge better than the wisest lawyers;
a brute beast to reprehend the folly of a prophet; and
poor fishers to confound the great clerks of the world
—cannot I make a woman to be a good ruler over
you?"

This is the last word of his reasoning. Although he
was not altogether without Puritanic leaven, shown particularly in what he says of the incomes of Bishops,
yet it was rather loyalty to the old order of things than
any generous belief in the capacity of women, that
raised up for them this clerical champion. His courtly
spirit contrasts singularly with the rude, bracing repub-
licanism of Knox. "Thy knee shall bow," he says,
"thy cap shall off, thy tongue shall speak reverently of
thy sovereign." For himself, his tongue is even more
than reverent. Nothing can stay the issue of his eloquent adulation. Again and again, "the remembrance
of Elizabeth's virtues" carries him away; and he has
to hark back again to find the scent of his argument.
He is repressing his vehement adoration throughout, until, when the end comes, and he feels his business at
an end, he can indulge himself to his heart's content
in indiscriminate laudation of his royal mistress. It
is humorous to think that this illustrious lady, whom
he here praises, among many other excellences, for
the simplicity of her attire and the "marvelous meek-
ness of her stomach," threatened him, years after,
in no very meek terms, for a sermon against female

vanity in dress, which she held as a reflection on herself.*

Whatever was wanting here in respect for women generally, there was no want of respect for the Queen; and one cannot very greatly wonder if these devoted servants looked askance, not upon Knox only, but on his little flock, as they came back to England tainted with disloyal doctrine. For them, as for him, the occidental star rose somewhat red and angry. As for poor Knox, his position was the saddest of all. For the juncture seemed to him of the highest importance; it was the nick of time, the flood water of opportunity. Not only was there an opening for him in Scotland, a smoldering brand of civil liberty and religious enthusiasm which it should be for him to kindle into flame with his powerful breath; but he had his eye seemingly on an object of even higher worth. For now, when religious sympathy ran so high that it could be set against national aversion, he wished to begin the fusion together of England and Scotland, and to begin it at the sore place. If once the open wound were closed at the Border, the work would be half done. Ministers placed at Berwick and such places might seek their converts equally on either side of the march; old enemies would sit together to hear the gospel of peace, and forget the inherited jealousies of many generations in the enthusiasm of a common faith; or—let us say better—a common heresy. For people are not most conscious of brotherhood when they continue languidly together in one creed, but when, with some doubt, with

---

* Hallam's "Const. Hist. of England," i. 225, note m.

some danger perhaps, and certainly not without some
reluctance, they violently break with the tradition of
the past, and go forth from the sanctuary of their
fathers to worship under the bare heaven. A new
creed, like a new country, is an unhomely place of
sojourn; but it makes men lean on one another and
join hands. It was on this that Knox relied to begin
the union of the English and the Scotch. And he had,
perhaps, better means of judging than any even of his
contemporaries. He knew the temper of both nations;
and already, during his two years' chaplaincy at Berwick, he had seen his scheme put to the proof. But
whether practicable or not, the proposal does him much
honor. That he should thus have sought to make a
love-match of it between the two peoples, and tried to
win their inclination toward a union instead of simply
transferring them, like so many sheep, by a marriage,
or testament, or private treaty, is thoroughly characteristic of what is best in the man. Nor was this all.
He had, besides, to assure himself of English support,
secret or avowed, for the reformation party in Scotland; a delicate affair, trenching upon treason. And so
he had plenty to say to Cecil, plenty that he did not
care to "commit to paper, neither yet to the knowledge
of many." But his miserable publication had shut the
doors of England in his face. Summoned to Edinburgh
by the confederate lords, he waited at Dieppe, anxiously
praying for leave to journey through England. The
most dispiriting tidings reach him. His messengers,
coming from so obnoxious a quarter, narrowly escape
imprisonment. His old congregation are coldly received,
and even begin to look back again to their place of

exile with regret. "My First Blast," he writes rue-
fully, "has blown from me all my friends of England." And then he adds, with a snarl, "The Second
Blast, I fear, shall sound somewhat more sharp, except
men be more moderate than I hear they are." * But
the threat is empty; there will never be a second blast
—he has had enough of that trumpet. Nay, he begins
to feel uneasily that, unless he is to be rendered useless for the rest of his life, unless he is to lose his
right arm and go about his great work maimed and
impotent, he must find some way of making his peace
with England and the indignant Queen. The letter just
quoted was written on the 6th of April, 1559; and on
the 10th, after he had cooled his heels for four days
more about the streets of Dieppe, he gave in altogether, and writes a letter of capitulation to Cecil. In
this letter,† which he kept back until the 22d, still hop-
ing that things would come right of themselves, he
censures the great secretary for having "followed the
world in the way of perdition," characterizes him as
"worthy of hell," and threatens him, if he be not
found simple, sincere, and fervent in the cause of
Christ's gospel, that he shall "taste of the same cup
that politic heads have drunken in before him." This
is all, I take it, out of respect for the Reformer's own
position; if he is going to be humiliated, let others be
humiliated first; like a child who will not take his medi-
cine until he has made his nurse and his mother drink
of it before him. "But I have, say you, written a

---

* Knox to Mrs. Locke, 6th April 1559. Works, vi. 14.
† Knox to Sir William Cecil, 10th April 1559. Works, ii. 16, or vi. 15

treasonable book against the regiment and empire of women. . . . The writing of that book I will not deny; but to prove it treasonable I think it shall be hard. . . . It is hinted that my book shall be written against. If so be, sir, I greatly doubt they shall rather hurt nor (than) mend the matter." And here come the terms of capitulation; for he does not surrender unconditionally, even in this sore strait: "And yet if any," he goes on, "think me enemy to the person, or yet to the regiment, of her whom God hath now promoted, they are utterly deceived in me, *for the miraculous work of God, comforting His afflicted by means of an infirm vessel, I do acknowledge, and the power of His most potent hand I will obey. More plainly to speak, if Queen Elizabeth shall confess, that the extraordinary dispensation of God's great mercy maketh that lawful unto her which both nature and God's law do deny to all women*, then shall none in England be more willing to maintain her lawful authority than I shall be. But if (God's wondrous works set aside) she ground (as God forbid) the justness of her title upon consuetude, laws, or ordinances of men, then"—Then Knox will denounce her? Not so; he is more politic nowadays—then, he "greatly fears" that her ingratitude to God will not go long without punishment.

His letter to Elizabeth, written some few months later, was a mere amplification of the sentences quoted above. She must base her title entirely upon the extraordinary providence of God; but if she does this, "if thus, in God's presence, she humbles herself, so will he with tongue and pen justify her authority, as

the Holy Ghost hath justified the same in Deborah,
that blessed mother in Israel." * And so, you see, his
consistency is preserved; he is merely applying the doctrine of the "First Blast." The argument goes thus:
The regiment of women is, as before noted in our
work, repugnant to nature, contumely to God, and a
subversion of good order. It has nevertheless pleased
God to raise up, as exceptions to this law, first Deborah, and afterward Elizabeth Tudor—whose regiment
we shall proceed to celebrate.

There is no evidence as to how the Reformer's explanations were received, and indeed it is most probable
that the letter was never shown to Elizabeth at all.
For it was sent under cover of another to Cecil, and
as it was not of a very courtly conception throughout,
and was, of all things, what would most excite the
Queen's uneasy jealousy about her title, it is like
enough that the secretary exercised his discretion (he
had Knox's leave in this case, and did not always
wait for that, it is reputed) to put the letter harm-
lessly away beside other valueless or unpresentable
State Papers. I wonder very much if he did the same
with another,† written two years later, after Mary had
come into Scotland, in which Knox almost seeks to
make Elizabeth an accomplice with him in the matter
of the "First Blast." The Queen of Scotland is going
to have that work refuted, he tells her; and "though
it were but foolishness in him to prescribe unto her
Majesty what is to be done," he would yet remind

---

* Knox to Queen Elizabeth, July 20th, 1559. Works, vi. 47, or ii. 26.
† Knox to Queen Elizabeth, August 6th, 1561. Works, vi. 126.

her that Mary is neither so much alarmed about her own security, nor so generously interested in Elizabeth's, "that she would take such pains, *unless her crafty counsel in so doing shot at a further mark.*" There is something really ingenious in this letter; it showed Knox in the double capacity of the author of the "First Blast" and the faithful friend of Elizabeth; and he combines them there so naturally, that one would scarcely imagine the two to be incongruous.

Twenty days later he was defending his intemperate publication to another queen — his own queen, Mary Stuart. This was on the first of those three interviews which he has preserved for us with so much dramatic vigor in the picturesque pages of his history. After he had avowed the authorship in his usual haughty style, Mary asked: "You think, then, that I have no just authority?" The question was evaded. "Please your Majesty," he answered, "that learned men in all ages have had their judgments free, and most commonly disagreeing from the common judgment of the world; such also have they published by pen and tongue; and yet notwithstanding they themselves have lived in the common society with others, and have borne patiently with the errors and imperfections which they could not amend." Thus did "Plato the philosopher": thus will do John Knox. "I have communicated my judgment to the world: if the realm finds no inconvenience from the regiment of a woman, that which they approve, shall I not further disallow than within my own breast; but shall be as well content to live under your Grace, as Paul was to live under Nero. And my hope is, that so long as ye defile not your hands with the

blood of the saints of God, neither I nor my book
shall hurt either you or your authority." All this is
admirable in wisdom and moderation, and, except that
he might have hit upon a comparison less offensive than
that with Paul and Nero, hardly to be bettered. Having said thus much, he feels he need say no more;
and so, when he is further pressed, he closes that part
of the discussion with an astonishing sally. If he has
been content to let this matter sleep, he would recommend her Grace to follow his example with thankful-
ness of heart; it is grimly to be understood which of
them has most to fear if the question should be reawakened. So the talk wandered to other subjects.
Only, when the Queen was summoned at last to dinner ("for it was afternoon"), Knox made his salutation
in this form of words: "I pray God, Madam, that you
may be as much blessed within the Commonwealth of
Scotland, if it be the pleasure of God, as ever Deborah
was in the Commonwealth of Israel."* Deborah again.

But he was not yet done with the echoes of his
own "First Blast." In 1571, when he was already
near his end, the old controversy was taken up in one
of a series of anonymous libels against the Reformer
affixed, Sunday after Sunday, to the church door. The
dilemma was fairly enough stated. Either his doctrine
is false, in which case he is a "false doctor" and sedi-
tious; or, if it be true, why does he "avow and approve the contrare, I mean that regiment in the Queen
of England's person; which he avoweth and approveth,
not only praying for the maintenance of her estate, but

---

* Knox's Works, ii. 278-80.

also procuring her aid and support against his own
native country?" Knox answered the libel, as his wont
was, next Sunday, from the pulpit. He justified the
"First Blast" with all the old arrogance; there is no
drawing back there. The regiment of women is repugnant to nature, contumely to God, and a subversion
of good order, as before. When he prays for the
maintenance of Elizabeth's estate, he is only following
the example of those prophets of God who warned and
comforted the wicked kings of Israel; or of Jeremiah,
who bade the Jews pray for the prosperity of Nebu-
chadnezzar. As for the Queen's aid, there is no harm
in that: *quia* (these are his own words) *quia omnia
munda mundis:* because to the pure all things are
pure. One thing, in conclusion, he "may not pre-
termit"; to give the lie in the throat to his accuser,
where he charges him with seeking support against his
native country. "What I have been to my country,"
said the old Reformer, "What I have been to my country, albeit this unthankful age will not know, yet the
ages to come will be compelled to bear witness to the
truth. And thus I cease, requiring of all men that
have anything to oppone against me, that he may
(they may) do it so plainly, as that I may make myself and all my doings manifest to the world. For to
me it seemeth a thing unreasonable, that, in this my
decrepit age, I shall be compelled to fight against
shadows, and howlets that dare not abide the light."[*]

Now, in this, which may be called his "Last Blast,"

---

[*] Calderwood's "History of the Kirk of Scotland," edition of the
Wodrow Society, iii. 51-54.

there is as sharp speaking as any in the "First Blast"
itself. He is of the same opinion to the end, you see,
although he has been obliged to cloak and garble that
opinion for political ends. He has been tacking indeed,
and he has indeed been seeking the favor of a queen;
but what man ever sought a queen's favor with a
more virtuous purpose, or with as little courtly policy?
The question of consistency is delicate, and must be
made plain. Knox never changed his opinion about female rule, but lived to regret that he had published
that opinion. Doubtless he had many thoughts so far
out of the range of public sympathy that he could
only keep them to himself, and, in his own words,
bear patiently with the errors and imperfections that
he could not amend. For example, I make no doubt
myself that, in his own heart, he did hold the shocking dogma attributed to him by more than one calum-
niator; and that, had the time been ripe, had there
been aught to gain by it, instead of all to lose, he
would have been the first to assert that Scotland was
elective instead of hereditary—"elective as in the days
of paganism," as one Thevet says in holy horror.*
And yet, because the time was not ripe, I find no
hint of such an idea in his collected works. Now, the
regiment of women was another matter that he should
have kept to himself; right or wrong, his opinion did
not fit the moment; right or wrong, as Aylmer puts
it, "the 'Blast' was blown out of season." And this
it was that he began to perceive after the accession of
Elizabeth; not that he had been wrong, and that fe-

---

* Bayle's "Historical Dictionary," art. Knox, remark G.

male rule was a good thing, for he had said from the first that "the felicity of some women in their empires" could not change the law of God and the nature of created things; not this, but that the regiment of women was one of those imperfections of society which must be borne with because yet they cannot be remedied. The thing had seemed so obvious to him, in his sense of unspeakable masculine superiority, and his fine contempt for what is only sanctioned by antiquity and common consent, he had imagined that, at the first hint, men would arise and shake off the debasing tyranny. He found himself wrong, and he showed that he could be moderate in his own fashion, and understood the spirit of true compromise. He came round to Calvin's position, in fact, but by a different way. And it derogates nothing from the merit of this wise attitude that it was the consequence of a change of interest. We are all taught by interest; and if the interest be not merely selfish, there is no wiser preceptor under heaven, and perhaps no sterner.

Such is the history of John Knox's connection with the controversy about female rule. In itself, this is obviously an incomplete study; not fully to be understood, without a knowledge of his private relations with the other sex, and what he thought of their position in domestic life. This shall be dealt with in another paper.

II.—PRIVATE LIFE

To those who know Knox by hearsay only, I believe the matter of this paper will be somewhat astonishing. For the hard energy of the man in all public
matters has possessed the imagination of the world; he
remains for posterity in certain traditional phrases, brow-
beating Queen Mary, or breaking beautiful carved work
in abbeys and cathedrals, that had long smoked themselves out and were no more than sorry ruins, while
he was still quietly teaching children in a country gentleman's family. It does not consist with the common
acceptation of his character to fancy him much moved,
except with anger. And yet the language of passion
came to his pen as readily, whether it was a passion
of denunciation against some of the abuses that vexed
his righteous spirit, or of yearning for the society of
an absent friend. He was vehement in affection, as in
doctrine. I will not deny that there may have been,
along with his vehemence, something shifty, and for the
moment only; that, like many men, and many Scotchmen, he saw the world and his own heart, not so
much under any very steady, equable light, as by extreme flashes of passion, true for the moment, but not
true in the long run. There does seem to me to be
something of this traceable in the Reformer's utterances:
precipitation and repentance, hardy speech and action
somewhat circumspect, a strong tendency to see himself

in a heroic light and to place a ready belief in the disposition of the moment. Withal he had considerable confidence in himself, and in the uprightness of his own disciplined emotions, underlying much sincere aspiration after spiritual humility. And it is this confidence that makes his intercourse with women so interesting to a modern. It would be easy, of course, to make fun of the whole affair, to picture him strutting vaingloriously among these inferior creatures, or compare a religious friendship in the sixteenth century with what was called, I think, a literary friendship in the eighteenth. But it is more just and profitable to recognize what there is sterling and human underneath all his theoretical affectations of superiority. Women, he has said in his "First Blast," are "weak, frail, impatient, feeble, and foolish"; and yet it does not appear that he was himself any less dependent than other men upon the sympathy and affection of these weak, frail, impatient, feeble, and foolish creatures; it seems even as if he had been rather more dependent than most.

Of those who are to act influentially on their fellows, we should expect always something large and public in their way of life, something more or less urbane and comprehensive in their sentiment for others. We should not expect to see them spend their sympathy in idyls, however beautiful. We should not seek them among those who, if they have but a wife to their bosom, ask no more of womankind, just as they ask no more of their own sex, if they can find a friend or two for their immediate need. They will be quick to feel all the pleasures of our association—not the great ones alone, but all. They will know not love only, but

all those other ways in which man and woman mutually make each other happy—by sympathy, by admiration, by the atmosphere they bear about them—down to
the mere impersonal pleasure of passing happy faces in
the street. For, through all this gradation, the difference of sex makes itself pleasurably felt. Down to the
most lukewarm courtesies of life, there is a special
chivalry due and a special pleasure received, when the
two sexes are brought ever so lightly into contact. We
love our mothers otherwise than we love our fathers;
a sister is not as a brother to us; and friendship between man and woman, be it never so unalloyed and
innocent, is not the same as friendship between man
and man. Such friendship is not even possible for all.
To conjoin tenderness for a woman that is not far short
of passionate with such disinterestedness and beautiful
gratuity of affection as there is between friends of the
same sex, requires no ordinary disposition in the man.
For either it would presuppose quite womanly delicacy
of perception, and, as it were, a curiosity in shades of
differing sentiment; or it would mean that he had accepted the large, simple divisions of society: a strong
and positive spirit robustly virtuous, who has chosen a
better part coarsely, and holds to it steadfastly, with
all its consequences of pain to himself and others; as
one who should go straight before him on a journey,
neither tempted by wayside flowers nor very scrupulous
of small lives under foot. It was in virtue of this
latter disposition that Knox was capable of those intimacies with women that embellished his life; and we
find him preserved for us in old letters as a man of
many women friends; a man of some expansion toward

the other sex; a man ever ready to comfort weeping women, and to weep along with them.

Of such scraps and fragments of evidence as to his private life and more intimate thoughts as have survived to us from all the perils that environ written paper, an astonishingly large proportion is in the shape of letters to women of his familiarity. He was twice married, but that is not greatly to the purpose; for the Turk, who thinks even more meanly of women than John Knox, is none the less given to marrying. What is really significant is quite apart from marriage. For the man Knox was a true man, and woman, the *ewigweibliche*, was as necessary to him, in spite of all low theories, as ever she was to Goethe. He came to her in a certain halo of his own, as the minister of truth, just as Goethe came to her in a glory of art; he made himself necessary to troubled hearts and minds exercised in the painful complications that naturally result from all changes in the world's way of thinking; and those whom he had thus helped became dear to him, and were made the chosen companions of his leisure if they were at hand, or encouraged and comforted by letter if they were afar.

It must not be forgotten that Knox had been a presbyter of the old Church, and that the many women whom we shall see gathering around him, as he goes through life, had probably been accustomed, while still in the communion of Rome, to rely much upon some chosen spiritual director, so that the intimacies of which I propose to offer some account, while testifying to a good heart in the Reformer, testify also to a certain survival of the spirit of the confessional in the Reformed Church, and are not properly to be judged without this idea. There is no friendship so noble, but it is the product of the time; and a world of little finical observances, and little frail proprieties and fashions of the hour, go to make or to mar, to stint or to perfect, the union of spirits the most loving and the most intolerant of such interference. The trick of the country and the age steps in even between the mother and her child, counts out their caresses upon niggardly fingers, and says, in the voice of authority, that this one thing shall be a matter of confidence between them, and this other thing shall not. And thus it is that we must take into reckoning whatever tended to modify the social atmosphere in which Knox and his women friends met, and loved and trusted each other. To the man who had been their priest and was now their minister, women would be able to speak with a confidence quite impossible in these latter days; the women would be able to speak, and the man to hear. It was a beaten road just then; and I daresay we should be no less scandalized at their plain speech than they, if they could come back to earth, would be offended at our waltzes and worldly fashions. This, then, was the footing on which Knox stood with his many women friends. The reader will see, as he goes on, how much of warmth, of interest, and of that happy mutual dependence which is the very gist of friendship, he contrived to ingraft upon this somewhat dry relationship of penitent and confessor.

It must be understood that we know nothing of his intercourse with women (as indeed we know little at all about his life) until he came to Berwick in 1549,

when he was already in the forty-fifth year of his age.
At the same time it is just possible that some of a
little group at Edinburgh, with whom he corresponded
during his last absence, may have been friends of an
older standing. Certainly they were, of all his female
correspondents, the least personally favored. He treats
them throughout in a comprehensive sort of spirit that
must at times have been a little wounding. Thus, he
remits one of them to his former letters, "which I
trust be common betwixt you and the rest of our sisters, for to me ye are all equal in Christ." * Another
letter is a gem in this way. "Albeit" it begins, "albeit
I have no particular matter to write unto you, beloved
sister, yet I could not refrain to write these few lines
to you in declaration of my remembrance of you. True
it is that I have many whom I bear in equal remembrance before God with you, to whom at present I
write nothing, either for that I esteem them stronger
than you, and therefore they need the less my rude
labors, or else because they have not provoked me by
their writing to recompense their remembrance." † His
"sisters in Edinburgh" had evidently to "provoke" his
attention pretty constantly; nearly all his letters are,
on the face of them, answers to questions, and the
answers are given with a certain crudity that I do not
find repeated when he writes to those he really cares
for. So when they consult him about women's apparel
(a subject on which his opinion may be pretty correctly
imagined by the ingenious reader for himself) he takes
occasion to anticipate some of the most offensive matter

---

* Works, iv. 244.   † Ib. iv. 246.

of the "First Blast" in a style of real brutality.* It
is not merely that he tells them "the garments of
women do declare their weakness and inability to exe-
cute the office of man," though that in itself is neither
very wise nor very opportune in such a correspondence
one would think; but if the reader will take the trouble
to wade through the long, tedious sermon for himself,
he will see proof enough that Knox neither loved, nor
very deeply respected, the women he was then addressing. In very truth, I believe these Edinburgh sisters
simply bored him. He had a certain interest in them
as his children in the Lord; they were continually "pro-
voking him by their writing"; and, if they handed his
letters about, writing to them was as good a form of
publication as was then open to him in Scotland. There
is one letter, however, in this budget, addressed to the
wife of Clerk-Register Mackgil, which is worthy of some
further mention. The Clerk-Register had not opened his
heart, it would appear, to the preaching of the Gospel,
and Mrs. Mackgil has written, seeking the Reformer's
prayers in his behalf. "Your husband," he answers,
"is dear to me for that he is a man indued with some
good gifts, but more dear for that he is your husband.
Charity moveth me to thirst his illumination, both for
his comfort and for the trouble which you sustain by
his coldness, which justly may be called infidelity."
He wishes her, however, not to hope too much; he
can promise that his prayers will be earnest, but not
that they will be effectual; it is possible that this is to
be her "cross" in life; that "her head, appointed by

---

* Works, iv. 225.

God for her comfort, should be her enemy." And if this be so, well, there is nothing for it; "with patience she must abide God's merciful deliverance," taking heed only that she does not "obey manifest iniquity for the pleasure of any mortal man." * I conceive this epistle would have given a very modified sort of pleasure to the Clerk-Register, had it chanced to fall into his hands. Compare its tenor—the dry resignation not without a hope of merciful deliverance therein recommended—with these words from another letter, written but the year before to two married women of London: "Call first for grace by Jesus, and thereafter communicate with your faithful husbands, and then shall God, I doubt not, conduct your footsteps, and direct your counsels to His glory."† Here the husbands are put in a very high place; we can recognize here the same hand that has written for our instruction how the man is set above the woman, even as God above the angels. But the point of the distinction is plain. For Clerk-Register Mackgil was not a faithful husband; displayed, indeed, toward religion a "coldness which justly might be called infidelity." We shall see in more notable instances how much Knox's conception of the duty of wives varies according to the zeal and orthodoxy of the husband.

As I have said, he may possibly have made the acquaintance of Mrs. Mackgil, Mrs. Guthrie, or some other, or all, of these Edinburgh friends while he was still Douglas of Longniddry's private tutor. But our certain knowledge begins in 1549. He was then but newly escaped from his captivity in France, after pull-

---

ing an oar for nineteen months on the benches of the
galley "Nostre Dame"; now up the rivers, holding
stealthy intercourse with other Scottish prisoners in the
castle of Rouen; now out in the North Sea, raising his
sick head to catch a glimpse of the far-off steeples of
St. Andrews. And now he was sent down by the
English Privy Council as a preacher to Berwick-upon-
Tweed; somewhat shaken in health by all his hardships, full of pains and agues, and tormented by gravel,
that sorrow of great men; altogether, what with his
romantic story, his weak health, and his great faculty
of eloquence, a very natural object for the sympathy
of devout women. At this happy juncture he fell into
the company of a Mrs. Elizabeth Bowes, wife of Richard Bowes, of Aske, in Yorkshire, to whom she had
borne twelve children. She was a religious hypochondriac, a very weariful woman, full of doubts and
scruples, and giving no rest on earth either to herself
or to those whom she honored with her confidence.
From the first time she heard Knox preach she formed
a high opinion of him, and was solicitous ever after of
his society.* Nor was Knox unresponsive. "I have
always delighted in your company," he writes, "and
when labors would permit, you know I have not spared
hours to talk and commune with you." Often when
they had met in depression he reminds her, "God hath
sent great comfort unto both."† We can gather from
such letters as are yet extant how close and continuous
was their intercourse. "I think it best you remain till
the morrow," he writes once, "and so shall we com-

---

mune at large at afternoon. This day you know to be
the day of my study and prayer unto God; yet if your
trouble be intolerable, or if you think my presence may
release your pain, do as the Spirit shall move you.
. . . Your messenger found me in bed, after a sore
trouble and most dolorous night, and so dolour may
complain to dolour when we two meet. . . . And
this is more plain than ever I spoke, to let you know
you have a companion in trouble."* Once we have the
curtain raised for a moment, and can look at the two
together for the length of a phrase. "After the writing
of this preceding," writes Knox, "your brother and
mine, Harrie Wycliffe, did advertise me by writing, that
your adversary (the devil) took occasion to trouble you
because that *I did start back from you rehearsing
your infirmities. I remember myself so to have done,
and that is my common consuetude when anything
pierceth or toucheth my heart. Call to your mind what
I did standing at the cupboard at Alnwick.* In very
deed I thought that no creature had been tempted as
I was; and when I heard proceed from your mouth the
very same words that he troubles me with, I did wonder and from my heart lament your sore trouble, knowing in myself the dolour thereof."† Now intercourse of
so very close a description, whether it be religious intercourse or not, is apt to displease and disquiet a husband; and we know incidentally from Knox himself
that there was some little scandal about his intimacy
with Mrs. Bowes. "The slander, and fear of men," he
writes, "has impeded me to exercise my pen so oft as

* Works, iii. 352, 353.   † Ib. iii. 350.

I would; *yea, very shame hath holden me from your
company, when I was most surely persuaded that
God had appointed me at that time to comfort and
feed your hungry and afflicted soul.   God in his infinite mercy,*" he goes on, "*remove not only from me
all fear that tendeth not to godliness, but from others
suspicion to judge of me otherwise than it becometh
one member to judge of another.*"* And the scandal,
such as it was, would not be allayed by the dissension
in which Mrs. Bowes seems to have lived with her
family upon the matter of religion, and the countenance
shown by Knox to her resistance. Talking of these con-
flicts, and her courage against "her own flesh and most
inward affections, yea, against some of her most natural
friends," he writes it, "to the praise of God, he has
wondered at the bold constancy which he has found in
her when his own heart was faint." †

Now, perhaps in order to stop scandalous mouths,
perhaps out of a desire to bind the much loved evan-
gelist nearer to her in the only manner possible,
Mrs. Bowes conceived the scheme of marrying him to
her fifth daughter, Marjorie; and the Reformer seems
to have fallen in with it readily enough. It seems to
have been believed in the family that the whole matter had been originally made up between these two,
with no very spontaneous inclination on the part of the
bride.‡ Knox's idea of marriage, as I have said, was
not the same for all men; but on the whole, it was
not lofty. We have a curious letter of his, written at
the request of Queen Mary, to the Earl of Argyle, on

---

* Works, iii. 390, 391.   † Ib. iii. 142.   ‡ Ib. iii. 378.

very delicate household matters; which, as he tells us, "was not well accepted of the said Earl."* We may suppose, however, that his own home was regulated in a similar spirit. I can fancy that for such a man, emotional, and with a need, now and again, to exercise parsimony in emotions not strictly needful, something a little mechanical, something hard and fast and clearly understood, would enter into his ideal of a home. There were storms enough without, and equability was to be desired at the fireside even at a sacrifice of deeper pleasures. So, from a wife, of all women, he would not ask much. One letter to her which has come down to us is, I had almost said, conspicuous for coldness.† He calls her, as he called other female correspondents, "dearly beloved sister"; the epistle is doctrinal, and nearly the half of it bears, not upon her own case, but upon that of her mother. However, we know what Heine wrote in his wife's album; and there is, after all, one passage that may be held to intimate some tenderness, although even that admits of an amusingly opposite construction. "I think," he says, "I *think* this be the first letter I ever wrote to you." This, if we are to take it literally, may pair off with the "two *or three* children" whom Montaigne mentions having lost at nurse; the one is as eccentric in a lover as the other in a parent. Nevertheless, he displayed more energy in the course of his troubled wooing than might have been expected. The whole Bowes family, angry enough already at the influence he had obtained over the mother, set their faces ob-

---

* Works, ii. 379.　　　　† Ib. iii. 394.

durately against the match. And I daresay the opposition quickened his inclination. I find him writing to
Mrs. Bowes that she need no further trouble herself
about the marriage; it should now be his business altogether; it behooved him now to jeopard his life "for
the comfort of his own flesh, both fear and friendship
of all earthly creature laid aside." * This is a wonder-
fully chivalrous utterance for a Reformer forty-eight
years old; and it compares well with the leaden co-
quetries of Calvin, not much over thirty, taking this
and that into consideration, weighing together dowries
and religious qualifications and the instancy of friends,
and exhibiting what M. Bungener calls "an honorable
and Christian difficulty" of choice, in frigid indecisions
and insincere proposals. But Knox's next letter is in
a humbler tone; he has not found the negotiation so
easy as he fancied; he despairs of the marriage altogether, and talks of leaving England—regards not "what
country consumes his wicked carcass." "You shall understand," he says, "that this sixth of November, I
spoke with Sir Robert Bowes" (the head of the family,
his bride's uncle) "in the matter you know, according
to your request; whose disdainful, yea, despiteful, words
hath so pierced my heart that my life is bitter to me.
I bear a good countenance with a sore troubled heart,
because he that ought to consider matters with a deep
judgment is become not only a despiser, but also a
taunter of God's messengers—God be merciful unto him!
Amongst others his most unpleasing words, while that I
was about to have declared my heart in the whole

---

* Works, iii. 376.

matter, he said, 'Away with your rhetorical reasons! for I will not be persuaded with them.' God knows I did use no rhetoric nor colored speech; but would have spoken the truth, and that in most simple manner. I am not a good orator in my own cause; but what he would not be content to hear of me, God shall declare to him one day to his displeasure, unless he repent." * Poor Knox, you see, is quite commoved. It has been a very unpleasant interview. And as it is the only sample that we have of how things went with him during his courtship, we may infer that the period was not as agreeable for Knox as it has been for some others.

However, when once they were married, I imagine he and Marjorie Bowes hit it off together comfortably enough. The little we know of it may be brought together in a very short space. She bore him two sons. He seems to have kept her pretty busy, and depended on her to some degree in his work; so that when she fell ill, his papers got at once into disorder.† Certainly she sometimes wrote to his dictation; and, in this capacity, he calls her "his left hand."‡ In June 1559, at the headiest moment of the Reformation in Scotland, he writes regretting the absence of his helpful colleague, Goodman, "whose presence" (this is the not very grammatical form of his lament) "whose presence I more thirst, than she that is my own flesh."§ And this, considering the source and the circumstances, may be held as evidence of a very tender sentiment. He tells us himself in his history, on the occasion of a certain

---

* Works, iii. 378.   † Ib. vi. 104.   ‡ Ib. v. 5.   § Ib. vi. 27.

meeting at the Kirk of Field, that "he was in no small heaviness by reason of the late death of his dear bedfellow, Marjorie Bowes."* Calvin, condoling with him, speaks of her as "a wife whose like is not to be found everywhere" (that is very like Calvin), and again, as "the most delightful of wives." We know what Calvin thought desirable in a wife, "good humor, chastity, thrift, patience, and solicitude for her husband's health," and so we may suppose that the first Mrs. Knox fell not far short of this ideal.

The actual date of the marriage is uncertain; but by September 1566, at the latest, the Reformer was settled in Geneva with his wife. There is no fear either that he will be dull; even if the chaste, thrifty, patient Marjorie should not altogether occupy his mind, he need not go out of the house to seek more female sympathy; for behold! Mrs. Bowes is duly domesticated with the young couple. Dr. M'Crie imagined that Richard Bowes was now dead, and his widow, consequently, free to live where she would; and where could she go more naturally than to the house of a married daughter? This, however, is not the case. Richard Bowes did not die till at least two years later. It is impossible to believe that he approved of his wife's desertion, after so many years of marriage, after twelve children had been born to them; and accordingly we find in his will, dated 1558, no mention either of her or of Knox's wife.† This is plain sailing. It is easy enough to understand the anger of Bowes against this inter-

---

* Works, ii. 138.
† Mr. Laing's preface to the sixth volume of Knox's Works, p. lxii.

loper, who had come into a quiet family, married the daughter in spite of the father's opposition, alienated the wife from the husband and the husband's religion, supported her in a long course of resistance and rebellion, and, after years of intimacy, already too close and tender for any jealous spirit to behold without resentment, carried her away with him at last into a foreign land. But it is not quite easy to understand how, except out of sheer weariness and disgust, he was ever brought to agree to the arrangement. Nor is it easy to square the Reformer's conduct with his public teaching. We have, for instance, a letter addressed by him, Craig, and Spottiswood, to the Archbishops of Canterbury and York, anent "a wicked and rebellious woman," one Anne Good, spouse to "John Barron, a minister of Christ Jesus his evangel," who, "after great rebellion shown unto him, and divers admonitions given, as well by himself as by others in his name, that she should in no wise depart from this realm, nor from his house without his license, hath not the less stubbornly and rebelliously departed, separated herself from his society, left his house, and withdrawn herself from this realm." * Perhaps some sort of license was extorted, as I have said, from Richard Bowes, weary with years of domestic dissension; but setting that aside, the words employed with so much righteous indignation by Knox, Craig, and Spottiswood, to describe the conduct of that wicked and rebellious woman, Mrs. Barron, would describe nearly as exactly the conduct of the religious Mrs. Bowes. It is a little bewil-

* Works, vi. 534.

dering, until we recollect the distinction between faithful and unfaithful husbands; for Barron was "a minister of Christ Jesus his evangel," while Richard Bowes, besides being own brother to a despiser and taunter of God's messengers, is shrewdly suspected to have been "a bigoted adherent of the Roman Catholic faith," or, as Knox himself would have expressed it, "a rotten Papist."

You would have thought that Knox was now pretty well supplied with female society. But we are not yet at the end of the roll. The last year of his sojourn in England had been spent principally in London, where he was resident as one of the chaplains of Edward the Sixth; and here he boasts, although a stranger, he had, by God's grace, found favor before many.* The godly women of the metropolis made much of him; once he writes to Mrs. Bowes that her last letter had found him closeted with three, and he and the three women were all in tears.† Out of all, however, he had chosen two. "*God*," he writes to them, "*brought us in such familiar acquaintance, that your hearts were incensed and kindled with a special care over me, as a mother useth to be over her natural child; and my heart was opened and compelled in your presence to be more plain than ever I was to any.*"‡ And out of the two even he had chosen one, Mrs. Anne Locke, wife to Mr. Harry Locke, merchant, nigh to Bow Kirk, Cheapside, in London, as the address runs. If one may venture to judge upon such imperfect evidence, this was the woman he loved best. I have a difficulty in quite form-

---

* Works, iv. 220. † Ib. iii. 380. ‡ Ib. iv. 220.

ing to myself an idea of her character. She may have been one of the three tearful visitors before alluded to; she may even have been that one of them who was so profoundly moved by some passages of Mrs. Bowes's letter, which the Reformer opened, and read aloud to them before they went. "O would to God," cried this impressionable matron, "would to God that I might speak with that person, for I perceive there are more tempted than I."* This *may* have been Mrs. Locke, as I say; but even if it were, we must not conclude from this one fact that she was such another as Mrs. Bowes. All the evidence tends the other way. She was a woman of understanding, plainly, who followed political events with interest, and to whom Knox thought it worth while to write, in detail, the history of his trials and successes. She was religious, but without that morbid perversity of spirit that made religion so heavy a burden for the poor-hearted Mrs. Bowes. More of her I do not find, save testimony to the profound affection that united her to the Reformer. So we find him writing to her from Geneva, in such terms as these: "You write that your desire is earnest to see me. *Dear sister, if I should express the thirst and languor which I have had for your presence, I should appear to pass measure. . . . Yea, I weep and rejoice in remembrance of you;* but that would evanish by the comfort of your presence, which I assure you is so dear to me, that if the charge of this little flock here, gathered together in Christ's name, did not impede me, my coming should prevent my letter." † I

---

* Works, iii. 380.   † Ib. iv. 238.

say that this was written from Geneva; and yet you
will observe that it is no consideration for his wife or
mother-in-law, only the charge of his little flock, that
keeps him from setting out forthwith for London, to
comfort himself with the dear presence of Mrs. Locke.
Remember that was a certain plausible enough pretext
for Mrs. Locke to come to Geneva—"the most perfect
school of Christ that ever was on earth since the days
of the Apostles"—for we are now under the reign of
that "horrible monster Jezebel of England," when a
lady of good orthodox sentiments was better out of
London. It was doubtful, however, whether this was
to be. She was detained in England, partly by circumstances unknown, "partly by empire of her head," Mr.
Harry Locke, the Cheapside merchant. It is somewhat
humorous to see Knox struggling for resignation, now
that he has to do with a faithful husband (for Mr.
Harry Locke was faithful). Had it been otherwise, "in
my heart," he says, "I could have wished—yea," here
he breaks out, "yea, and cannot cease to wish—that
God would guide you to this place."* And after all,
he had not long to wait, for, whether Mr. Harry Locke
died in the interval, or was wearied, he too, into giving permission, five months after the date of the letter
last quoted, "Mrs. Anne Locke, Harry her son, and
Anne her daughter, and Katharine her maid," arrived
in that perfect school of Christ, the Presbyterian paradise, Geneva. So now, and for the next two years, the
cup of Knox's happiness was surely full. Of an afternoon, when the bells rang out for the sermon, the

---

* Works, iv. 240.

shops closed, and the good folk gathered to the
churches, psalm-book in hand, we can imagine him
drawing near to the English chapel in quite patriarchal
fashion, with Mrs. Knox and Mrs. Bowes and Mrs.
Locke, James his servant, Patrick his pupil, and a due
following of children and maids. He might be alone
at work all morning in his study, for he wrote much
during these two years; but at night, you may be sure
there was a circle of admiring women, eager to hear
the new paragraph, and not sparing of applause. And
what work, among others, was he elaborating at this
time, but the notorious "First Blast"? So that he may
have rolled out, in his big pulpit voice, how women
were weak, frail, impatient, feeble, foolish, inconstant,
variable, cruel, and lacking the spirit of counsel, and
how men were above them, even as God is above the
angels, in the ears of his own wife, and the two dear-
est friends he had on earth. But he had lost the sense
of incongruity, and continued to despise in theory the
sex he honored so much in practice, of whom he chose
his most intimate associates, and whose courage he was
compelled to wonder at, when his own heart was faint.

We may say that such a man was not worthy of
his fortune; and so, as he would not learn, he was
taken away from that agreeable school, and his fellowship of women was broken up, not to be reunited.
Called into Scotland to take at last that strange position in history which is his best claim to commemora-
tion, he was followed thither by his wife and his
mother-in-law. The wife soon died. The death of her
daughter did not altogether separate Mrs. Bowes from
Knox, but she seems to have come and gone between

his house and England. In 1562, however, we find him
characterized as "a sole man by reason of the absence
of his mother-in-law, Mrs. Bowes," and a passport is
got for her, her man, a maid, and "three horses,
whereof two shall return," as well as liberty to take
all her own money with her into Scotland. This looks
like a definite arrangement; but whether she died at
Edinburgh, or went back to England yet again, I cannot find. With that great family of hers, unless in
leaving her husband she had quarreled with them all,
there must have been frequent occasion for her presence, one would think. Knox at least survived her;
and we possess his epigraph to their long intimacy,
given to the world by him in an appendix to his latest
publication. I have said in a former paper that Knox
was not shy of personal revelations in his published
works. And the trick seems to have grown on him.
To this last tract, a controversial onslaught on a Scottish Jesuit, he prefixed a prayer, not very pertinent to
the matter in hand, and containing references to his
family which were the occasion of some wit in his adversary's answer; and appended what seems equally ir-
relevant, one of his devout letters to Mrs. Bowes, with
an explanatory preface. To say truth, I believe he had
always felt uneasily that the circumstances of this intimacy were very capable of misconstruction; and now,
when he was an old man, taking "his good-night of
all the faithful in both realms," and only desirous "that
without any notable sclander to the evangel of Jesus
Christ, he might end his battle; for as the world was
weary of him, so was he of it;"—in such a spirit it
was not, perhaps, unnatural that he should return to

this old story, and seek to put it right in the eyes of all men, ere he died. "Because that God," he says, "because that God now in His mercy hath put an end to the battle of my dear mother, Mistress Elizabeth Bowes, before that He put an end to my wretched life, I could not cease but declare to the world what was the cause of our great familiarity and long acquaintance; which was neither flesh nor blood, but a troubled conscience upon her part, which never suffered her to rest but when she was in the company of the faithful, of whom (from the first hearing of the word at my mouth) she judged me to be one. . . . Her company to me was comfortable (yea, honorable and profitable, for she was to me and mine a mother), but yet it was not without some cross; for besides trouble and fashery of body sustained for her, my mind was seldom quiet, for doing somewhat for the comfort of her troubled conscience."* He had written to her years before, from his first exile in Dieppe, that "only God's hand" could withhold him from once more speaking with her face to face; and now, when God's hand has indeed interposed, when there lies between them, instead of the voyageable straits, that great gulf over which no man can pass, this is the spirit in which he can look back upon their long acquaintance. She was a religious hypochondriac, it appears, whom, not without some cross and fashery of mind and body, he was good enough to tend. He might have given a truer character of their friendship, had he thought less of his own standing in public estimation, and more of the dead woman.

---

* Works, vi. 513, 514.

But he was in all things, as Burke said of his son in that ever memorable passage, a public creature. He wished that even into this private place of his affections posterity should follow him with a complete approval; and he was willing, in order that this might be so, to exhibit the defects of his lost friend, and tell the world what weariness he had sustained through her unhappy disposition. There is something here that reminds one of Rousseau.

I do not think he ever saw Mrs. Locke after he left Geneva; but his correspondence with her continued for three years. It may have continued longer, of course, but I think the last letters we possess read like the last that would be written. Perhaps Mrs. Locke was then remarried, for there is much obscurity over her subsequent history. For as long as their intimacy was kept up, at least, the human element remains in the Reformer's life. Here is one passage, for example, the most likable utterance of Knox's that I can quote— Mrs. Locke has been upbraiding him as a bad correspondent. "My remembrance of you," he answers, "is not so dead, but I trust it shall be fresh enough, albeit it be renewed by no outward token for one year. *Of nature, I am churlish; yet one thing I ashame not to affirm, that familiarity once thoroughly contracted was never yet broken on my default. The cause may be that I have rather need of all, than that any have need of me.* However it (*that*) be, it cannot be, as I say, the corporal absence of one year or two that can quench in my heart that familiar acquaintance in Christ Jesus, which half a year did engender, and almost two years did nourish and confirm. And there-

fore, whether I write or no, be assuredly persuaded that
I have you in such memory as becometh the faithful
to have of the faithful."* This is the truest touch of
personal humility that I can remember to have seen in
all the five volumes of the Reformer's collected works:
it is no small honor to Mrs. Locke that his affection
for her should have brought home to him this unwonted
feeling of dependence upon others. Everything else in
the course of the correspondence testifies to a good,
sound, downright sort of friendship between the two,
less ecstatic than it was at first, perhaps, but serviceable and very equal. He gives her ample details as to
the progress of the work of reformation; sends her the
sheets of the "Confession of Faith," "in quairs," as he
calls it; asks her to assist him with her prayers, to
collect money for the good cause in Scotland, and to
send him books for himself—books by Calvin especially,
one on Isaiah, and a new revised edition of the "Insti-
tutes." "I must be bold on your liberality," he writes,
"not only in that, but in greater things as I shall
need."† On her part she applies to him for spiritual
advice, not after the manner of the drooping Mrs.
Bowes, but in a more positive spirit—advice as to practical points, advice as to the Church of England, for
instance, whose ritual he condemns as a "mingle-man-
gle."‡ Just at the end she ceases to write, sends him
"a token, without writing." "I understand your impedi-
ment," he answers, "and therefore I cannot complain.
Yet if you understood the variety of my temptations,
I doubt not but you would have written somewhat."§
One letter more, and then silence.

---

* Works, vi. 11. † Ib. vi. pp. 21, 101, 108, 130. ‡ Ib. vi. 83. § Ib. vi. 129.

And I think the best of the Reformer died out with
that correspondence. It is after this, of course, that he
wrote that ungenerous description of his intercourse with
Mrs. Bowes. It is after this, also, that we come to the
unlovely episode of his second marriage. He had been
left a widower at the age of fifty-five. Three years
after, it occurred apparently to yet another pious parent
to sacrifice a child upon the altar of his respect for the
Reformer. In January 1563, Randolph writes to Cecil:
"Your Honor will take it for a great wonder when I
shall write unto you that Mr. Knox shall marry a very
near kinswoman of the Duke's, a Lord's daughter, a
young lass not above sixteen years of age."* He adds
that he fears he will be laughed at for reporting so
mad a story. And yet it was true; and on Palm Sunday, 1564, Margaret Stewart, daughter of Andrew Lord
Stewart of Ochiltree, aged seventeen, was duly united
to John Knox, Minister of St. Giles's Kirk, Edinburgh,
aged fifty-nine—to the great disgust of Queen Mary
from family pride, and I would fain hope of many
others for more humane considerations. "In this," as
Randolph says, "I wish he had done otherwise." The
Consistory of Geneva, "that most perfect school of Christ
that ever was on earth since the days of the Apostles,"
were wont to forbid marriages on the ground of too
great a disproportion in age. I cannot help wondering
whether the old Reformer's conscience did not uneasily
remind him, now and again, of this good custom of
his religious metropolis, as he thought of the two-and-
forty years that separated him from his poor bride.

* Works, vi. 532.

Fitly enough, we hear nothing of the second Mrs. Knox until she appears at her husband's deathbed, eight years after. She bore him three daughters in the interval; and I suppose the poor child's martyrdom was made as easy for her as might be. She was "extremely attentive to him" at the end, we read; and he seems to have spoken to her with some confidence. Moreover, and this is very characteristic, he had copied out for her use a little volume of his own devotional letters to other women.

This is the end of the roll, unless we add to it Mrs. Adamson, who had delighted much in his company "by reason that she had a troubled conscience," and whose deathbed is commemorated at some length in the pages of his history.*

And now, looking back, it cannot be said that Knox's intercourse with women was quite of the highest sort. It is characteristic that we find him more alarmed for his own reputation than for the reputation of the women with whom he was familiar. There was a fatal preponderance of self in all his intimacies: many women came to learn from him, but he never condescended to become a learner in his turn. And so there is not anything idyllic in these intimacies of his; and they were never so renovating to his spirit as they might have been. But I believe they were good enough for the women. I fancy the women knew what they were about when so many of them followed after Knox. It is not simply because a man is always fully persuaded that he knows the right from the wrong and

---

* Works, i. 246.

sees his way plainly through the maze of life, great
qualities as these are, that people will love and follow
him, and write him letters full of their "earnest desire
for him" when he is absent. It is not over a man,
whose one characteristic is grim fixity of purpose, that
the hearts of women are "incensed and kindled with a
special care," as it were over their natural children. In
the strong quiet patience of all his letters to the weariful Mrs. Bowes we may perhaps see one cause of the
fascination he possessed for these religious women. Here
was one whom you could besiege all the year round
with inconsistent scruples and complaints; you might
write to him on Thursday that you were so elated it
was plain the devil was deceiving you, and again on
Friday that you were so depressed it was plain God
had cast you off forever; and he would read all this
patiently and sympathetically, and give you an answer
in the most reassuring polysyllables, and all divided
into heads—who knows?—like a treatise on divinity.
And then, those easy tears of his. There are some
women who like to see men crying; and here was this
great-voiced, bearded man of God, who might be seen
beating the solid pulpit every Sunday, and casting
abroad his clamorous denunciations to the terror of all,
and who on the Monday would sit in their parlors by
the hour, and weep with them over their manifold
trials and temptations. Nowadays, he would have to
drink a dish of tea with all these pentients. . . . It
sounds a little vulgar, as the past will do, if we look
into it too closely. We could not let these great folk
of old into our drawing-rooms. Queen Elizabeth would
positively not be eligible for a housemaid. The old

manners and the old customs go sinking from grade
to grade, until, if some mighty emperor revisited the
glimpses of the moon, he would not find any one of
his way of thinking, any one he could strike hands
with and talk to freely and without offense, save perhaps the porter at the end of the street, or the fellow
with his elbows out who loafs all day before the public-
house. So that this little note of vulgarity is not a
thing to be dwelt upon; it is to be put away from
us, as we recall the fashion of these old intimacies; so
that we may only remember Knox as one who was
very long suffering with women, kind to them in his
own way, loving them in his own way—and that not
the worst way, if it was not the best—and once at
least, if not twice, moved to his heart of hearts by a
woman, and giving expression to the yearning he had
for her society in words that none of us need be
ashamed to borrow.

And let us bear in mind always that the period I
have gone over in this essay begins when the Reformer
was already beyond the middle age, and already broken
in bodily health: it has been the story of an old man's
friendships. This it is that makes Knox enviable. Unknown until past forty, he had then before him five-
and-thirty years of splendid and influential life, passed
through uncommon hardships to an uncommon degree
of power, lived in his own country as a sort of king,
and did what he would with the sound of his voice
out of the pulpit. And besides all this, such a following of faithful women! One would take the first forty
years gladly, if one could be sure of the last thirty.
Most of us, even if, by reason of great strength and

the dignity of gray hairs, we retain some degree of public respect in the latter days of our existence, will find a falling away of friends, and a solitude making itself round about us day by day, until we are left alone with the hired sick-nurse. For the attraction of a man's character is apt to be outlived, like the attraction of his body; and the power to love grows feeble in its turn, as well as the power to inspire love in others. It is only with a few rare natures that friendship is added to friendship, love to love, and the man keeps growing richer in affection—richer, I mean, as a bank may be said to grow richer, both giving and receiving more—after his head is white and his back weary, and he prepares to go down into the dust of death.

END OF VOLUME SEVEN

300